Year 2000 Personal Computer Fix-It Guide

Year 2000 Personal Computer Fix-It Guide

JD Consulting

CHARLES RIVER MEDIA, INC.
Rockland, Massachusetts

Publisher: David F. Pallai
Production: Reuben Kantor
Cover Design: The Printed Image
Artist: Justin S. Faucher
Printer: InterCity Press

CHARLES RIVER MEDIA, INC.
P.O. Box 417
403 VFW Drive
Rockland, Massachusetts 02370
781-871-4184
781-871-4376 (FAX)
chrivmedia@aol.com
http://www.charlesriver.com

This book is printed on acid-free paper.

Year 2000 Personal Computer Fix-It Guide
By JD Consulting
   ISBN 1-886801-94-0
   Printed in the United States of America

98 99 00 01 02 03 7 6 5 4 3 2

CHARLES RIVER MEDIA titles are available for site license or bulk purchase by
institutions, user groups, corporations, etc. For additional information, please contact
the Special Sales Department at (781) 871-4184.

DEDICATION

This book is dedicated to Peter and Valentina McGrail (Pete and Toni). If not for them, we and this book would never be!

Table of Contents

Acknowledgments

DAN. . . .

I would like to thank all the folks at the different software companies for working with me and providing excellent tools and testers to help our readers work through their year 2000 problems.

Thank you to my family, friends, fellow team members, and most importantly my sweetheart Jackie, for putting up with me through 8 months of grouchy days and sleepless nights.

ELLEN. . . .

A special thanks to the rest of the Team — John, Julie, Dan and Justin — and especially my husband Steve for keeping me going, tolerating my stressful moments, and making this book a reality. You guys are the greatest!

I also want to sincerely thank my friends and associates in Connecticut and Florida for their encouragement, input, and willing support.

JOHN. . . .

Special thanks to my co-authors for working so hard and keeping me motivated throughout this project. Additional thanks go out to all my family and friends, especially to Jeff, Renée, and Lynn, who helped in their own special way.

JULIE. . . .

Thanks to the special man in my life, Dan Reed, for all of his support and understanding of my goals.

I would like to thank my family, friends, and co-workers for all of their moral support and positive attitudes. And a special thanks to my mother, brothers, and cousin Dan for making this book possible!

TEAM. . . .

A huge thank you to Justin Faucher from the rest of the team for coming through on short notice with his terrific graphics. Super Job Jay!

About the Authors

Dan McGrail is an IT professional whose experience includes customer support, system analysis and design, and project management. His hardware focus is PC based LANs and UNIX, while his software development focus is in PC-COBOL, Visual BASIC, and various other languages. Dan is a "technology" junkie who loves the internet, GUI, and everything about computers. He is a partner of Coordinated Systems Inc., an East Hartford Connecticut based manufacturing and accounting software firm. He is also a partner of JD Consulting LLC, an East Hartford Connecticut based computer consulting firm specializing in the year 2000 problem.

Ellen Faucher holds a bachelor's degree in computer information science from Nova Southeastern University. She has been a systems professional for more than 25 years and has spent her entire career working in the insurance industry. She is currently a part owner of JD Consulting LLC, and is also a Vice President of Technology at PRC Corporation in Hartford, Connecticut. Before returning to Connecticut in 1997, Ellen was a senior-level manager at a Florida-based insurance company, where she successfully initiated and lead their corporate-wide year 2000 problem solution project. She knows the "Millennium Bug" is real and is determined to help others understand its impact and cure.

John Gasparini holds a bachelor's degree in computer engineering from Syracuse University. Upon graduating in 1987, he was employed by the State of Connecticut's Division of Special

Revenue, where he spent the majority of his career developing minicomputer- and PC-based applications to accommodate the agency's distinct business needs. As well as being a principal of JD Consulting, he is currently employed by the Connecticut-based firm Advanced Technologies & Services, LLC, as a Senior Technical Consultant. John is the quintessential weekend warrior, whose motto is "Work hard and play even harder!"

Julie Rozek is presently a senior office systems analyst at Lincoln Financial Group of CT. Her 16 years of IT work experience have provided her with a strong understanding of all areas of LAN and desktop PC support. One of Julie's views of keys to successful customer service is: "Never cut a customer off. In PC support you learn that listening to the customer is one of the most important aspects of troubleshooting. Ninety percent of the time, they will identify the cause of their problem."

Preface

It's a widely known fact the turn of the Millennium will cause major problems for computers and computer systems. However, a large portion of the general public believes this phenomenon will not affect them. In fact, it's commonly thought that this problem exists only in large main frame computer systems used by corporate America and government agencies. In actuality this problem can exist in every size computer system. It is our goal to help you understand what the "year 2000" problem is, how it affects your personal computer, and how to fix it.

We also focus your attention on the fact that businesses and government agencies that hold your personal data, or those you rely on for products and services to run your business, may not be addressing their year 2000 problems. As a result they are placing your financial security and well- being at risk. Just ask yourself what you would do if you suddenly stopped receiving your monthly retirement benefits checks or if your bank notified you that they had no record showing that you had paid your mortgage for the past 15 years. We offer advice on some actions you should be taking now to avoid or minimize the chances of this happening.

This book is designed for the individual home user and small business owner who needs help evaluating and solving the year 2000 problem on desktop personal computers or small Local Area Networks. It is also designed for those who may not even own a computer but who are worried that they will be affected if government agencies, banks and other institutions begin storing or processing their personal information incorrectly after December 31, 1999. In plain easy to understand terms, this book will discuss the problem, how to evaluate whether you have it, and how to fix it. We offer basic advice on protecting your assets and also discuss how to contact various companies, institutions and government agencies to learn how they are handling the problem and whether your information is safe.

In reality this problem affects everyone. We live in the "Information Age." Computer technology dominates and automates every facet of business and personal information, from the day our foot is stamped on the birth certificate to the day we are marked deceased in the local hall of records. Hardware and software of all kinds is affected by this problem. Even newly purchased desktop PC applications may have problems dealing with dates into and beyond the year 2000. It would be foolish to ignore the problem.

Our book walks you through the problem causes and their possible solutions. We discuss how to take a complete inventory of your computer system and include worksheets to help you organize your testing, problem identification and solution needs. We provide extensive information on how to test and evaluate all pieces of the problem. For those who decide to seek outside professional help, we talk about hiring contractors and consultants, what you can expect to pay and how to ensure you get what you pay for. We discuss legal issues related to your software licenses, as well as other service and insurance contracts to help you understand your rights and obligations. We provide information about how to contact your vendors and service providers, and what information you need to obtain to determine your solution path and risks of failure. We include Web site addresses, phone support numbers, and sample letters to make this an easy process. We also provide other sources of information and assistance and we discuss tools and testers which can help automate and simplify different pieces of the problem identification and solution effort. A CD-ROM which contains various tools and testers accompanies our book. All of the information provided is focused on our goal of ensuring that when the clock turns 12:00 am on January 1, 2000, your computer will continue to be a useful tool for you and your business.

Do yourself a favor and take our tour. Get all the facts about the infamous "Millennium Bug."

How This Book Is Organized

We have designed this book as an easy-to-use guide to "year 2000" compliance. However, it is critical that you follow this book step-by-step. Missing one step may lead to inadequate results.

UNDERSTANDING THE "YEAR 2000" PROBLEM
☆ Provides an overview of the problem and the different areas of concern.

CREATING AN INVENTORY
☆ Lists the various areas of your computer that need to be inventoried.

🏢 An "Inventory Worksheet" can be found in Appendix A.

HARDWARE, FIRMWARE, AND PERIPHERALS
☆ Gives you an overview of the various hardware components.

☆ Helps you create an inventory of the hardware components.

☆ Discusses various tests for determining if problems exist.

☆ Discusses automated testers.

🏢 A hardware manufacturer list can be found in Appendix B.

OPERATING SYSTEMS
☆ Gives you an overview of the various operating systems.

☆ Helps you identify what type of operating system you are running.

☆ Helps you create an inventory of the operating system components.

☆ Discusses various tests for determining if problems exist.

☆ Discusses automated testers.

⊞ Operating system titles can be found in Appendix C.

HOME AND OFFICE SOFTWARE APPLICATIONS

☆ Gives you an overview of the different types of software applications.

☆ Helps you create an inventory of your software applications.

☆ Discusses various tests for determining if problems exist.

☆ Provides you with steps on how to determine software title, manufacturer, and version number.

☆ Discusses the need to contact manufacturers.

⊞ Software application titles can be found in Appendix D .

⊞ Software manufacturer contact information can be found in Appendix E.

DATA FILES

☆ Gives you an overview on how to pinpoint the data files, fields, and macros presenting inconsistencies and migration problems.

☆ Helps you identify and evaluate your data files.

☆ Assists you in creating your file inventory.

☆ Helps you review file content.

☆ Discusses field expansion and migration needs.

COMMERCIAL OFF-THE-SHELF PRODUCTS—TIPS AND TECHNIQUES

☆ Discusses software and data interdependency issues for commercial off-the-shelf products.

☆ Pinpoints the problem areas and offers tips and techniques for spreadsheets, databases, word processors, groupware, and other common applications.

⊞ Software application titles can be found in Appendix D.

⊞ Software manufacturer contact information can be found in Appendix E.

SERVERS AND THE YEAR 2000

☆ Discusses the impact the year 2000 has on servers.

☆ Lists year 2000 compliance status for Novell Netware, Windows NT, and Windows for Workgroups, as well as LANtastic.

HIRING CONSULTANTS AND CONTRACTORS

☆ Discusses the availability of resources.

☆ Lists what qualities and credentials you should look for.

☆ Provides an example of a good proposal and methodology.

☆ Explains how to be sure you get what you pay for.

☆ Estimates what it will cost for services.

LEGAL CONCERNS

☆ Discusses the need for diligence.

☆ Explains how to take advantage of product and service guarantees and warranties.

☆ Helps you examine software licenses, contracts, and insurance coverage.

SOURCES FOR THE YEAR 2000 INFORMATION

☆ Discusses informational web sites and user groups.

⊞ A U.S. user group listing can be found in Appendix J.

OTHER COMPANIES AND GOVERNMENT AGENCIES

☆ Explains who is important to you, why, and how to contact them.

☆ Provides you with information on how to contact them.

⊞ Sample information request letters can be found in Appendix H.

INFORMATION REQUEST LETTERS

☆ Overviews the importance of information request letters and how they can help you.

☆ Lists what questions you should ask.

☆ Explains options and next steps.

▦ Sample information request letters can be found in Appendix H.

TOOLS AND TESTERS

☆ Overviews the pros and cons of tools and testers.

☆ Discusses their purpose and how to put them to use.

☆ Lists steps to take before purchasing tools and testers.

☆ Explains different types.

☆ Details the tools included on the CD-ROM.

▦ Tool and Tester information can be found in Appendix G.

▦ An overview of the contents of the CD-ROM is given in Appendix I.

DETERMINING AND IMPLEMENTING SOLUTIONS

☆ Gives you an overview of determining and implementing solutions.

☆ Discusses reviewing the results of the inventory worksheet and determining the best solutions.

▦ An "Inventory Worksheet" can be found in Appendix A.

CHAPTER

1

The Problem and
The Solution

The year 2000 problem, known as the "Millennium Bug," exists because of an early design shortcoming that persists in a majority of computers today. When computers were first designed, memory and storage space were costly. Computer designers decided to save some of that space by using a six-digit date format. Dates were stored and processed as YYMMDD, or Year Year Month Month Day Day. The two-digit century was assumed to be 19. Therefore, a date of December 25, 1997, was stored as 971225. For years this proved successful. As time went on, this technique became an industry standard for designers of hardware and software.

This technique of storing and processing dates works fine until the century changes from 19 to 20.

> December 25, 1997, in computer code is programmed as 971225.
>
> January 2, 2000, in computer code is programmed as 000102.

As you can see in this example, the number 000102 sequentially comes before the number 971225. If we look at this in calendar date calculations, we really need 971225 to come before 000102. So, this is where the problem arises. A calculation or sorting function would not produce the correct result when processing these two dates.

For example, suppose you paid a full-year insurance premium due on October 1, 1999. The insurance company's billing system applies your premium and calculates that you are paid through October 1, 2000. This date is stored in the computer as 001001. During the November 1, 1999, billing cycle, the insurance company's billing system compares the current date, which is stored as 991101, to your "paid-through" date, which is 001001. Because 991101 is greater than 001101, it decides your payment is more than 30 days late and it cancels your policy. Obviously, this is an error.

The solution is simple. Store and process dates in an eight-digit format, including the two-digit century in the year. The new eight-digit format would be YYYYMMDD, or Year Year Year Year Month Month Day Day.

> November 01, 1999, in 8-digit format computer code is 19991101.
> October 1, 2000, in 8-digit format computer code is 20001001.

Now when processing the dates above, November 01, 1999, or 19991101, mathematically comes before October 1, 2000, or 20001001. A calculation or sorting function would produce the correct results.

Hardware and software designers have since produced "year 2000 versions" of their products. This means one of two things.

1. They no longer use the six-digit date format. Instead, they use the new eight-digit format including the two-digit century.

2. They still allow use of the six-digit date format, but apply a formula to calculate the correct century before performing date calculations and comparisons to ensure the correct results.

However, old versions of hardware and software which are not "year 2000 compliant" still dominate home and business computing. The world has not yet upgraded.

Six Areas of Concern

The year 2000 problem or Millennium Bug exists in both hardware and software products. To better explain and understand the problem, we will start by defining what we see as the six areas of concern: the system clock, the basic input/output system, the operating system, software applications, data files, and peripherals.

The System Clock

The system clock is a physical chip inside the computer, usually referred to as the CMOS/RTC (Complementary Metal Oxide Semiconductor/Real Time Clock). The CMOS chip is powered by a battery to keep track of the date and time and to hold the system setup information when the computer is powered off.

The BIOS

The BIOS (Basic Input/Output System) is a small program that loads into memory when you turn on the computer. It recognizes and controls access to various components such as the keyboard, display screen, and disk drives, as well as the system clock.

The Operating System

The operating system is the most important program running on the computer. It communicates with the BIOS and runs the other general software applications. It coordinates the interaction and sharing of all the system components so that they do not interfere with each other while the computer is running.

Software Applications

A software application is any program that executes under the control of the operating system. An application may be a program written by a computer's user, a shrink-wrapped program (such as Microsoft Word or Microsoft Excel), or a program developed by a third party to suit a user's specific needs.

Data Files
Data files are information previously entered by a computer's user. They are stored and accessed by software applications as needed and usually reside on fixed or removable disks.

Peripherals
A peripheral is any hardware device externally attached to a computer, such as a printer, backup unit, modem, scanner, or fax machine. Some of these devices may contain date-dependent control logic that cannot handle the eight-digit date format.

ORIGIN AND PATH OF THE PROBLEM

The CMOS/RTC holds the date when the computer is powered off. When the computer is powered on, the BIOS wakes up and asks the CMOS/RTC for the date. After the BIOS goes through its start-up functions, the operating system loads and asks the BIOS for the date. When software applications that require the date are executed, they get it from the operating system. There are some exceptions to the rule, but this is normally the chain of command.

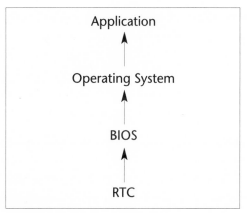

FIGURE *Normal Chain of Command.*
1-1

Some software applications may jump over the operating system and go directly to the BIOS.

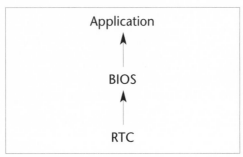

Figure
1-2 *Application to BIOS.*

Some applications may go directly to the CMOS/RTC for date information. This scenario is extremely rare.

Figure
1-3 *Application to CMOS/RTC.*

In any event, you can see how the interaction between components requires that they all handle dates in a consistent manner. We must recognize the problem and begin to resolve it at the source.

The problem starts at the CMOS/RTC. In many older and some newer computers, the CMOS/RTC maintains a two-digit year. The problem presents itself when the BIOS tries to interpret the two-digit year. When the system clock rolls over from the year 99 (1999) to the year 00 (2000), any requests from the BIOS for a date may result in the CMOS/RTC returning a year value of "00". The BIOS must interpret the century based on the two-digit year. Many BIOSs fail at this task due to a programming oversight. Some BIOSs can handle the century rollover, some set the year to 1900, and others set the year to 1980.

Another problem to be concerned with is the rare occurrence of a leap year at the turn of a century, which does happen in the year 2000. Some BIOSs do not recognize this fact and will incorrectly set the date for February 29, 2000, to March 1, 2000.

The problem presents itself again when the operating system performs a BIOS call for the date and time. If the BIOS passes an improper date, the operating system will not obtain the correct date. The user may manually reset the operating system date by using a date command; however, this date may be lost when the computer is powered off.

The problem surfaces again when a software application makes a call to the operating system to get the current date and time information. Furthermore, even if your operating system contains the proper date, the way the software application is written or used may still cause a failure in the handling of dates. Many applications only recognize the two-digit portion of the year. So when the date changes from year 1999 to 2000, the application will no longer function correctly because year 00 sequentially comes before, instead of after, 99. Therefore, arithmetic operations and sorting functions using this date will generate invalid results.

IS IT REAL?

As a home PC user or small business owner, you may feel that the year 2000 problem won't have as drastic an impact or isn't as great a concern for you as it is for private industry or government agencies. Yes, this may be true. However, if you do nothing to correct your year 2000 date problem, or pressure others on whom you rely for goods and services to fix theirs, you or your business will certainly be affected. You need to plan, take action, and make certain your business and external business interfaces are year 2000 compliant.

If, suddenly, you can no longer reliably provide the services or goods your customers desire, we guarantee they will switch to other companies who can satisfy their needs. And if your bank or investment firm starts to miscalculate what you owe them or what they've invested for you, we're willing to guarantee you will be more than a little upset.

Perhaps the following examples will give you a better sense of how this problem may affect you.

"What do you mean I don't qualify for Social Security?"

The Social Security Administration (SSA) is an example of an agency that is extremely date sensitive. Much of the agency's millions of lines of computer code revolve around the eligibility of recipients, which is based on age. If their computer system's have a problem processing the year 2000 date change, many individuals receiving regularly scheduled Social Security checks may stop receiving those checks. Even worse, it could take months to get the problem resolved and receive the money you are owed.

Imagine This Scenario. . . .

You are out to dinner with your family and have enjoyed a lovely meal. The waitress brings your check and suddenly you realize you're short on cash. You figure, "No problem. I'll just use my charge card." To your dismay the waitress comes back and tells you your credit card was denied. Will this be an awkward moment? Possibly. . . .

Some of the chips and micro-code in certain card-reading machines cannot recognize the year 2000 and therefore won't accept a card with an expiration date later than December 31, 1999. In reality, this card reader problem has already surfaced. Last year a couple of the major credit card companies actually had to recall cards they had issued with expiration dates later than 1999. They replaced them with cards having a 1999 expiration date. They then initiated a massive effort to contact businesses who used their card readers to test and correct the reader problems. By now most of the card reader problems are probably fixed, but who knows?

Actually, this simple example illustrates just how heavily the banking industry relies on information technology, which in itself is a cause for concern. What if their systems fail and you don't have access to your accounts? How long will it take to regain access to your money? What about the aggravation involved in trying to straighten out interest or loan balance problems? It could be a nightmare, and you'd better make sure you have records of what you paid and deposited.

"What do you mean my insurance costs have increased by $1000?"	Insurance companies track a great amount of information based on a client's birth date. Insurance providers showing a birth date of 01/01/00 would not know if a person was just born or was 100 years old. Actuarial systems, which are highly oriented toward age-related risk factors, are particularly vulnerable if they misinterpret birth dates. Age miscalculations in these systems may result in higher premiums for young people and lower premiums for older individuals.
Imagine This Scenario. . . .	You're the owner of a small business and your sitting at your desk on Tuesday, February 1st, of the year 2000, when all of a sudden your switchboard lights up like Rockefeller Center. Every one of your customers is calling up to complain about bills that include 99 years of late charges and service fees. In a panic, you log onto your system, and within minutes you realize that your billing application was not year 2000 compliant. The system has incorrectly updated your customer files. It may take months to correct the problem. You may find your company losing customers, and the loss or delay of incoming revenue could cripple, if not bankrupt, your business.

HOW DO I FIX IT?

The problem is quite simple: six-digit date formats. The solution is quite simple: eight-digit date formats. The process of evaluating your systems, determining if you have a problem, and following a path to resolution is not so simple. Let's break it down into manageable steps.

- First, take a complete inventory of all your hardware, software and peripherals.
- Test or evaluate each hardware, software, and data component to identify date-related problems.
- Review your license agreements to determine vendor responsibilities and actions needed to resolve problems.
- Identify vendors and agencies you conduct business with or rely on for data, products, or services.
- Request compliance information.
- Formulate solution options.
- Implement selected solutions.

Create an Inventory

Chapter 2 discusses the various areas that need to be inventoried and how they are important to ensuring a thorough year 2000 problem resolution process. This is the first and most important step for analyzing and solving your year 2000 problems. How to complete a thorough inventory is discussed in more detail in subsequent chapters.

Evaluate and Test for Compliance

Chapters 3 through 8 discuss how to test and evaluate hardware and software. Testing is a very important process, as it will help you determine where you have problems. Regardless of your test results, you should always contact manufacturers to obtain confirmation of each product's year 2000 date handling status.

Review Legal Documents	Chapter 10 addresses the need to review legal agreements and contracts to ensure you are taking the required steps to secure manufacturer support for resolution of your problems. You need to understand what the product warranties and limitations are, as well as the liabilities the vendor or you will assume if their products fail to operate correctly. Auditing your legal documents to clearly understand their terms and conditions is an important step in the year 2000 problem solution process.
Identify Vendors and Agencies	Chapter 12 explains how to identify those companies and agencies that are important to your personal and business security, and how to contact them to obtain the information you need to assess their year 2000 readiness. If you are provided with invalid date information or faulty products, you will have problems.
Request Compliance Information	Chapter 13 walks you through the process of creating year 2000 information request letters. It provides guidance on the types of questions and information you should request to determine where vendors, businesses, and government agencies stand on resolution of their year 2000 problems. Once you learn certain products are not going to work or a company you rely on is at risk, you must figure out what your options are and determine an appropriate course of action.
Identify and Implement Solutions	Chapter 15 discusses how to determine and implement solutions for the problem areas. Different components of your system may require different fixes. You may be able to simply upgrade your BIOS to satisfy hardware compliance. However, you may need to

install a software patch to fix your operating system, or completely replace your billing application if it is not compliant and the vendor does not have a year 2000 compliant version. As you progress through the problem evaluation and research steps discussed throughout this book, you will gather the information you need to determine your options and help you select the most reasonable solution path.

COMPLIANT VS READY

There is a significant difference between being year 2000 *compliant* and year 2000 *ready*. This difference is important to understand, especially when you determine your information technology's ability to handle the year 2000 change.

To be fully year 2000 *compliant* means that the specific information technology can and *always will* accurately process date and time data from the year 1900 into and beyond the year 2000 (including the leap year). Such processing includes date and time calculations, comparisons, and sequencing. Information technology's compliance also relies on valid acquisition and exchange of date and time data from and with dependent information technologies.

To be year 2000 *ready* means that the specific information technology has the capability of being year 2000 compliant; however, improper use of such technology would prevent it from being compliant. In other words, year 2000 *ready* technologies allow the user to define and process date information in either a six-digit or eight-digit date format. This is referred to as the "short date" and "long date" formats, respectively. When the six-digit format is used, the user must take care to ensure the software application code will always interpret the correct century. The user must also make certain the "short date" information will not be stored on files or passed to other programs that expect the "long date" format.

| **Example of Year 2000 Ready** | Here's an example that should help to clarify this distinction and why it is important for you to understand the difference. |

Suppose you are running Microsoft Access 97 and have set up your Windows 95 operating system to accept a full eight-digit (long date) format as follows:

Month	2 digits
Day	2 digits
Century	2 digits
Year	2 digits

However, the Access software still allows you to enter date information in a short date format, which is MMDDYY.

If you enter a date of January 1, 2030, as "010130" while processing a database record entry and then retrieve the record from your database, you will get January 1, 1930. If you enter a date of December 31, 2029, as "123129" and then retrieve it, you will get December 31, 2029. This happens because Microsoft Access 97 uses a *windowing* technique to interpret the correct century. If you do not specifically enter all eight digits of the date, the software applies this technique to calculate the century before storing the date on the database.

The way it does this is by assuming the century starts in the year 1930 instead of the year 1900. When the two-digit year is typed in, Access compares it to the base year of 30. If the year you type in is less than 30, it assumes the century value is "20". If you type in a two-digit year whose value is greater than 29, it assumes the century is "19".

Suppose you're using the database to store birth dates and other personal information about your clients. If some of your clients were born before December 31, 1929, you need to ensure that the person maintaining the database enters a full eight-digit date format. If you do not, the wrong century will be stored in your database file.

Many vendors have opted to use this windowing technique to make their products *year 2000 ready*. They assume it is the responsibility of software users to understand and use their products in a year 2000 compliant manner. This is why it is important for you to investigate the method your software vendors have chosen to make their products year 2000 compliant. Any time they mention *base years* or *pivot years*, you know they are using a windowing approach. You need to know what base year they are using and then evaluate whether this will present a problem for your intended use of the software.

2

Creating an Inventory

THE CHECKLIST

Creating an inventory checklist is the most important piece of the entire year 2000 evaluation and fix process. You must carry out this step thoroughly to ensure that you identify and deal with all areas related to your computers, your company, and other areas of your life that could be affected by year 2000 date problems.

Creating a thorough inventory is not rocket science, but it does require some organization and some tools. You need to gather information on the four components of the computer: hardware, software, the operating system, and data files. Data files includes files you may be receiving or sending to another user or company. You also need to inventory peripherals that are attached to your computer, as well as your critical service or product providers, government agencies, and other institutions that may be important to some aspect of your life. We know this process can be confusing, and so we recommend using the Inventory Checklist in Appendix A as a guide. We created this checklist to ensure that you can organize all information in one work area.

It is important to get as much information about each component as possible. Some of the inventory information will be unknown to you, but don't worry. As you work through Chapters 3, 4, 5, 6, and 7, you will learn how to perform a proper inventory, including how and where to obtain the information you need.

AREAS TO INVENTORY

Hardware, Firmware, and Peripherals

Any computer component containing a chip or any device that stores and executes electronic instructions may pose a date problem and is classified as hardware.

Some of these components contain data or instructions that cannot be modified. This type of hardware is referred to as *firmware*. Firmware is actually a combination of hardware and software that are manufactured together.

Peripherals are external hardware devices that are attached to your computer. There are two classifications of peripherals. The first includes devices that are attached to your computer with cables, but physically reside outside of the computer. The second includes devices such as sound cards or modems that are placed inside your computer system.

You might be asking yourself, "Why should I be concerned about my hardware, once I know the Basic Input Output System (BIOS) and Real Time Clock (CMOS/RTC) are OK? My fax modem can't cause me any date problems. There's no need to worry about my CD-ROM drive." In most cases probably not, but don't be so sure. Many individual components and their drivers have built-in programs that allow the user to change internal configurations and settings. The component may use an internal date to interact with another component. Don't assume anything. All hardware, firmware, and peripherals need to be listed in the hardware section of the Inventory Worksheet. Chapter 3 is designed to walk you through the process of gathering the needed information.

Operating System

Why should you worry about your operating system? The operating system is considered the "boss" because all applications rely on its functions in order to run. Most software applications get the date by making a call to the operating system. If there's a date problem with your operating system, chances are the software on your computer will fail. Refer to Chapter 4 to determine what operating system information needs to be entered into your Inventory Worksheet.

Software Applications

Any software application that reads, stores, or processes date information may pose a problem. Why should you be concerned about your software? Maybe you have a spreadsheet you use to track due dates or to calculate interest payments over time. If it's not date compliant, you may be late on some payments or miss early discounts. Do not assume anything. Any software application that uses a date should be listed in the software section of the Inventory Worksheet. This includes commercial off-the-shelf software such as spreadsheets, word processors, and database applications, as well as software developed by end users, or written by third parties to perform unique business functions. Chapter 5 helps you identify what software you are running to ensure completion of a thorough inventory.

Data Files

Do your software applications create or retrieve information from files that contain date fields? This includes files containing general data records as well as those containing "macros" and "functions." Macros and functions are lists of program instructions or commands that are read into the computer's memory and executed when called by a user or another program. If your data files contain date information, or if the macros and functions manipulate date information, they need to be checked out. It is important to note these files on your inventory. You may need to expand or convert these date fields to another format if the software application has to be changed or upgraded to a year 2000 compliant version that cannot read or correctly interpret the old format. Chapter 6 suggests processes for gathering your file inventory.

Other Businesses and Institutions

Why should you be concerned about businesses and other institutions? "The bank won't lose my money. My 401K and IRA are safe." "My investment company won't lose my stocks or funds." "Our vendors won't be late on our shipments." Don't be so sure.

After all, this information is just numbers in a database. If the computer system managing that database fails, you may be temporarily unable to access your funds or receive goods. Chapters 9 and 12 provide information and guidance on how to identify those companies you are most dependent on for services and financial security.

Government Agencies	Why should you be concerned with the government and its individual agencies? "The government wouldn't let anything happen to their system." Once again, don't be so sure. Our research leaves us quite concerned about the lack of attention and late start many local, state and federal agencies have given the year 2000 problem. If your date of birth is improperly stored in the Social Security database, you may suddenly not be eligible for benefits even though you've been receiving a monthly check for a number of years. Scheduled payments may not arrive on time as agencies scramble to figure out who gets what. Veterans' pensions, disability benefits, IRS returns, and many others may not process when they're supposed to. Who can afford to wait for these errors to be corrected? Chapter 12 will help you to think through who must be contacted and included in this inventory.

INVENTORY METHODS

Some of the information on the inventory will have to be completed manually. However, you may want to use some sort of automated tool to assist in completing the various Hardware, Software, and Data File inventory components. A variety of tools are available to scan your system and look for hardware, software, operating systems, and files. Some are available in single-user versions; others are capable of scanning a network. Refer to Chapter 14 and Appendix G to obtain information about these tools and how they may help. However, even if you use a "Tool Man" approach, remember that tools won't provide all the inventory information that you need.

BACKING UP YOUR DATA

Once you've gathered the inventory information, you will be ready to move into the testing phase. Before you make any date changes or start testing, it is *critical* that you back up your computer system, or at least your important data files. Many computer users who complete testing without backing up their systems find they have lost valuable data. Don't let this happen to you. By using a simple DOS or Windows Explorer COPY command, you can perform a backup to a floppy diskette or other external disk device. Refer to your operating system manuals or on-line help for proper use of these commands.

In the event you encounter problems and need to restore from the backup device, first make sure the computer system dates have been changed back to the current date. The steps needed to modify the hardware and operating system dates are described in the next two chapters.

Since we are discussing the importance of backups, this seems like an appropriate time to explain how the year 2000 date can affect your normal backup and restore processes, if you are using special backup software.

Does your backup program prompt you to enter a two-digit or four-digit year? If your answer is two digits, think about whether the year comparison will perform correctly, and what the consequences will be if it doesn't. Imagine this scenario. You complete a backup of your critical files on December 29th, 1998. Your backup process is set to append files to a backup medium each time it runs. You tell your program to save the backup files for a five-year period. The retention date that gets written to the files will be 122903. The next time you run your backup process it checks to see if the expiration date on the file is exceeded. Since 122903 is calculated as being 95 years earlier than 123098, it assumes the file is more than five years old, and all the information from the prior backup will be written over.

Again, if you routinely use special backup software, bear this in mind and adjust your normal backup procedures as needed. Now let's move forward with the inventory and testing steps outlined in the next several chapters.

CHAPTER

3

Hardware, Firmware, and Peripherals

THIS CHAPTER CONTAINS:

- Overview
- Peripheral Inventory
- Year 2000 Rollover
- Automated Tester

- Hardware and Firmware Inventory
- Testing for Year 2000 Problems
- Leap Year Test

OVERVIEW

Think about your daily life for a moment and how many electronic devices you depend on. How many of them have the ability to display a date or use date functionality? Hardware technology such as computers, printers, fax machines, scanners, credit card readers, security systems, automated teller machines (ATMs), advanced phone systems, personal digital assistants (PDAs), automobile clocks, and alarm clocks are just a few examples of electronic devices that will be a concern at the turn of the year 2000. It is amazing how technology-dependent our society has become.

The first step in identifying and resolving your hardware year 2000 date handling problem is to create an inventory of the various hardware components that need to be tested or checked. This chapter is designed to walk you through the hardware inventory and BIOS testing process.

It's important to complete as much of the inventory checklist as possible before contacting any manufacturers regarding year 2000 problems, fixes, concerns, or general questions. They will ask you specific questions about your system's components and configuration. Without this information, the manufacturer might give you incorrect answers. Your inventory checklist will help you to answer these questions

HARDWARE AND FIRMWARE INVENTORY

It is important to document the following information about your computer. Most of this information is typically listed on the purchase invoice or packing slip, which you received when you purchased your computer.

- Manufacturer, model, and serial number
- Total random access memory (RAM)
- Total hard disk space and available hard disk space
- CPU (central processing unit) manufacturer, type, and speed
- BIOS manufacturer and version number

If you don't have any invoices or slips, read on. There are other ways to obtain this information.

Manufacturer, Model, and Serial Number

Most computers are imprinted with their manufacturer's name, model, and serial number.

MANUFACTURER, MODEL, AND SERIAL NUMBER
STEPS

1. Look at the front and back of your CPU (central processing unit) or computer case for this information. Remember, this is not your monitor screen, but the box that your monitor is physically connected to. You are looking for the following three pieces of information:

   (a) Manufacturer. Example manufacturers are IBM, Hewlett Packard, Compaq, AST, or Gateway.

   (b) Model number. This typically starts with Model No., Model, or M/N.

   (c) Serial number. This typically starts with Serial No., Serial, or S#.

2. If you can't find this information, consult the computer manuals.

3. Fill this information in on the inventory worksheet.

Total Random Access Memory

Most computers count the amount of RAM installed when the computer is powered on. This memory is used to store and run your software applications.

Ways to determine this information:

> 1. Computer purchase invoice
> 2. Power up process
> 3. Through the operating system
> 4. CMOS setup information

POWER UP PROCESS

1. Turn on your computer and immediately look at the upper left-hand corner of the monitor screen. You will see a number counting up. Write down the last number displayed. For example, the number 4096 translates into 4 megabytes of memory. If you were to read this, you would think it means "four thousand and ninety-six." In memory terms it really means "four million ninety-six thousand," or 4,096,000 bytes or characters of memory.

2. Fill in the amount of memory on the inventory worksheet.

Operating Systems

MS-DOS AND WINDOWS 3.11 PROCESS

STEPS

The MS-DOS and Windows 3.11 operating system will report this information when a user types in the MEM DOS command.

1. Go to a C: prompt.

    If you have Windows 3.11 you will need to click on Main, Control Panel, MS-DOS. This will bring you to the c:\windows directory.

2. Type in MEM and press ENTER.

3. You will see something similar to what is shown in the example displayed below. To read this screen and determine the total amount of random access memory, look at the line that starts with "Total memory." The total, which is 16,384K, means that this computer has 16 megabytes of RAM.

4. Write in the amount of memory on the inventory worksheet.

5. To return to Windows 3.11, type in EXIT and press ENTER.

Memory Type	Total	Used	Free
Conventional	640K	28K	612K
Upper	95K	95K	0K
Reserved	384K	384K	0K
Extended (XMS)	15,265K	153K	15,112K
Total memory	16,384K	660K	15,724K
Total under 1 MB	735K	122K	612K
Largest executable program size	612K (627,136 bytes)		

WINDOWS 95 PROCESS

STEPS

1. Turn on your computer.

2. Once Windows 95 loads, you will see an icon on your desktop called My Computer. Right-click your mouse button on My Computer.

3. Click on the Properties Menu option. It will display a screen that has an area labeled COMPUTER:. Underneath the COMPUTER: area it will display xxx.xMB. The xxx.x represents the amount of memory your computer contains.

4. Fill in this information on the inventory worksheet.

5. Click on Cancel to exit from the Properties screen.

CMOS SETUP INFORMATION
STEPS

Note. This process should be used as a last resort. You must be careful not to alter any settings in the procedure described below. Accidentally changing a setting in the setup area could result in complete system failure. If you are not comfortable with entering into the CMOS setup area, consult a professional for help.

1. Turn on your computer and enter into the CMOS Setup Utility. Access to your CMOS setup screen varies. However, many systems display the keystrokes needed to enter the Setup Utility in the upper left-hand corners of their screens. If your system does not display this information, consult the manual that came with your computer. Don't be afraid to call your computer manufacturer for assistance if you are unable to locate this information.

2. Once you have entered into the Setup area, you need to find out where the memory information is located. Computer CMOS Setup menus are different, so you might have to look around at different menu options to determine the memory information.

3. Fill in the amount of memory on the inventory worksheet.

4 When you are done you should exit the Setup Utility, but please do not save any changes..

Total Hard Disk Space and Available Hard Disk Space

Total hard disk space refers to the size of all hard drives combined. Most computers have one hard drive, but some have more. Don't confuse a 3.5 inch floppy diskette with a hard drive. The hard drive is inside your computer and is considered a fixed disk. It cannot be removed without disassembling your system. Available hard disk space is the amount of total hard disk space not being used. If you have 500 megabytes of total hard disk space and have 300 megabytes of data loaded on your machine, you have 200 megabytes of free hard disk space.

Ways to determine the total amount of hard disk space and available hard disk on your computer are as follows:

1. Invoice or purchase slip
2. MS-DOS
3. Windows 3.11
4. Windows 95

MS-DOS 6.22 PROCESS

STEPS

1. Turn on your computer and wait for a command prompt.

2. Type in `c:\` and press ENTER. That will bring you to the C:\ prompt.

3. Type in `MSD` (for Microsoft Diagnostics) and press ENTER.

4. Continue to press ENTER until the Main menu appears.

5. Press Alt D to view disk drive information. A screen will appear displaying your drive types.

Below is an example of a drives screen. This reports that a floppy disk drive exists, which is the A: drive. It also reports that there is a fixed disk, which is a hard disk drive. This is the C: drive. The C: drive has a total of 695 megabytes of disk space and 188 megabytes of free or available space. A CD-ROM drive also exists, which is the D: drive.

6. You should enter both the total and free fixed disk information on the inventory worksheet.

Note. You will see that the MSD utility also provides you with other needed inventory worksheet information. It includes the type, model, or version of the computer/BIOS, total amount of memory, video classification, network adapter type, mouse, and other adapters

7. To quit this screen and return to DOS, press the F3 key at the main menu.

Drive Type	Free Space	Total Size
A: Floppy Drive, 3.5" 1.44M, 80 Cylinders, 2 Heads, 512 Bytes/Sector, 18 Sectors/Track		
C: Fixed Disk, CMOS Type 1 707 Cylinders, 32 Heads, 512 Bytes/Sector, 63 Sectors/Track	188M	695M
D: CD-ROM Drive		

WINDOWS 3.11 PROCESS

To determine total and available hard disk space in Windows 3.11, you need to complete the following steps.

STEPS

1. Turn on your machine and start up Windows 3.11.

2. The Program Manager screen should display. If the Program Manager has been minimized, you will need to double-click and reopen that screen.

3. Click on File/Run.

4. On the run line, type in C:\WINDOWS\WINFILE.EXE and press ENTER. This will open the File Manager utility.

5. On the File Manager screen, click on Options.

6. Make sure the Status Bar option is turned on. If it is turned on there will be a ✓ mark next to "Status Bar." If there is no check, then click it to turn it on.

7. This option will display a bar on the bottom of the File Manager screen. Click on the different drive letters, starting with the C: drive, and read the information displayed in the bar area. Note the total and free drive space and enter it on the inventory worksheet. Complete the same steps if you have a D:, E:, or F: drive.

WINDOWS 95 PROCESS

STEPS

1. Turn on your computer.

2. Once Windows 95 loads, you will see an icon on your desktop labeled My Computer. Double-click your mouse button on My Computer.

3. A screen will open up and display all drives installed on your computer. Start by right-clicking on your C: drive, and then click on Properties. This will display information on the screen and will report used space and free space.

4. Fill in this information on the inventory worksheet.

5. If you have other hard drives such as D: or E:, repeat steps 3 and 4 for each drive.

Don't confuse a CD-ROM drive with a hard drive. The CD-ROM drive has a picture of a hard drive with a compact disk on top of it next to the drive letter.

Central Processing Unit Manufacturer Type and Speed

Many people think the CPU is the entire computer case. In fact, the computer case holds many different components. The CPU is a processor chip that resides on the main board or motherboard. The CPU is equivalent to the fuel injection kit on a race car. Most CPUs have a numbering scheme. Typically, the bigger the number, the faster the processor executes instructions.

To determine the CPU processor speed you have a few options.

> 1. The invoice or purchase slip
> 2. Manual inspection
> 3. The operating system

MANUAL INSPECTION

STEPS

1. Look at your computer cover. Many computers systems have numbers on the front of them.

   (a) Example: AST 4/66. This means the computer manufacturer is AST Corporation, and the machine is a 486 processor running at 66 megahertz.

   (b) Example: Gateway 2000 P5-90. This means that the computer manufacturer is Gateway Corporation and the machine is a Pentium processor running at 90 megahertz.

2. Write down the processor speed on your inventory worksheet.

MS-DOS AND WINDOWS 3.11 PROCESS

STEPS

1. Turn on your computer and wait for a command prompt. Type in c:\ and press ENTER. This will bring you to the C:\ prompt. (Note: If you are running Windows 3.11, you

must close the operating system by pressing ALT F4. This will bring you to a DOS prompt.)

2. Type in MSD (for Microsoft Diagnostics) and press ENTER.

3. Continue to press ENTER until the Main menu appears.

4. Press Alt-P to select Computer, and a screen will appear displaying information. Go to the line that is labeled Processor and copy this information on the inventory worksheet.

5. Press ENTER to exit back to the Main menu, and then press F3 to exit back to DOS.

WINDOWS 95 PROCESS

STEPS

1. Turn on your computer.

2. Once Windows 95 loads, you will see an icon labeled My Computer. Right-click your mouse button on My Computer.

3. The System Properties screen will be displayed. On this first screen is an area called COMPUTER:. Underneath the COMPUTER: area is the CPU information.

4. Enter this information on the inventory worksheet.

5. Click on Cancel to exit My Computer.

Read the documentation or contact the manufacturer if you have any questions or problems.

BIOS Manufacturer and Version Number

1. Power-on process
2. Operating system
3. CMOS setup

POWER-ON PROCESS

STEPS

Most computers list BIOS information on the screen when the system is powered on. This is the easiest way to determine BIOS manufacturer and version number.

1. Turn on your computer and read the upper left-hand corner of the screen.

2. If the BIOS information is displayed, write it down and enter it on the inventory sheet.

MS-DOS AND WINDOWS 3.11 PROCESS

STEPS

1. Turn on your computer and wait for a command prompt. Type in c:\ and press ENTER. This will bring you to the C:\ prompt. (Note: If you are running Windows 3.11, you must close the operating system by pressing Alt-F4. This will bring you to a DOS prompt.)

2. Type in MSD (for Microsoft Diagnostics) and press ENTER.

3. Press ENTER until the Main menu appears.

4. Press Alt C for Computer, and a screen displaying computer information will appear as shown below.

5. Copy the BIOS information onto your inventory worksheet.

6. Press ENTER to return to the Main menu, and then press F3 to exit to DOS.

Computer	
Computer Name:	American Megatrends
BIOS Manufacturer:	American Megatrends
BIOS Version:	BIOS Version 1.00.09.AX1
BIOS Version	1.00.09.AX1
BIOS Category:	IBM PC/AT
BIOS ID Bytes:	FC 01 00
BIOS Date:	07/25/94
Processor:	486DX
Math Coprocessor:	Internal
Keyboard:	Enhanced
Bus Type:	ISA/AT/Classic Bus

CMOS SETUP INFORMATION:

Please note the previous warning regarding modifications to the CMOS setup.

STEPS

1. Turn on your computer and enter into the CMOS Setup Utility. Access to your CMOS Setup screen varies. However, many systems display the keystrokes needed to enter the Setup Utility in the upper left-hand corners of their screens. If your system does not display this information, consult the manual that came with your computer. Don't be afraid to call your computer manufacturer for assistance if you are unable to locate this information.

2. Once you have entered the Setup area, you need to find out where the BIOS information is located. Computer CMOS Setup menus are different, so you might have to look around at different menu options to discover the BIOS information.

3. When you are done, you should exit the Setup Utility, but please *do not save any changes*.

PERIPHERALS INVENTORY

Hardware components other than the ones listed above are considered peripherals. These additional components may or may not be installed on your personal computer. Such peripherals include printers, scanners, fax machines, modems, backup devices, and many others. Although the majority of these peripherals will not be threatened by the year 2000 date problem, it is important to include them in the inventory checklist and test them for compliance. Consult the documentation or utility disks that came with the peripheral for more information. Make sure to include the manufacturer, model, serial number, version, and any other information that may prove useful when contacting the manufacturer.

TESTING FOR HARDWARE PROBLEMS

To ensure year 2000 compliance, even on a new computer, it is important to test all components. Remember, your personal computer is assembled from components that have been manufactured by different vendors. Some of these parts may have date problems. The only way to be absolutely sure all hardware, firmware, and peripherals are compliant is to manually test them. Although such testing is time-consuming and tedious, we cannot stress enough how important it is. Also, please don't assume a newer computer will not have any problems. No two computers are alike.

Hardware and Firmware

There are two very important tests that will check the ability of your hardware and firmware to correctly recognize and handle dates beyond December 31, 1999. The first is called the "Year 2000 Rollover Test." This test is done by changing the system clock, turning off your computer, and allowing the Real Time

Clock to pass into January 1, 2000, while your system is powered down. The second is a "Leap Year Test." This test is done by completing the same process, but rolling from February 28, 2000, into February 29, 2000, once again while the system is powered down.

Note. We highly recommend that you back up your computer system before you perform these tests.

YEAR 2000 ROLLOVER

STEPS

1. If you are connected to a network, turn off your PC and physically disconnect it from the network. You want your computer to run in standalone mode so your BIOS and operating system clocks are not being overwritten by a server's date or time.

2. Turn on your computer and enter into the CMOS Setup Utility. Access to your CMOS setup screen varies. However, many systems display the keystrokes needed to enter into the Setup Utility in the upper left-hand corners of their screens. If your system does not display this information, consult the manual that came with your computer. Don't be afraid to call your computer manufacturer for assistance if you are unable to locate this information.

3. Once you are at the CMOS Setup menu, locate the Date and Time option.

4. Change the date field to the following month/day/year setting: Dec 31 1999.

5. Change the time field to five minutes before midnight, using the following hours/minute/seconds settings: 23:55:00.

6. Exit the Setup screen, saving your changes. Your computer will then automatically complete the startup process.

7. After startup is complete, shut down your computer for at least 10 minutes.

8. Turn on the computer and issue the operating system command to view the date and time. The DOS DATE command will work for DOS, Windows 3.11, and Windows 95. It should report the date as 01-01-2000. If any other date is displayed your BIOS is not year 2000 compliant. You need to report the results of this test on your inventory sheet.

In step 8, the moment of truth has arrived. If the date and time settings reveal that it is a few minutes after midnight on January 1, 2000, your BIOS has successfully crossed the year 2000 barrier. If your settings report anything else, i.e., the year 1900 or 00 or 1980, your hardware/firmware has failed and is not year 2000 compliant. It is estimated that nearly 60% of existing PCs will fail this test. Also, the fact that you have a newly purchased PC does not guarantee it will have a compliant BIOS. Computers are assembled from many parts, some of which may have been manufactured well before they were installed in the system that you purchased. Don't worry; a BIOS fix may well be available that will save you from replacing the entire PC.

The Leap Year Test

Some programs may have problems with February 29, 2000, because they will incorrectly assume that 2000 is not a leap year. (Years divisible by 100 are not leap years, unless the year is also divisible by 400. This is referred as the "quad centennial leap year rule.") The year 2000 is a leap year.

To test for leap year compliance, complete the above PC test procedure, changing the System Setup date to 02-28-2000 and the time to 12:55:00, and power off your computer for 10 minutes. When you power back up, your computer should display 02-29-2000. If it displays 03-01-2000 or anything else, it has not passed the test.

Peripherals
With literally thousands of different types of peripherals and manufacturers, it is impossible for us to list all the possible test processes. If your system passes the year 2000 BIOS rollover test, one option is to test these peripherals while the BIOS date is still advanced into the year 2000. Do this by performing some normal processes involving use of these peripherals. However, the best course of action is to contact the manufacturers and ask them about the devices and their year 2000 compliance. At least pay attention to each component; put some thought into its importance and how it interacts with other devices.

 Note. Don't forget to change your date and time back to their original settings through CMOS/SETUP at the conclusion of your hardware tests.

AUTOMATED TESTER

Another way to test your computer's hardware/firmware for potential year 2000 problems is to use an automated diagnostic tool. Most of these tools allow you to insert a disk into your floppy drive and boot the computer. Upon bootup, the computer reads the disk and runs a program that performs multiple tests. These tests usually include the Year 2000 Rollover and the Leap Year Test. Such a tool is on the CD-ROM included with this book. Information about the use of the tool is detailed in Appendix I.

If Your Hardware Fails the Test
If your computer's BIOS fails the year 2000 rollover test, you must fix it before completing any further operating system, application, or data file tests. This is the only problem area that must be immediately addressed. If the hardware cannot process dates beyond the

year 2000 correctly, there is no assurance that any of your other testing will produce valid results.

At this point in the process you need to complete the hardware inventory and then contact the hardware manufacturer to obtain BIOS update options.

Refer to Appendixes B and E for manufacturer contact information. Also, see Chapter 15 to determine and implement solutions.

There are three possible options.

1. The manufacturer will provide you with a software fix, if one is available.

2. If a software fix is not available, a hardware fix may exist, such as the Millennium BIOS Board™. These boards are physically installed inside the computer box, and their function is to override the noncompliant BIOS. This type of fix usually costs less than $100.

3. A third, and certainly less attractive, option is to replace your system's motherboard. If this is the only option available, research the price of purchasing a new computer, because the cost may be comparable.

Usually, installing a BIOS software fix is much easier than installing a physical board into a computer. Many BIOS fixes are as simple as downloading a file onto a floppy diskette and then running a command that will cause the downloaded file to extract file information. From there you typically have to power off your computer, insert the diskette into your floppy disk drive, and then boot up your computer.

Please follow the detailed instructions provided by the manufacturer. We suggest you perform any of these update processes during the manufacturer's technical support phone hours. If you have any problems or questions during the process, contact them, and they can assist you in completing the process.

4 Operating System "The Boss"

THIS CHAPTER CONTAINS:

OPERATING SYSTEM DATE HANDLING

The operating system is the program that allows the computer to execute applications and manage data. In plain English, it's the piece of software that runs your computer.

When you start your computer, the operating system loads a portion of itself into memory and stays there the entire time your computer is running. While in memory, the operating system monitors your computer and acts like a traffic cop controlling all activity. It directs requests to/from software applications, hardware/firmware components, peripheral devices, and memory. Basically, the operating system is the boss.

Even so, the operating system does rely on other software programs and hardware components to help carry out its duties. The Real Time Clock (CMOS/RTC) and Basic Input/Output System (BIOS) help the operating system perform specific tasks. For example, creating a new file on a hard disk or copying a file to and from floppy drives requires assistance from the BIOS. The BIOS and CMOS/RTC were previously discussed, and you should already have checked them for year 2000 compliance.

When your computer is powered off, the operating system is not running. It is not loaded or present in memory and therefore is incapable of performing any tasks. The operating system relies on the Real Time Clock (RTC) to keep track of the date and time while the system is not running. The RTC uses an internal battery for power to continue to count seconds, minutes, hours, and days while the computer is powered down.

When your computer is powered on, the RTC passes the date to the BIOS, which passes it to the operating system. From that point forward while the computer is running, the operating system maintains its own clock and counts seconds, minutes, hours, and days. The operating system comes with functions for maintaining and changing the date and time. Therefore, a user may change the date, and the operating system will turn around and update the BIOS, which will turn around and update the RTC. When this is done, the date setting is permanently changed.

Software applications get their date from making a call to the operating system. In rare instances an application may jump over the operating system and make a direct call to the BIOS or RTC. The majority of the software on your computer is relying on the operating system for the current date and time. If there's a problem with your operating system, there's a good chance all software on your computer will fail. However, each software application is different and needs specific attention. Make sure you read Chapter 5, "Home and Office Software Applications," and test all applications independently.

Here's a review of the process:

- The computer is turned on, which makes the date and time information held in the CMOS/RTC Settings accessible to the BIOS.
- The operating system then loads and asks the BIOS for the date and time.
- Applications ask the operating system for the date and time.

OPERATING SYSTEM INVENTORY

As your computer powers on and the operating system starts to load, the operating system will display its name. Some will report Windows 95, Windows NT, MS-DOS, Windows 98, or Windows 3.11. Many operating systems have a Help area where you can select an About option. This option will report the operating system name, manufacturer, and version.

Many operating systems have different version numbers. This information is important when dealing with vendors regarding fix options. Use one of the following steps to determine the computer operating system version information.

DETERMINING OPERATING SYSTEM VERSIONS

MS-DOS PROCESS

STEPS

1. Turn on your computer and wait for a DOS prompt.

2. Type in the command VER and press the ENTER key. This will display what version of DOS you are running.

3. Record this on the inventory worksheet.

WINDOWS 3.11 PROCESS

STEPS

1. Start up Windows 3.11. The first screen that will open is the Program Manager Window. This is the main window that holds other program groups and application options.

2. Click the Help option on the menu.

3. Click on About to display the Windows version.

4. Record this on the inventory worksheet.

WINDOWS 95 PROCESS

STEPS

1. Turn on your machine, and the Windows 95 main desktop screen will appear.

2. Right—click on the My Computer icon.

3. Select the Properties menu option.

4. This will display the System Properties screen. The screen will display "Microsoft Windows 95™" and below that line will report the version information. Record this information on your Inventory Worksheet.

TESTING FOR OPERATING SYSTEM PROBLEMS

Testing the operating system is the only real way to determine if there's a problem. There are two very important tests that will check your operating system's ability to recognize dates in the year 2000. The first, called the "Year 2000 Rollover Test," is done by changing the operating system's date and time and passing into January 1, 2000, while the system is powered on. The second, the "Leap Year Test," is done by changing the operating system's date and time and passing into March 1, 2000, while the system is powered on.

Year 2000 Rollover Test

To do the Rollover Test, use the operating system command to change the date and time. Set the date to December 31, 1999, and the time to 23:55:00. After 10 minutes, check the operating system's date and time. It should be January 1, 2000, 12:05am. If the operating system is not year 2000 compliant, you will get incorrect year information such as 1900 or 1980.

CHANGING THE OPERATING SYSTEM'S DATE AND TIME

MS-DOS PROCESS

STEPS

1. Turn on your computer and wait for a command prompt.

2. Type in the command DATE and press the ENTER Key.

3. Type in 12-31-1999 and press ENTER. Note: Earlier versions of DOS may require you to type in 12-31-99.

4. Type in the command TIME and press the ENTER key.

5. Type in 23:55:00 and press ENTER.

6. Wait 10 minutes and then type in the command DATE and press the ENTER key. The date should display 01-01-2000.

7. After the test, do not forget to change the system back to the current date and time.

WINDOWS 3.11 PROCESS

To change the Date for Windows 3.11, you need to complete the following steps.

 Note. Windows 3.11 requires a date change at the DOS level to process four-digit year changes. You cannot change the date in the Windows 3.11 Control Panel Date area, because it only supports two-digit years.

STEPS

1. Start up Windows 3.11. The first screen that opens is the Program Manager Window, the main window that holds other program groups and application options.

2. Double-click on the group Main.

3. Double-click on Control Panel.

4. Double-click on MS-DOS prompt.

5. This will bring you to a command prompt.

6. Type in the command DATE and press the ENTER key.

7. Type in 12-31-1999 and then press the ENTER key.

8. Type in TIME and press the ENTER key.

9. Type in 23:55:00 and press the ENTER Key.

10. Wait 10 minutes, then type in the command DATE and press the ENTER key. Check and see if the date is correctly reporting 01-01-2000.

11. After the test is complete, do not forget to change the system back to the current date/time.

12. Record the operating system pass/fail status on the inventory.

13. Type in EXIT and press the ENTER key to return to Windows 3.11.

WINDOWS 95 PROCESS

STEPS

1. Turn on your computer and the Windows 95 main desktop screen will appear.

2. Click on Start/Settings/Control Panel.

3. Double-click on the Regional Settings Option.

4. Click on the Date Tab option.

5. Two date formats are presented on the screen. Change the Short Date Style to "M/d/yyyy". Change the Long Date Style to "dddd,mmmm,dd,yyyy".

6. Click on Apply and then click on OK.

7. This will return you to the Control Panel Group. Click on the Date/Time icon.

8. Change the month to January, change the year to 1999, and click on the 31st day. Change the time to 11:55:00 pm. Then click on Apply and OK.

9. Wait 10 minutes and then click on the Date/Time icon. Check to see if the date is January 1, 2000.

10. Record the operating system pass/fail status on the inventory worksheet.

11. Then set your time back to the current date and time.

Leap Year Test

The year 2000 is a leap year, so we recommend setting your current date and time to February 28, 2000, 23:55:00, and waiting 10 minutes. Again check the operating system's date and time and verify that it reads February 29, 2000, 12:05am. Refer to the above operating system steps for changing the date and time to February 28, 2000, and the time to 23:55:00.

Do not confuse the preceding two tests with the Rollover and Leap Year Test in the Hardware/Firmware section. One tests the hardware while the other tests the operating system. There is a big difference.

Refer to Appendixes C and E for manufacturer contact information. Also, see Chapter 15, which will help you determine and implement solutions.

AUTOMATED TESTER

Another way to test your computer's operating system for potential year 2000 problems is to use an automated diagnostic tool. Most of these tools allow you to insert a disk into your floppy drive and boot the computer. Upon bootup, the computer reads the disk and runs a program that performs multiple tests. These tests usually include the "Year 2000 Rollover" and "Leap Year" tests. Such a tool has been included on the CD that accompanies this book. Information about the use of the tool is given in Appendix I.

OPERATING SYSTEM YEAR 2000 STATUS

Regardless of whether your operating system passed the rollover and leap year tests, most still have year 2000 issues. Known problems exist even in the latest versions of these products that could result in application processing or command errors. The only way to be certain is to contact the manufacturer or visit its Web site for a complete list of all known problems.

Here are a few of the MS-DOS 6.22 problems:

- Four-digits cannot be displayed using the DIR command.
- The DATE command won't allow you to enter two-digit year values between 00 and 79. It forces you to enter a four-digit year.

The Windows 3.11 problems include these:

- A new version of WINFILE.EXE is needed to support year 2000 date preparation. This can be obtained from the net address *ftp://ftp.microsoft.com/softlib/mslfiles*.
- The DATE/TIME property inside the Control Panel does not allow you to change the date beyond the year 99.

A few of the Windows 95 problems are as follows:

- A new version of WINFILE.EXE is needed to support year 2000 date preparation. This can be obtained from the net address *ftp://ftp.microsoft.com/softlib/mslfiles*.
- Explorer (EXPLORER.EXE) will not display a four-digit year unless the Short Date in the Control Panel has been set to a four-digit year.
- The DATE command won't allow you to enter two-digit year values between 00 and 79. It forces you to enter a four-digit year.

Here is a Windows 98 problem:

- When the Regional Settings from Control Panel are set to use two-digit years, the DATE/TIME Picker function may not return the proper date.

You have two options to fix this last problem. Set the regional settings to four-digit date handling, or update COMCTL32.DLL to the latest version. You can obtain this updated file by going to the following Web address:

http://www.microsoft.com/msdownload/ieplatform/ie/comctrl.asp

 Note. A Windows 98 "date rollover" problem was recently reported by Microsoft. As of the time that research for this book was completed a solution had not been posted on the Microsoft web site. The problem could cause the operating system's calendar date to incorrectly jump ahead or backwards by 1or 2 days when the date rollover occurs. Check the Microsoft web address listed in Apprendix C for more current information about this problem and its fix.

CHAPTER

5 Home and Office Software Applications

THIS CHAPTER CONTAINS:

- Software Application and Dates
- Version Information
- Determining Software Compliance
- Different Types of Software
- Software Inventory
- Summary

51

Software applications are a predefined set of instructions that can perform a certain set of functions or activities when loaded into a computer's memory. Software applications cannot run without computer hardware.

It is common practice to refer to a personal computer as a "computer system." A computer system actually includes the central processing unit, hard drive, CMOS/RTC and BIOS, monitor, keyboard, and other peripherals, along with the operating system, which is a unique class of software. We addressed the operating system software in the previous chapter. This chapter focuses on other classes of software.

SOFTWARE APPLICATION AND DATES

When an application is first executed or loaded, it is unaware of the current date and time. In order to obtain the current date and time, applications make a call to the operating system or BIOS, which returns the date and time information. Once this information is retrieved, the application may store and run its own clock, or it may continually make calls to the operating system and/or BIOS. In Chapter 3 and 4 we discussed the operating system and BIOS and explained how to test them for problems. By now you should have already inventoried and evaluated your CMOS/RTC, BIOS, and operating system.

As mentioned earlier, memory and storage restrictions forced software developers to store dates in a six-digit format. It was, and in many cases still is, common practice to use a two-digit representation for the year. As memory and storage technologies progressed, so did software. Developers saw the year 2000 coming and knew they must store dates in an eight-digit format. New versions of software were produced and upgrades became available. However, many software applications continue to use six-digit dates even though they are capable of getting eight-digit dates from the operating system or BIOS. Unless these applications are identified and upgraded to recognize the correct century, errors or incorrect processing results may occur.

Some questions you should be asking yourself are:

- Is the software I'm using year 2000 compliant?
- If it's not, is a compliant version available that I can upgrade to?
- How do I determine if my software is or isn't compliant?
- How do I determine what upgrade options are available?

We will soon show you how to answer these questions.

DIFFERENT TYPES OF SOFTWARE

Aside from your operating system, each software application you are using can be categorized as one of the following:

- Commercial off-the-shelf software (COTS)
- Industry-specific software
- Custom-developed software
- Homegrown software

Commercial Off-the-Shelf Software (COTS)

This is the most widely used type of software and is available in electronic, computer, and media stores. Major manufacturers such as Microsoft, Lotus, Corel, IBM, and many others develop these titles. This type of software includes such products as spreadsheets, word processors, database tools, personal organizers, and desktop publishers. Most of these are now available in suite packages such as

Microsoft Office, Lotus SmartSuite, and Corel Suite. The majority of your home and office software will fall into this category.

Industry-Specific Software	This is software designed specifically for a single industry. Example applications are medical billing or claims processing, commercial insurance policy issue, gasoline consumption, manufacturing, and professional services. The developers of these applications are not broadly known to the general public, but are better known within their industry.
Custom-Developed Software	This is software designed by a developer specifically for you. Either it's designed from the ground up, or it's a prepacked application that has been modified to fit your needs. Development of this type of software would have required a close relationship between you/your company and a software developer.
Homegrown Software	This software is usually developed in-house by an end user with some programming skills using development tools such as BASIC, C/C++, COBOL, Fortran, Pascal, database managers, or any line of visual tools. It may have undergone extensive modification over a number of years.

VERSION INFORMATION

Most software applications are developed using a version numbering scheme. The first release of an application may be version 1. The next release may be version 2, then 3 and so on. Each manufacturer or developer should publish, or be able to provide you with, information regarding the year 2000 and when (at what version) their software became compliant.

It is very important that you determine the name, manufacturer, and version number of all applications you use. After you complete your testing you may find some software to be noncompliant. When you deal with manufacturers, they will ask you for the following information:

- The application's name and version number
- The operating system name and version
- How much memory, processor speed, and hard-disk space you have available

This information is essential because the upgrade and migration path to year 2000 compliance may require a change in hardware, operating system, and software. Also, you must ensure that one product's environment requirements do not conflict with what's needed to continue running other software products that check out okay.

SOFTWARE INVENTORY

Let's start with the software inventory. Determine the title, manufacturer and version for all applications and enter this information on your inventory worksheet. The simplest way for finding this information is by reading the Technical Manuals that came with the software. Other areas which list this information are the application startup screen or "splash screen," on-line help text, and the "About" function.

Application Startup Screen or Splash Screen

This is a window, box, or a few lines of text that are automatically displayed when the software is first executed. These screens are sometimes called splash screens. They usually stay on the computer monitor for a few seconds and list valuable information about the application and the manufacturer. This typically includes the product title and version/release number.

On-Line Help Text

On-line help text usually mirrors the information contained in the technical manual documentation that came with your software. Help text is most commonly invoked by selecting the Help Command off the menu bar at the top of your screen, or by pressing the F1 key or a hot key while running your application. A hot key is a combination of keystrokes that invokes a function, for example, CNTRL+F1 or SHIFT+F2. Once inside the help text, look for information regarding title, manufacturer, and version number.

"About" Function

In some newer products, when you select the Help command, it provides a menu option called "About." This is a function that displays a window or box with information concerning the application and manufacturer.

DETERMINING SOFTWARE COMPLIANCE

After you have identified all of your software applications, you need to test them to find out if they can correctly handle dates beyond December 31, 1999. If you do not have the time or patience to test each of your software products, you should at least research vendor claims about whether or not the products are compliant. You must also determine whether they achieved "year 2000 readiness" by using some sort of base-year or century windowing technique. You can then assess whether this will affect the way you use the software and the results it might generate. Chapter 7 provides tips and techniques on how some popular products recognize and handle date information and will help you to determine how or if your usage of these products will result in problems. For now, let's focus on testing tips and techniques to help you plan and execute a thorough test.

Since you may or may not know if your software is year 2000 compliant, the best way to determine this is to test it yourself. It's impossible for us to give an example for every application ever designed, but we can explain what a good test would involve and suggest some testing approaches and techniques to help you complete your year 2000 problem determination efforts.

DATE-SENSITIVE TESTING

A good test is one that involves *date-sensitive* testing. Planning and executing thorough date-sensitive tests includes the following:

Note. If your computer is connected to a network, then you must disconnect it and reboot before executing any tests.

STEPS

1. Define actual test case scenarios that involve processing date information. This information may be entered from the keyboard, or by reading a file residing on disk. If you are using the software product, think about how you normally rely on it to process date data. Do you input, sort, or display date information anywhere? Do you execute some series of functions based on date values? Do you use it to call a macro or function that uses or returns date information? Think about what would happen if the software were to erroneously interpret a year of "00" as 1900 instead of 2000. Write down these scenarios.

2. Establish a series of date values with which to test each of these scenarios. Refer to the following tables for a list of test dates that will help you develop a thorough test plan. It may

also be helpful to create an actual test matrix that identifies each test scenario and the various date conditions that you will input and validate results for.

3. Complete date testing for each of the identified scenarios without making any changes to your operating system or BIOS date. Review results to determine whether they are accurate. Record the results on the inventory worksheet.

4. Your next step is to complete the same tests after you have changed your operating system or BIOS date beyond the year 2000. Refer to the previous chapter for steps needed to change this date. Once again, validate results and record them on the inventory worksheet.

5. For industry-specific or custom-developed software, consider contacting the developer to request a copy of their year 2000 test case conditions. This of course assumes the developer has taken steps to ensure the product is year 2000 compliant.

Note. Remember to change your operating system date back to the current date after testing is complete. Also, delete any files that were created during the testing process because you do not know what impact they might have on your normal operating conditions.

Figure 5-1 will identify dates you should incorporate into your test process because they help you pinpoint common failure points when a product in not year 2000 compliant.

Transition Date Table

If year 2000 dates are not being processed correctly, you will be able to identify this by their inability to pass from one date to the appropriate next date on several key transition dates. Table 5-1 lists these dates.

Make sure you include all of these in your test scenarios.

Transition Start Date	Expected Next Date
6/30/99	7/1/99
9/9/99	10/1/99
12/31/99	1/1/2000
2/28/2000	2/29/2000
2/29/2000	3/1/2000
6/30/2000	7/1/2000
12/30/2000	12/31/2000
12/31/2000	1/1/2001
2/28/2001	3/1/2001
2/29/2004	3/1/2004

FIGURE *Transition date table.*
5-1

Cross-Millennium Tests

It is also important your tests include cross-millennium test conditions.

There are two different forms of cross-millennium testing that you will be concerned with. The first is a sorting situation where the input data contains dates both before and after the year 2000. The second involves date calculations in which the input contains dates that should be advanced from the 20th to the 21st century. An example of this is a billing system test in which you enter a customer record with a bill date of December 12, 1999. The next bill due date is in 30 days. See if the system calculates the next due date as January 11, 2000. If your software is not year 2000 compliant, many different dates may result. Most likely you will get a date in 1900.

Regardless of the outcome of your testing, you should also contact the manufacturer for additional compliance information. Chapter 13 provides further guidance on the types of information you need to request.

Remember, manufacturers and their resellers will provide information regarding an upgrade or migration path to fix any problems you may have found. There are various ways to contact a software vendor:

- Technical support phone number
- Internet Web site
- E-mail
- Postal mail

Refer to Appendixes C and E for manufacturer contact information.

SUMMARY

The steps outlined in this chapter were designed to assist you in creating your software application inventory, developing a thorough test plan, and executing date-sensitive test scenarios to pinpoint year 2000 date-handling problems. Each application will have different problems and require different solutions. The paths to resolution of these problems will be addressed in Chapter 15. However, we must first identify and evaluate files containing date information. To achieve year 2000 compliance, the date information on these files may need to be expanded from six- to eight-digit formats or converted into a format required by the year 2000 compliant version of the software application. Identification and evaluation of these files is addressed in the next chapter. Let's proceed.

CHAPTER

Data Files

THIS CHAPTER
CONTAINS:

- Overview
- Creating Your File Inventory
- Reviewing File Content

- Steps to Identify and Evaluate Your Data Files
- Evaluating Field Expansion and Migration Needs

OVERVIEW

Before you consider upgrading your software to make it year 2000 compliant, you need to determine whether the data files you expect to use with the upgraded software require any type of conversion or date field expansions. How date information is stored in a file and how a software application interprets that data are highly interdependent. The next chapter more thoroughly explores the software and date data interdependency issues for commercial off-the-shelf software products. It also provides examples that should help you to understand why there must be consistency between how date information is stored on a file and how it is interpreted by the software product that reads it as input.

This chapter focuses on the steps you can take to pinpoint files that may present inconsistencies and migration problems. It outlines inventory and evaluation techniques. It also discusses some of the issues and pitfalls you need to be aware of in deciding how to handle associated date field format modifications.

This is an aspect of the year 2000 problem resolution effort that requires your close attention. How do you determine what files are used or accessed by which software products? Why is it important to understand how your software interprets date information? Are there any products or techniques that will assist you in your file inventory and evaluation efforts? Will you need to expand date fields in every situation? These are the questions that will be examined and addressed in the following material.

STEPS TO IDENTIFY AND EVALUATE YOUR DATA FILES

Once you've determined that a particular software product is noncompliant, your next step is to determine whether any files created or accessed by the noncompliant version of the product will need to be modified. Of course, if you aren't going to use the files that were developed by the old version of the software, then there is absolutely no need to inventory or review these files.

However, before you can make decisions about which files need to be modified, you first need to do the following:

1. Determine what files, macros, or external functions were created or are accessed by each of the software products previously found to be noncompliant.

2. Identify which ones are going to be read or accessed by a modified version of the software.

3. Test or review the contents of those files to identify any date fields that do not contain four-digit century values or formats.

4. Evaluate how the replacement or upgraded software will interpret and use the date field input identified in step 3.

CREATING YOUR FILE INVENTORY

Steps 1 and 2 involve creating an inventory of the files that may require date field conversion work. You need to be as thorough as possible in identifying all of the files that will be accessed by the software you plan to upgrade, modify, or replace.

We have not been able to find a tool that can scan a personal computer or Local Area Network server file directory and automatically associate *every single file* listed in the directory with the software products that read or use them. A couple of vendors offer tools with scanning and file-matching capabilities that work well for some of the more common software products. If you followed the file naming standards provided by your software manufacturer, then you can rely on such a tool to automate some of your inventory work. Refer to Chapter 14 and Appendix G for more information regarding these tools. However, if you are running industry-specific or homegrown applications on your computer, you will have to use some manually assisted techniques to complete your file identification and review process.

Obviously, knowing the names of the files you are looking for or having some other means of identifying which files were produced or accessed by a given software product will help tremendously. Personal computer and server operating system software, as well as most commercial off-the-shelf software, uses standard file-name extensions to differentiate their files from products' files. A file-name extension consists of a "." usually followed by three alphanumeric characters, which is added to the end of the file name defined by the user. Typically these file extensions also identify the type of information contained in the file or they designate a file format type that is common to a variety of products.

For example, Microsoft Word will automatically append a ".doc" extension to whatever unique document file name you assign. So if you created a document and saved it with the name "file1," Word stores it with the name "file1.doc." An ".xls" file extension contains Excel spreadsheet information. A ".com" file usually contains operating system commands. Files with a ".txt" extension contain information that is stored in text file format. Some products use different file-name extensions for different versions or releases of the same product. Most software products also allow you to override their standard three-letter extensions. In those cases, you should know the file names and extensions you assigned.

Start the inventory process by first identifying which software products were found to be noncompliant. Then identify where the files associated with each of these software products are physically stored. They may be on your computer's hard drive, on a separate shared file server that your personal computer is connected to, or on some type of external storage device such as a floppy disk or CD. You will need to review the directory associated with each physical storage location to obtain a complete list of files.

Let's take a moment to explain what a directory is and its use. Think of the directory as a file cabinet. Each branch of the directory equates to a file cabinet drawer, which may contain a variety of different files or folders. On your personal computer, each directory points to an area of computer storage that contains files related to software products. Like a file cabinet, most directories have some type of logical organization. Some users organize their directory structures by product type so they can quickly identify and easily select any needed data files when running the software. If you've done this, then your inventory process should be quite simple. If you haven't done this, and also have no idea which directories contain the files you need, then you are going to have to review all the directories one by one.

Another technique to determine directory file locations for a specific application is to start the application and then complete a file save process. The application will typically display the default directory location where it saves files created by the user. Please note that some older applications will not provide the directory default location when you complete the file save process.

If you have actively used a product to create or store files containing data or macros, you are probably familiar with that product's standard set of file-name extensions, or you know what file names you used. If not, review the product manual or contact the manufacturer to find out what default extensions your product uses for various types of file information.

Once you have an idea of what you're looking for, use the appropriate operating system commands to view your computer hard-disk file directory structure. Fully expand each directory branch to its lowest level and scan the lists of files one by one to identify files with the names or extensions you are looking for. If you aren't sure whether a file contains date fields, values, or functions, then record its full directory path/file name on your inventory worksheet. Please note that a Software File Inventory Worksheet is included in Appendix A for your use.

There are also two other pieces of information that you need to record on the worksheet along with each file entry:

- One is the name of any other software applications that also read this file. This is important because, if you eventually determine you need to convert or expand some date field information contained on the file, then you also need to assess the impact this will have on the other software product. For example, suppose you have a Word document with an embedded Excel worksheet. When you make changes to the Excel worksheet, those changes are automatically passed to the Word document. In this scenario, you will need to be concerned with both applications. Another situation is if this file is used to pass data electronically to another party, i.e., an electronic data interchange. If it contains date information whose format must be changed, this will need to be coordinated with the party who is receiving and processing the file information.

- The second piece of information you need to record is the file's format type. You will need to know this in order to evaluate how the upgraded software will interpret the date information contained in the file. As you will learn in the next chapter, software products have different ways of interpreting date information presented in various formats. The following table identifies some common file format types and associated file-name extensions.

Don't forget, if your computer is connected to a file server and you save files to the network, then you also need to inventory these directories. Scan each one and record any files meeting your established review criteria.

Once again, if you know which directories contain your candidate files, then you don't need to perform the full directory structure search. Just go straight to the directories that contain your lists of files and review what's there. Repeat this process for each product. When you're finished with the inventory process your worksheet will contain a list of files associated with each software application.

Once you've identified all possible candidate files associated with each piece of software, you are ready to move on to the content review and evaluation phase.

File Extension	File Format Type
.doc	Microsoft Word
.doc	Word Perfect
.wpd	Word Perfect
.dot	Microsoft Word Template file
.xls	Microsoft Excel
.ppt	Microsoft PowerPoint
.wk1 .wk2 .wk3 .wk4	Lotus
.txt	Text file
.wps	Works
.csv	Comma Delimited file
.wq1	Quattro Pro
.dbf	DBASE
.bmp	Bit map
.rtf	Rich Text Format
.prn	Print File (space delimited text)
.xlw	Microsoft Excel Worksheet

FIGURE *File extension identification table.*
6-1

REVIEWING FILE CONTENT

This is where you really get under the hood and examine what's there. You must review the content of each file to determine if it has date-related information and how the information is stored and defined. Depending on the product or file type, different tools or methods can be used. Following are some suggested techniques for examining your file data.

- Files associated with a commercial off-the-shelf software product can be manually reviewed by running the software, opening the file, and fully examining its contents. Note: If you are running an operating system that has the File Manager or Windows Explorer utilities, you should be able to go straight to the file directory and double-click on the file you want to review. This automatically launches the software and opens and loads the selected file.

- Visually scan the data:

  1. If it's a spreadsheet application, move from cell to cell and check all information displayed with a date format. If the cell contains any functions or macros that involve date processing calculations or sorts, check to ensure that they correctly process century information. Any cell locations displaying two-digit years or involving macros or functions that compute two-digit year values should be recorded on your Software File Inventory Worksheet.

  2. If it's a database file, look at all fields to see if they contain date information and also review any stored queries, views, forms, reports, macros, or called modules associated with the database. If a field contains a two-digit year, record it on your Software File Inventory Worksheet.

Obviously this manual file review approach can be time-consuming but it is thorough. If you prefer some automated assistance, our research uncovered a couple of tools advertised as being designed to scan files for date-specific items. Again, refer to Chapter 14 and Appendix G for more information on tools and testers. Evaluation copies of some of these products are included on our enclosed CD.

We realize some vendors may still be developing or are just now introducing new tools to help their customers deal with their date identification and year 2000 migration efforts. Therefore, you may want to visit your software manufacturer's Web site to search for availability of other date analysis tools before you begin your file content review and evaluation.

For files created or accessed by industry-specific or custom-developed software products, first review the product documentation material provided by the developer. It should identify and include the record layouts for each file created, stored, or accessed by the software product. If any of the files have fields containing date information, review the format to ensure that it accommodates a four-digit year. If not, document the name of the noncompliant date fields on your Software File Inventory Worksheet.

If the file information is not available, contact the vendor. Request that they provide you with this information, or else give you a tool or some guidance on how to scan for and evaluate dates contained in their software files.

EVALUATING FIELD EXPANSION AND MIGRATION NEEDS

The final step is to understand how a modified or compliant version of the software might interpret and process the two-digit date information contained in these files, so you can determine whether the date fields need to be converted or expanded. This also involves assessing whether the date information is really important to the process you expect the software to perform. For example, the software may print a two-digit date at the top of a memo or a report. If it prints "1/1/00," it's unlikely that anyone will imagine this means the year 1900.

The next chapter is designed to help you complete the final step of the file evaluation process. Read the chapter to understand how some common software products handle date information. Also, if a compliant version of the software is available, try to obtain and review migration-related documentation provided by the manufacturer. Try to understand how different file format types, macros, and functions manipulate date information. Once you do this, go back to your file inventory worksheet and evaluate field expansion and macro or function replacement needs.

CHAPTER

7

Commercial Off-the-Shelf Products: Tips and Techniques

THIS CHAPTER CONTAINS:

- Overview
- Database Software
- General Groupware

- Spreadsheet Software
- Word-Processing Software
- Other COTS: Financial, Payroll and Mail

OVERVIEW

As described in Chapter 1, there is a significant difference between being year 2000 compliant and year 2000 ready, especially in the realm of commercial off-the-shelf products, or COTS as they are commonly called. Many manufacturers claim that their products are year 2000 compliant, but very few, if any, will back this claim with a warranty or guarantee. In fact, most will identify their product as being compliant and in the next breath say, "But if you don't use our product properly, we bear no responsibility for any losses and/or damages." For the most part, a manufacturer that makes the claim of compliance is simply saying, "Our product can handle four-digit years into the 21st century."

As a personal computer user, you may not see which COTS might be affected by the "Millennium Bug." In fact, any product is susceptible, whether the manufacturer claims it is compliant or not.

As stated in Chapter 1, there are six areas of concern when you are dealing with the year 2000 problem. If any one of these areas fails to accommodate the transition into the year 2000, the compliance of your products could be jeopardized. Here is the simplest of examples. Your PC's BIOS is not compliant and rolls over to 1980 (if you're lucky) on the turn of the century. Now any software that retrieves a date stamp from your system will be using the invalid current date.

So, before you attempt to verify that your COTS are compliant, it is important to verify that your system's clock, BIOS, operating system and any peripherals are compliant. The other areas of concern, data files and other interactive software, can be addressed while evaluating your COTS.

Here is one last important fact that very often gets overlooked. Even if every piece of hardware and software on your computer is compliant, the way a product is used can affect its compliance as much as any external factors.

The objective of this chapter is to provide you, as a personal computer user, with simple tips and techniques to ensure that your COTS are being utilized in a truly compliant manner. Some of the more popular software titles are covered; however, the provided tips and techniques should apply to almost any year 2000 compliant COTS. When you've finished this chapter, you should be able to identify and correct many of the common date problems affecting your products.

The Products

This chapter covers six different categories of commercial off-the-shelf products: spreadsheet, database, word processing, groupware, mail, financial, and payroll software. In each of these categories, some of the industry's most popular titles will be covered.

For each title covered, information about the manufacturer and different versions will be discussed. Additionally, tips, techniques, and suggestions will be provided wherever possible.

SPREADSHEET SOFTWARE

What Is a Spreadsheet?

A spreadsheet or worksheet is a document consisting of a grid of cells arranged in rows and columns. These cells contain four types of information: text, numeric, and date values, as well as formulas that define how one cell relates to other cells. This design was originally developed for maintaining financial information, but the possible applications for documents of this type are endless.

Spreadsheet software such as Excel, LOTUS 1-2-3, and Quattro Pro provide a means of creating and updating such documents. Each of these products has a set of functions and tools that let the user quickly and easily populate and tailor spreadsheets to accomplish any number of tasks

	A	B	C	D
1	12/31/29	47483	12/31/2029	12/31/29
2	1/1/30	10959	1/1/1930	1/1/30
3	1/1	35796	1/1/1998	1/1/98
4	1/1/1990 12:20 AM	32874.01389	1/1/1990	1/1/90
5	0	0	1/0/1900	1/0/00
6	1/1/1900	1	1/1/1900	1/1/00
7	1-1-2000	36526	1/1/2000	1/1/00

FIGURE *Examples of how data is input, stored, and displayed in Excel 97.*
7-1

How Is Data Handled by Spreadsheets?

Values are input, stored, and displayed in spreadsheets in very different ways. When a value is entered into a cell, the spreadsheet application first attempts to interpret the entered value as a number or date. If the entered value is in a valid date or numeric format, the spreadsheet application converts and stores the cell contents in a format it will recognize; otherwise, the result is left as text. After storage, the spreadsheet application then displays the cell contents using either a default format or a format the user has assigned to the cell. This process is demonstrated in Figure 7.1.

The values in Column A represent the actual data entered by the user. Upon pressing the ENTER or Tab key, the spreadsheet application interprets the entry and stores the values represented in Column B. Columns C and D illustrate how the cells would be displayed if the cells default formats were set at "m/d/yyyy" and "m/d/yy", respectively.

Pinpointing the Problem Areas

The majority of spreadsheet applications have an internal date format that will handle dates in both the 20th and 21st centuries, leading most manufacturers to claim that their products are compliant. However, the manufacturers make it clear that all dates must be expanded to include a four-digit year to ensure compliance. Unfortunately, this alone does not guarantee that your dates are stored with the correct century.

There are three problem areas:

1. User entry of two-digit years
2. Entry of two-digit years from text or comma-delimited files
3. Date functions and macros

Problem: User entry of two-digit years

Even with the expansion to a four-digit year, the user is generally not restricted from entering a two-digit year. If a two-digit year is entered, the spreadsheet application will apply its rules of interpretation to determine the default century. Therefore, you, as the user, must understand how your product makes this interpretation.

This may not seem like a major problem, especially when the derived century will be displayed upon completion of a date entry. However, it provides the opportunity for unintended errors.

Problem: Entry of two-digit years from text or comma-delimited files

Text or comma-delimited file formats save only the text and values as they would be displayed in cells of an active spreadsheet. Unlike true spreadsheets, these files don't retain the internal date formats. Figure 7-2 demonstrates how a comma-delimited file containing dates will be saved.

	A	B
1	12/31/2029	12/31/29
2	1/1/2030	1/1/30
3	12/31/1929	12/31/29
4	1/1/1930	1/1/30

```
12/31/2029,12/31/29
1/1/2030,1/1/30
12/31/1929,12/31/29
1/1/1930,1/1/30
```

Figure *Example of a spreadsheet saved as a comma-delimited file.*
7-2

As you can see, all the dates were written to the file just as they were displayed in the spreadsheet cell. The dates in column A were expanded to display the century; thus, the comma-delimited file retained the century. However, the dates in column B didn't retain the century.

When files of this type are read in or imported into a spreadsheet, they are handled as if the user keyed each cell in. Thus, as each cell is populated, the loaded value will be interpreted, stored, and displayed. Therefore, if the file contains dates without century information, such as the values in column B in the figure, the spreadsheet application will be forced to determine the century. For this reason, you need to ensure either that dates in the text file contain century information, or that the correct century will be interpreted in all situations.

PROBLEM: DATE FUNCTIONS AND MACROS

Each spreadsheet product lets you automate tasks and formulate complex calculations by using functions and macros. Among these are various date functions, which may or may not interpret two-digit years by the same rules the spreadsheet application uses to evaluate entered date data.

Additionally, the most recent releases of products such as Excel and Lotus 1-2-3 provide rich macro programming environments containing their own sets of date functions. These date functions don't necessarily follow the same windowing rules as the spreadsheet software or its date functions.

This problem is the most difficult of the three to correct, especially for users with limited technical skills. If you're using a spreadsheet supplied by someone else, you may have to go to the source for help in identifying any date calculations. However, if you created the spreadsheet, you should be able to identify the date functions and any macros that might be susceptible to the "Millennium Bug."

General Spreadsheet Tips and Techniques

WHAT YOU SEE IS WHAT YOU GET!

Expanding dates to include the century should be the first step in ensuring you're using your spreadsheet application in a compliant manner. This practice accomplishes two important tasks: letting you see the century of your date data, and guaranteeing that any text output of your date data will include the century.

Three areas must be addressed to accomplish date expansion. The first is the operating system default date format (steps to change this setting are detailed in Chapter 4). The second and third areas are the default date formats applied to whole worksheet and those applied to each cell in a worksheet. The cell formats override the worksheet formats, and the worksheet formats override the operating system settings. To easily identify cells with date display formats, first change your system setting to display the long date, then open your worksheet and change its default date format to one that displays the full year. All the cells containing dates should now show the full year. If the date displays with two-digit years, the cell must have a format applied to it.

Even though date expansion is probably the easiest of the steps to year 2000 compliance, it introduces other problems. Expanding your dates means that all worksheets and reports displaying dates need space to show two more digits. Also, spreadsheets to be saved in a text format should be investigated to guarantee the expanded date can be handled.

Note. Some products don't utilize the operating system date settings, and others don't have the means to set defaults for the whole worksheet.

KNOW YOUR PRODUCT OR TYPE THE EXTRA TWO DIGITS

As stated earlier, spreadsheet software generally allows the user to enter a two-digit year regardless of the date format. So, as a user you have two options: either know the date interpretation rules your products employ, or enter the extra two digits of the year.

If your spreadsheet application isn't covered in this chapter, you should contact the manufacturer, refer to your user's manual, or simply test your software by entering two-digit years in a cell with a long date format and examining the results.

KNOW MORE ABOUT YOUR PRODUCT

Knowing how your product interprets short dates isn't always enough. Some of the older products might be able to handle dates into the 21st century, but some are greatly limited. It is important to identify the date restrictions of your product so you can ensure that date data integrity will be maintained.

You can find these limitations by methods similar to those you used to determine your products' interpretation of short dates.

KNOW YOUR DATA

In the prior section, "Pinpointing the Problem Areas," all text data, both incoming and outgoing, should be analyzed. Once you identify date data without century information, you should contact the source and request that the dates be expanded. If this can be accomplished, no other action on your part is required. However, if the source can't or won't cooperate, it becomes your task to verify that all dates are interpreted correctly.

KNOW YOUR FUNCTIONS AND MACROS

In the prior section, "Pinpointing the Problem Areas," the problem with functions and macros was discussed and identified as the most difficult to correct. The reason for this is simple: the ease with which you as the user can accomplish this task comes down to your knowledge and the availability of tools.

There are three steps involved in resolving this problem.

1. First, research the date functions your spreadsheet software provides; see how they work, what they take for parameters,

and what values they return. Pay particular attention to functions that translate dates to text and vice versa.

2. Second, identify where these functions are used. To view functions in your worksheet, position on a suspect cell, and the equation contained in the cell will be displayed in the formula box. Also, some products provide a means to view all the formulas in your spreadsheet. In addition, you can view macro code through your product's macro editor.

3. Third, make sure the functions interpret the century in a manner consistent with your software: expand all parameters to use the century or apply a window by testing the two-digit year and setting the century.

Some resources for addressing these issues are your user's guide, monthly publications, on-line help, add-in software supplied by the manufacturer, and third-party tools.

Summing It Up

Each spreadsheet should be thought of as a stand-alone application. To correct any date problems, every aspect of every spreadsheet must be investigated. Unless you have access to technologies staff, it's your job to correct these problems. On the brighter side, your lack of knowledge usually corresponds to the complexity of your spreadsheets and use of functions and macros.

Excel

The main focus of this section is Microsoft Excel 97, which was also shipped with the Office 97 suite. The functionality of this product varies very little from version to version, so much of what is covered should apply to other versions as well.

Figure 7-3 gives compliance information for the Excel product line. If your version isn't identified, then Microsoft hasn't addressed

Manufacturer: Microsoft Corporation			
Version	**Compliant**	**Operational Range**	**Date Window for Two-Digit Years**
97, 97 SR-1	Yes	1/1/1900 through 12/31/9999	1/1/1930 through 12/31/2029
95	Yes	1/1/1900 through 12/31/2078	1/1/1920 through 12/31/2019
5	Yes	1/1/1900 through 12/31/2078	1/1/1920 through 12/31/2019

FIGURE 7-3 *Compliance table for Microsoft Excel products.*

its compliance. This information was obtained from the vendor Web site and may have changed since our research was completed.

EXCEL 97 INTERNAL DATE FORMAT

Excel stores dates as serial numbers with 1 representing January 1, 1900, and 2958465 representing December 31, 9999. To see what number a date is stored as, simply enter the date and format the cell with the General format.

In the earlier versions of Lotus 1-2-3, day 60 was erroneously interpreted as February 29, 1900. Since the year 1900 was not a leap year, this date does not exist. Note that, to ensure backward compatibility, Excel reproduced this Lotus 1-2-3 error.

DATE ENTRY AND INTERPRETATION

Excel 97 functions as previously described. When a user enters data into a cell, the program attempts to interpret what type of data it is. If the data entered could be a date, Excel will interpret and apply the format set for the current cell. If the cell isn't formatted, Excel applies the closest standard format it finds.

A common mistake many users make is to set a date format on a group of cells and then enter only part of the date, such as the two-digit year. Or they enter the date as it would appear upon being formatted. To ensure that your date data is interpreted correctly, always enter the date into the system as long date format. Regardless of what format is set on your cells, the date will be converted into the correct internal date format and will be displayed in the display format you desire.

When two-digit years are entered, Excel interprets the years from 00 to 29 as 2000 to 2029 and the years from 30 to 99 as 1930 to 1999. Additionally, if just the month and the two-digit year are entered into a cell, Excel might interpret the date as month and day. This will happen if the entered year is also a valid day in the entered month in the current year.

Figure 7-4 represents some examples of date entries, which will give you an idea of how Excel interprets and displays dates. Each row is a separate example showing what the cell display format is, what the user entered, and how Excel interpreted and then displayed the date.

	A	B	C	D
	Display format	What was entered	What was stored	What was displayed
2	d-mmm	1/3	1/3/1998	3-Jan
3	d-mmm	2/29	2/1/2029	1-Feb
4	d-mmm	5/0	5/1/2000	1-May
5	mmm-yy	May-01	5/1/1998	May-98
6	mmm-yy	5/1/2001	5/1/2001	May-01
7	mmm-yy	May-98	5/1/1998	May-98
8	m/d/yy	12/31/29	12/31/2029	12/31/29
9	m/d/yy	12/31/1929	12/31/1929	12/31/29
10	m/d/yy	1/1/30	1/1/1930	1/1/30
11	m/d/yy	1/1/2030	1/1/1930	1/1/30
12	m/d/yyyy	12/31/29	12/31/2029	12/31/2029
13	m/d/yyyy	12/31/1929	12/31/1929	12/31/1929
14	m/d/yyyy	1/1/30	1/1/1930	1/1/1930
15	m/d/yyyy	1/1/2030	1/1/2030	1/1/2030
16	d/m/yyyy	3/1/29	3/1/2029	1/3/2029
17	d/m/yyyy	13/3/30	13/3/30	13/3/30

FIGURE *Common data entry problems.*
7-4

As you can see from these examples, wherever the full date was entered, there was no confusion or inconsistencies between what was entered, stored, and displayed. However, the same can't be said for the other examples. The second row was interpreted as January 3rd of the current year, since the year portion of the date wasn't supplied. Since February 29th is not a valid day in 1998, Excel interprets 2/29 entered in the third row as the month and year and translates the date to February 1st of 2029. The fourth row was interpreted the same way as the third row. The fifth row is an example of how Excel translates the entered month and day regardless of the mmm-yy display format. The seventh row is translated as the intended month and year simply because 98 is not a valid day in May. Rows 8, 10, 12, 14, and 16 demonstrate how Excel's windowing technique converts two-digit years. The 16th row also illustrates that the display format, though set in the European d/m/yyyy format, does not affect how the entered date is converted. The final example in the 17th row shows that when Excel doesn't recognize the entry as a date, the result remains text. This is apparent from the left alignment of the displayed result, which is the default for text.

TEXT FILE FORMATS AND HOW THEY ARE HANDLED

Excel will save and import several text file formats: Data Interchange Format (*.dif), comma delimited (*.csv), tab delimited (*.txt), and formatted text (space-delimited). Each of these formats saves the worksheet data as it is displayed in the cell. Thus, if there is date data in your worksheet, you should change all formats to display the full date, including the month, day, year, and century.

The reason this should be done was described earlier. When text files are input into Excel or any other spreadsheet application, the data is treated as if it were keyed into cells. The spreadsheet software attempts to interpret the data type and then stores the interpreted value. If the display format of your date data was not changed before the file was saved, there is no guarantee your dates' integrity will be maintained.

Even if your dates display the full date, the use of text files should be avoided. Consider this scenario. You are saving a file with the full date displayed in the format m/d/yyyy and one of your cells contains the date 1/3/1999. You now send this file to a contact in a European country and they import the file into the spreadsheet software which looks for the date format d/m/yyyy. Now your cell that contained the date January 3, 1999, is interpreted as March 1, 1999, which obviously is not correct.

DATE DISPLAY FORMATS

If you have no intention or need to save or export your worksheets as text files, then date display formats will not affect the compliance of Excel. Regardless of the date display format, the date is internally stored as a serial number and will be saved that way as long as the standard spreadsheet format is used. Microsoft suggests date expansion and display of the year mainly to enable the user to see what date was stored in a cell.

DATE FUNCTIONS

There are several date functions in Excel 97 that you should be careful in using: DATE, DATEVALUE, YEAR, MONTH, and DAY. The DATE function accepts three parameters: the year, the month, and the day. It returns a serial number representing the Excel internal format for a date. All three parameters are numeric. The year parameter is a number from 0 to 9999. The month parameter is the elapsed months from the start of the year parameter. The day parameter is the elapsed days from the year and month parameters. When the year parameter is less than 1900, Excel doesn't use its windowing to determine the century; it interprets the year as the elapsed year from 1900. For example, the following function: DATE (29,1,1) returns a serial date number for January 1, 1929, instead of January 1, 2029.

The DATEVALUE function accepts one parameter, which is a date text string, and returns a serial number representing the Excel internal date format. The date text string, like any date entered by a user, must represent a valid date between January 1, 1900, and December 31, 9999. Now that's planning ahead — it will be able to handle dates up to the year 10,000! If the full date is not entered, Excel will attempt to translate the string using its windowing technique.

The YEAR, MONTH, and DAY functions accept one parameter, which is either a serial number or date text string, and return an integer. If the parameter is a serial number, Excel treats it as an internal date. If the parameter is a date text string, Excel will attempt to translate the string using its windowing technique. The returned integers range from 1900 to 9999, 1 to 12, and 1 to 31 for the YEAR, MONTH, and DAY functions, respectively.

When you view an Excel spreadsheet, it's not always clear what functions or formulas are utilized. All Excel 97 formulas used in a spreadsheet can be displayed if you select Tools from the menu bar, click on Options, click on the View tab, and then check ✓ the Formulas check box. Once the formulas are displayed, you should verify that all occurrences of the date functions are used in such a way that dates will be interpreted correctly.

MACROS

Excel 97 macros are written using a language called VBA, or Visual Basic for Applications. Internally, this language treats dates the same way as Excel. Therefore, date transfers from macros shouldn't be affected unless date text is utilized.

VBA permits the use of a m/d/yy format for date text. When this date format is used in your code the two-digit year translation is determined by the version of the OLE automation library. To avoid any misinterpretation in your macros, avoid all date text translations. If date text is required — for example, to pass dates from an external database that doesn't support the serial date format — you should make sure the century is passed, or else know how your version of the OLE automation library translates dates.

There are two different rules the OLE automation libraries apply to interpret the century of date text. An OLE library whose version is less than 2.20.4049 interprets the century part of the year as the current century. An OLE library whose version is greater than or equal to 2.20.4049 applies a sliding window that interprets two-digit years between 00 and 29 as 21st century years and all other years as 20th century years.

To determine which OLE automation library is installed on your computer, open Windows Explorer and go to the Windows|System directory. Then locate the file named "Oleaut32.dll" and right-click on it. From the pop-up menu select Properties to display the Properties dialog box. When the Properties dialog box appears, select the Version tab to see the version of this file, which is your OLE automation library.

SORTING

In Excel 97, dates are sorted based on their internal date format. For this reason, the date display format applied to a cell will not affect how that cell's row or column is sorted. Since the internal date format is just a serial number, any sorts will weight the cell accordingly. Numeric values are sorted with less weight than text values. Figure 7-5 is an example of how date, numeric, and text values are sorted.

	A	B	C
1	b	1/1/1999	b
2	1/1/00	36525	a
3	36525	1/1/00	36527
4	36527	36527	1/1/00
5	1/1/1999	a	36525
6	a	b	1/1/1999

FIGURE 7-5 *Sorting dates, numbers, and text.*

The figure displays three columns. The first contains random date, numeric, and text values. The second demonstrates the results after an ascending sort on the first column. The third shows the results after a descending sort on the first column. By observing this example you can see:

1. The date 1/1/1999 has a lesser value than the number 36525.

2. The number 36525 has a lesser value than the date 1/1/00 (1/1/2000).

3. The date 1/1/00 has a lesser value than the number 36526.

4. The text has a higher value than numbers.

Lotus 1-2-3

This section will cover Lotus 1-2-3 97, which is also shipped with Lotus SmartSuite 97. The operation of this product varies slightly from version to version, and much of what is covered will apply to other versions. Figure 7-6 provides compliance information for the Lotus 1-2-3 product line. If your version isn't identified, then the Lotus Development Corporation hasn't addressed its compliance.

LOTUS 1-2-3 INTERNAL DATE FORMAT

Like Excel, Lotus 1-2-3 stores dates as serial numbers, with 1 representing January 1, 1900, and 73050 representing December 31, 2099. You can view the stored serial number by setting the cells' display format.

As mentioned in the prior section, Lotus 1-2-3 erroneously calculates the year 1900 as a leap year and recognizes the date February 29, 1900, as a valid day. Thus, all days after this date are off by one serial number.

Manufacturer: Lotus Development Corporation			
Version	Compliant	Operational Range	Date Window for Two-Digit Years
97 12/31/1999	Yes	1/1/1900 through 12/31/2099	1/1/1900 through or 1/1/1950 through 12/31/2049 (depending on setup)
Less than 97	Yes	1/1/1900 through 12/31/2099	1/1/1900 through 12/31/1999

FIGURE 7-6 *Compliance table for Lotus 1-2-3 products.*

DATE ENTRY AND INTERPRETATION

Just as described previously, when data is entered in a worksheet cell, 1-2-3 attempts to interpret, translate, and store the data properly. The interpretation of dates and of two-digit years depends on how Lotus 1-2-3 has been set up on the user's computer.

By default, Lotus 1-2-3 will interpret two-digit years as being in the 20th century. However, two-digit years from 00 to 49 will be interpreted as 21st century dates when 1-2-3 user preferences are set up to do so. You can do this by selecting 1-2-3 Preferences off of the File|User Setup menu, clicking on the General tab, and checking the check box labeled "Interpret entry of years 00-49 as 21st century."

The following assumptions are made by Lotus 1-2-3 when parts of the date are not entered. When the day is not entered, the first day of the month is assumed. When the year is not entered, the current year is assumed.

Unlike Excel, Lotus 1-2-3 date display formats have an effect on date entry. There are four date formats that are always recognized as valid dates: DD-MMM-YY, DD-MMM, MMM-YY, and MM/DD/YY. Additional date formats will be recognized if they are promoted to the **Frequently Used** list on the status bar. Note that entered dates are interpreted by the preceding date formats or the display format set on the cell. If the entered date data is not recognized as one of these formats, then the date is interpreted as outside the date range. If no date display format is set on the cell and the entered data is not one of the formats on the **Frequently Used** list or one of the four formats just mentioned, 1-2-3 will interpret the entry either as text or as a calculation.

Figure 7-7 shows some examples of date entries, which will give you an idea of how 1-2-3 interprets and displays dates. Each row is a separate example showing what the cell display format is, what the user entered, and how 1-2-3 interpreted and then displayed the date. Note that all of these examples were done with 1-2-3 set to interpret the entry of all two-digit years as 20th-century dates.

As you can see from these examples, wherever the full date was entered, there is no confusion or inconsistency between what was entered, stored, and displayed. However, the same can't be said for the other examples. Row 2 is interpreted as January 3rd of the cur-

A	A	B	C	D
1	Display Format	What Was Entered	What Was Stored	What Was Displayed
2	d-mmm	1/3	1998/01/03	03-Jan
3	d-mmm	2/29	*************	*************
4	d-mmm	5/0	ERR	ERR
5	mmm-yy	May-01	1901/05/01	May-01
6	mmm-yy	5/1/2001	2001/05/01	May-01
7	mmm-yy	May-98	1998/05/01	May-98
8	dd-mm-yy	12/31/29	1929/12/31	12/31/29
9	dd-mm-yy	12/31/2029	2029/12/31	12/31/29
10	dd-mm-yy	1/1/01	1901/01/01	01/01/01
11	dd-mm-yy	1/1/2001	2001/01/01	01/01/01
12	yyyy-mm-dd	1/1/99	1999/01/01	1999/01/01
13	yyyy-mm-dd	1/1/199	2099/01/01	2099/01/01
14	yyyy-mm-dd	00/01/01	*************	*************
15	yy-mm-dd	00/01/01	1900/01/01	00/01/01

FIGURE *Date entry examples.*

7-7

rent year because the year portion of the date wasn't supplied. Since February 29th of the current year is not a valid day in 1998, 1-2-3 can't interpret the date 2/29 entered in row 3 and fills the cell with asterisks to signify an invalid date. Row 4 is treated in a slightly different manner. Since 5/0 could never be a valid date, 1-2-3 attempts to divide 5 by 0, which results in a divide-by-zero error, and the text "ERR" is then stored in the cell. Rows 5 and 7 are examples of the correct interpretation of the date because of the date format. Rows 5, 7, 8, 10, 12, and 15 are examples of how two-digit year entries are interpreted as years in the current century. Row 13 demonstrates that a year entered as an offset from the year 1900 will be interpreted exactly that way. Row 14 represents a situation where the entered date is not one of the four default date formats or the date format applied to the cell, causing the date to be interpreted as out of the valid date range. Row 15 is an example of the date being entered in the format set on the cell, resulting in the correct interpretation of the date.

DATE DISPLAY FORMATS

If you have no intention or need to save or export your worksheets as text files, then date display formats will not affect the compliance of 1-2-3. Regardless of the date display format, the date is internally stored as a serial number and will be saved that way as long as the standard spreadsheet format is used. Lotus Development Corporation suggests date expansion and display of the year mainly to enable the user to see what date was stored in a cell.

Lotus 1-2-3 allows the user to set date display formats on a cell, on a range of cells, and on a whole spreadsheet. There are several ways to view what display format is set on a cell. One way is to right-click on the desired cell and to select Range Properties off of the pop-up menu. When the Range Properties dialog box appears, select the "#" tab to view display formats. The format already applied to the cell is displayed.

TEXT FILE FORMATS AND HOW THEY ARE HANDLED

Lotus 1-2-3 saves worksheets in only one text file format, a space-delimited format, which outputs only the text and values as they are displayed in the cells of a worksheet. Thus, if there is date data in your worksheet, all formats should be changed to display the full date, including the month, day, year, and century.

You can display the full date by setting dates to always display four-digit year and by selecting cell display formats that display the month, day, and year. To set up 1-2-3 to display four-digit years, select 1-2-3 Preferences off of the File|User Setup menu and view the General tab. On the General tab, the check box labeled "Set dates to always display 4 digit years" should be checked.

Lotus also reads several text formats. When these files are input, all date data is interpreted as if you entered the data into unformatted cells. Thus, you should inspect all imported text files prior to input to verify that all dates will be interpreted correctly.

DATE FUNCTIONS

Most of the date functions provided by 1-2-3 accept the date number as a parameter. The date number is the serial number of stored date data. These functions won't have any date compliance issues, provided the source of the date number was interpreted correctly.

There are three functions which must be inspected to verify that they are used in a compliant fashion. These are the DATE, DATE-VALUE, and YEAR functions.

The DATE function accepts three parameters — the year, the month, and the day — and returns the date number. All three parameters are numbers. The year parameter can be numbers from 0 to 199, which represents the years 1900 to 2099. The month parameter is an integer from 1 to 12, and the day is an integer between 1 and 31. It is important to note that the day parameter must be a valid day for the supplied month and year.

The DATEVALUE function accepts one parameter and returns a serial date number. The passed parameter is a text value, a formula that results in text, or the address or name of a cell that contains text or a formula that results in text. This parameter's format must adhere to the rules for data entry of dates into cells.

The YEAR function accepts one or two parameters and returns a two- or four-digit number. The first parameter, which is required, is a serial date number that falls in the range of valid Lotus 1-2-3 dates. The second parameter is the integer 0 or 1. When the second parameter is 0 or omitted, the YEAR function returns the offset of the year from 1900. If the second parameter is 1, the YEAR function returns the four-digit year.

MACROS

Lotus 1-2-3 macros are written in a programming language called LotusScript. This language provides a set of functions that enable the macro programmer to enter, retrieve, and manipulate date and time values. Although LotusScript doesn't provide a predefined date data type, date values may be stored as 8-byte floating-point numbers.

LotusScript supports dates from January 1, 100 through December 31, 9999. Additionally, LotusScript functions can output years in two-digit and four-digit year formats. When a user enters dates via a macro routine, all two-digit years are assumed to be in the 20th century.

Even though cross-millennium date calculations are performed correctly by LotusScript, inconsistencies between dates entered via macros and dates entered directly into spreadsheets could occur. This would happen if the user set up 1-2-3 to interpret two-digit year entries 00 to 49 as 21st-century dates.

SORTING

In Lotus 1-2-3, dates are sorted based on their internal date format. For this reason, the date display format applied to a cell will not affect how that cell's row or column is sorted. Since the internal date

A	A	B	C
1	b	01/01/99	36527
2	2000/01/01	36525	2000/01/01
3	36525	2000/01/01	36525
4	36527	36527	01/01/99
5	01/01/99	a	b
6	a	b	a

FIGURE *Sorting dates, numbers, and text.*
7-8

format is just a serial number, any sorts will weight the cell accordingly. In ascending and descending sorts, the numeric and date values are grouped together and all text values are grouped together, and then sorted. Figure 7-8 is an example of how date, numeric, and text values are sorted.

The figure displays three columns. The first contains random date, numeric, and text values. The second demonstrates the results after an ascending sort on the first column. The third shows the results after a descending sort on the first column. From this example, you can see the following:

1. The date 1/1/1999 has a lesser value than the number 36525.

2. The number 36525 has a lesser value than the date 1/1/00 (1/1/2000).

3. The date 1/1/00 has a lesser value than the number 36527.

4. Ascending and descending sorts group the numeric and date values first; then the sort is applied to each group.

Quattro Pro

Corel's Quattro Pro 8, which is also part of the WordPerfect Suite 8, is covered in this section, which discusses this product's date compliance issues and possible problem areas. Figure 7-9 provides compliance information for the Quattro Pro product line. If your version isn't identified, Corel hasn't addressed its compliance.

Manufacturer: Corel Corporation			
Version	Compliant	Operational Range	Date Window for Two-Digit Years
7 and 8	Yes	1/1/1600 through 12/31/3199	1/1/1951 through 12/31/2050

FIGURE *Compliance table for Corel Quattro products.*
7-9

QUATTRO PRO 8 INTERNAL DATE FORMAT

Quattro Pro stores dates as serial numbers with –109,571 representing January 1, 1600, and 474,816 representing December 31, 3199. For compatibility with Lotus 1-2-3 and Excel, the serial number 61 represents March 1, 1900, even though it is really the 60th day of the 20th century.

To view the date number of a date entered in a spreadsheet cell, you must change the format of the cell to a normal numeric format. To change the format on a selected cell, right-click the cell and select Cell Properties off of the pop-up menu. Once the Cell Properties dialog box displays, click on the Numeric Format tab and the Normal format option button.

DATE ENTRY, INTERPRETATION, AND FORMATTING

Dates entered into Quattro Pro spreadsheets must be input in one of the following five formats: DD-MMM-YY, DD-MMM, MMM-YY, MM/DD/YY, and MM/DD. The last two formats represent the default long and short date formats, respectively. These two defaults may be changed by right-clicking the Quattro Pro title bar, and by selecting Application Properties off of the pop-up menu. Once the Application Properties dialog box is displayed, select the International tab to alter the default date formats.

Unlike Lotus 1-2-3 and Excel, Quattro Pro date formats limit what a user can enter into a cell and also determine how the entered dates will be displayed. The same steps to set a normal format on a cell may be utilized to set one of the valid date formats on a cell or block of cells.

It is important to note that dates entered without specifying a year are assumed to be dates in the current year. Furthermore, all dates entered with the two-digit years 00 to 50 are assumed to be 21st-century dates.

TEXT FILE FORMATS AND HOW THEY ARE HANDLED

Quattro Pro provides a means to save and input spreadsheets via two text file formats. The two file types are the Data Interchange Format (*.dif) and the tab-delimited format (*.txt). This product handles text files in the same manner as Excel and Lotus 1-2-3. Thus, you should take the same care when dealing with date data while importing and exporting these file types.

DATE FUNCTIONS AND MACROS

As identified in prior sections, date functions utilized in Quattro Pro are a possible compliance problem area. This product provides functions similar to its competitor's functions and their improper use could cause incorrect date calculations.

There are two places where you could apply these date functions, and you should investigate both to verify that all date calculations are done in a compliant manner. First, you can use date functions to build formulas that are stored in a spreadsheet cell. Second, you can store date functions in macros that are saved with the spreadsheet or as a separate file.

Quattro Pro supports two types of macros: keystroke or command macros, and programming language macros. You create a keystroke macro by recording your keystrokes while performing a task. Later you can repeat this task simply by running the macro. This type of macro can be saved in spreadsheet cells or in a library, making them available to all spreadsheets.

The programming language macro is written using Corel's own macro language, called PerfectScript. These types of macros are saved as separate files and may be executed while editing any spreadsheet. Additionally, this language supports its own set of functions to manipulate date data.

SORTING

The Quattro Pro application sorts in a fashion similar to Excel and Lotus 1-2-3. All dates are sorted based on their stored date number, regardless of the format applied to the cell. Since date numbers are just serial numbers, other numeric values are grouped and sorted together with dates.

When a column containing both numeric and text values is to be sorted, the different types of values are grouped before the sort is performed. Depending on the way you set up the sort, numeric values may be sorted before or after text values.

To execute a sort, select the block of cells to be sorted, then select Tools from the menu bar and choose Sort off of the Tools menu. The Sort dialog box is displayed allowing the sort specifications to be built. To sort numbers before text or vice versa, click on the Options button on the Sort dialog box.

DATABASE SOFTWARE

What Is a Database?

Whether or not people use computers, they do use databases, even if they don't realize it. Anyone who has ever used a phone book, a menu, a newspaper, or an address book has used a database.

Essentially, a database is a collection of information, usually separated and ordered by data type. Take the phone book, for example. A single phone listing has types of data such as the person's full name, phone number, city, and street address. Additionally, the phone book is grouped by city and sorted by last and first name.

Traditional database software or database management systems, as they are sometimes called, are distinguished by three components: fields, records, and files. A field is a piece of information, such as a name or a phone number. A record is a complete set of fields, such as a person's or business's phone listing (i.e., name, address, phone number). A file, which is sometimes referred to as a table, is a collection of records, such as the whole telephone directory.

A database management system, or DBMS, lets you enter, organize, and view the data in databases. All DBMS software stores various types of information such as character, numeric, or date data. Furthermore, all DBMS software provides a means of manipulating the database information.

How Is Date Data Handled by Database Software?

All database software has a way to handle date data. The software generally will provide a way of entering dates, will interpret or translate the entered information as valid dates, and will store the dates in an internal format. Just like spreadsheet software, when the full date is not entered, the database software will attempt to interpret the correct month, day, year, and century.

Pinpointing the Problem Areas

As mentioned earlier, all database applications can handle date data. However, how the date is stored and the valid date ranges differ from one DBMS to another. Since most database software can handle dates into the 21st century, the product manufacturers make the claim that their products are year 2000 compliant. All of these manufacturers also provide disclaimers warning the consumer that improper use of their product could affect its compliance.

Database applications have three problem areas when dealing with date data:

1. User entry of two-digit years.
2. Importing/exporting date data with two-digit years.
3. Date functions, procedures, and macros.

PROBLEM: USER ENTRY OF TWO-DIGIT YEARS

Just like spreadsheet applications, database applications are forced to interpret or assume the century when the user enters two-digit years. If database users are permitted to do this, then they must be aware of their products' rules for interpreting the century.

PROBLEM: IMPORTING/EXPORTING DATE DATA WITH TWO-DIGIT YEARS

All database products have a way to import and export data for sharing data with other applications. The most common method of passing data is through text files. These text file formats don't usually support a date data type. Imported date data is converted from text values to the internal date type as if it had been entered directly into the database. Furthermore, date data is exported into text files as text values. The century is output only if the export command is specified correctly.

PROBLEM: DATE FUNCTIONS, PROCEDURES, AND MACROS

All database software provides mechanisms to perform calculations on and to manipulate its data. It does so through the use of functions, procedures, and macros. Date functions are among those supplied by the DBMS. For the most part, these date functions perform calculations on the date data type, but some do convert dates to text values and vice versa. These are the functions that may cause incorrect date calculations.

Unlike spreadsheet applications, most database applications supply a way for you to manage how your databases will be maintained via procedures. These procedures can be thought of as blocks of code that are executed by a user action or an application event. The blocks of code may contain the previously described functions to manage date data.

As explained in the section on spreadsheets, a macro is an action or set of actions that enable a user to automate tasks. Some macros are created by recording keystrokes and others by using an editor and robust programming languages. These macro-programming languages usually supply their own set of functions to manipulate date data, and they don't always apply the same rules of date interpretation.

General Database Tips and Techniques

WHAT YOU SEE IS WHAT YOU GET!

Expanding displayed dates to include the century should be your first task. Although displaying the century doesn't keep users from entering two-digit years, it will let them see the century of their date data, making it easy to identify when incorrect dates are stored in their databases.

MORE IS BETTER!

Another technique that should be applied is the use of input masks. These masks can be set up to force the user to enter four-digit years instead of two-digit years. If this is not an option, the user should at least be able to enter the four-digit year. Thus, any input masks preventing the four-digit year entry should be removed.

KNOW YOUR PRODUCT

As mentioned previously, sometimes forcing the entry of the full year is not an option. In this case, it is a good idea to understand the assumptions the database software applies when interpreting entered date data.

If your database application isn't covered in this chapter, you should contact the manufacturer, refer to your user's manual, or simply test your software. Do this by entering two-digit years in a field with a four-digit year display format and examining the results.

KNOW MORE ABOUT YOUR PRODUCT

Knowing how your product handles the interpretation of entered dates isn't always enough. Some of the older products might be able to handle dates into the 21st century, but some are greatly limited. It is important to identify the date restrictions of your product so you can ensure that date data integrity will be maintained. You should apply a method similar to the one you used to determine your product's interpretation of short dates.

KNOW YOUR DATA

All text data, either incoming or outgoing, should be analyzed. Once you have identified date data without century information, you should contact the source and request that the dates be expanded. If this can be accomplished, no other action on your part is required. However, if the source can't or won't cooperate, it becomes your task to verify that all dates are interpreted correctly.

Refer to the Data Files chapter for more information on handling these types of data files.

IDENTIFY ALL DATE DATA

Although most databases have date data types, sometimes date information will be stored in text fields. You should avoid this practice, especially if calculations are performed on this data or if the data is exported to another application. Whenever dates are stored in this fashion, the possibility of incorrect interpretation of dates increases.

KNOW YOUR FUNCTIONS, PROCEDURES, AND MACROS

This is the most difficult task to accomplish. The ease with which you can identify problem functions, procedures, and macros depends directly on your knowledge of the product and the availability of tools.

There are three steps involved in resolving this problem:

1. Research the date functions your database software provides; see how they work, what they take for parameters, and what values they return. Pay particular attention to functions that translate dates to text and vice versa.

2. Identify where each function is utilized. Use your product's program editor to view procedures and macros.

3. Make sure the functions interpret the century in a manner consistent with your software. Do this by expanding all parameters to use the century, or apply a window by testing the two-digit year and setting the century.

Some resources for addressing these issues are your user's guide, monthly publications, online help, add-in software supplied by the manufacturer, and third-party tools.

Summing It Up

Addressing date compliance issues in databases you've developed should not present much of a problem. The complexity of these databases should be proportional to your knowledge of your DBMS.

On the other hand, a database written for you or canned databases purchased from a vendor may prove impossible to investigate, let alone fix. If these databases are critical, you may need to call on the original vendor to accomplish this task. In some rare cases, where the source code was purchased along with the database, you might use third-party tools to help with this effort.

Access

This section will cover Microsoft Access 97, which is also shipped with the Office 97 suite. The operation of this product varies slightly from version to version, and much of what is covered will apply to other versions. Figure 7-10 provides compliance information for the Access product line. If your version isn't identified, then the Microsoft Corporation hasn't addressed its compliance.

INTERNAL DATA STORAGE

Access 97 provides a date/time data type. This data type is a double-precision, floating-point number that can handle up to 15 decimal

Manufacturer: Microsoft Corporation			
Version	Compliant	Operational Range	Date Window for Two-Digit Years
97, 97 SR-1	Yes	1/1/100 through 12/31/9999	1/1/1930 through 12/31/2029
95	Yes	1/1/100 through 12/31/9999	Current century or 1/1/1930 through 12/31/2029 (depending on installed OLE; see Excel | Macro section above)
2	No	1/1/100 through 12/31/9999	1/1/1900 through 12/31/1999

FIGURE *Compliance table for Microsoft Access products.*
7-10

places. The integer portion of the number holds the date and the decimal portion of the number holds the time.

An Access date field can handle dates from 1/1/100 A.D., which is represented by the number −657434, to 12/31/9999, which is represented by the number 2958465. Unless a date field is converted to a number data type, through code or functions, stored numeric values will never be displayed.

ENTRY AND INTERPRETATION OF DATES

As a default, Access allows dates to be entered in a two-digit or four-digit year format. When a two-digit year between 00 and 29 is entered, the date is assumed to be in the 21st century. All other two-digit years are assumed to be in the 20th century. As described earlier, one of the ways to prevent users from entering two-digit years is to apply an input mask requiring four-digit year entry.

The Access DBMS lets you apply a set of standard input masks, as well as custom input masks, on tables, queries, forms, reports, and modules. Although you can force entry of four-digit years, this is not always desirable or required. However, you should investigate all instances of input masks to ensure that users are not forced to enter two-digit years, thus limiting the date range of entered dates from January 1, 1930, to December 31, 2029.

An additional feature supplied by Access is a means to validate entered data. This feature, which can be applied at the field level on tables, queries, and forms, may contain functions that utilize text date values. If these text date values contain two-digit years, the entry of dates may be limited. Entry of four-digit years might be allowed, but the validation will fail if the date's year is not between 1930 and 2029.

DISPLAYING DATES

Displaying a date in a four-digit year format is a good idea, because the user will always be sure what will be stored in the database.

However, unlike in Excel, the display of dates has no effect on how Access saves or exports text data.

You can set date display formats on fields in tables, queries, forms, and reports. Like input masks, display formats can be applied using the supplied set of predefined formats, as well as with custom formats. Also, when you use the system short date format, you can display the full four digits by adjusting the Regional settings in the Control Panel.

IMPORTING AND EXPORTING TEXT DATA

You can import and export database data using the Access menus, using the Transfer Text macro action, and using the Transfer Text method of the Visual Basic for Applications language.

When importing text files, you can specify whether the two-digit or four-digit year format will be utilized. If the two-digit format is used, the windowing rule for date entry will be applied.

When exporting text data, you can also specify a two-digit or four-digit date format. To ensure that all data passed to other applications includes the correct century, apply the four-digit format.

FUNCTIONS AND MODULES

Access 97, via Visual Basic for Applications, provides numerous functions that perform calculations on date data. These functions reside in modules of code, which are executed as a result of user action or application events. All modules should be investigated and all date functions interpreting date text values should be modified to include the four-digit year.

FoxPro   Microsoft's FoxPro database software fits under a category known as Xbase. Essentially, an Xbase database supports the .DBF format file and utilizes a programming language that supports similar, if

Manufacturer: Microsoft Corporation			
Version	Compliant	Operational Range	Date Window for Two-Digit Years
5.0	Yes	1/1/100 through 12/31/9999	Default is 20th century. Adjustable using the Set Century To... Rollover command.
3.0b, 2.6	Yes, with minor issues	1/1/100 through 12/31/9999	1/1/1900 through 12/31/1999

FIGURE *Compliance table for Microsoft FoxPro products.*
7-11

not identical, command sets. Other widely known Xbase products are Clipper and dBase.

This section focuses on Visual FoxPro 5.0. However, much of what is covered applies to earlier versions of this product line. Figure 7-11 summarizes Microsoft's stance on the compliance status of the FoxPro products.

INTERNAL DATE STORAGE

Visual FoxPro, like its competitors, provides a date data type. This data type is a numeric value representing the number of days from a fixed date. As is evident from Figure 7-11, the database tables and calculations can handle dates from January 1, 100, to December 31, 9999.

Besides providing a database date type, FoxPro provides a means to manipulate date information using date variables. These variables can be loaded with dates from the database, user entry, calculations, or date constants. Furthermore, these variables support the same date range as the database date type.

As mentioned earlier, an additional date source exists in the form of date constants. Date constants are usually declared in code and are utilized to set default dates, to execute date tests, or to perform date calculations. Date constants support the same date range as the date variable and the database date type. However, they may be declared using the two-digit year format, which causes FoxPro to interpret the century. Leaving the century interpretation to FoxPro means that date constant values may be altered by changing the setup of the FoxPro environment and then recompiling the code that contains the variable declaration.

DATE ENTRY, DISPLAY, AND INTERPRETATION

Similar to most database products, FoxPro permits the user to enter dates using both the two-digit and four-digit year formats. By default, all dates entered in the two-digit year format are interpreted as 20th century dates. However, FoxPro 5.0 provides the command Set Century To...Rollover that enables the user to adjust the date entry window. The following example, Set Century To 19 Rollover 60, causes dates entered with the two-digit years between 00 to 59 to be interpreted as 21st century dates and all others as 20th century dates.

You can adjust the display of the year portion of dates in FoxPro by using the Set Century On and Set Century Off commands. Once the Set Century On command has been executed, all dates are displayed in a four-digit year format and any date can be entered. On the other hand, the Set Century Off command allows only dates in the current date window to be entered. The adjustment of this date window was discussed previously.

Besides the Set Century and Set Century To...Rollover commands just described, Visual FoxPro 5 provides another means to alter the display and entry of dates. You can set up defaults using the Options dialog box from the Tools menu. In this dialog box, select the Regional tab. On this tab, three settings exist that affect dates. When the Use System Settings check box is checked, FoxPro uses the operating system default date format. If this check box isn't checked, a date format drop-down list lets you select the default date and time formats. Also, you can display the century by checking the check box labeled " Century (1998 vs. 98)."

Other than the settings just mentioned, FoxPro provides many other ways of limiting or forcing the entry of date fields. At the table and form level, formats and validations can be applied to date fields. Pay special attention to the Century and Format properties of text boxes in forms. These properties will override the environment settings.

DATE FUNCTIONS

The majority of date functions in FoxPro perform calculations correctly on the date data type. These functions shouldn't have any compliance issues, as long as the dates passed to the functions were calculated or interpreted correctly and the returned results are utilized correctly. For example, the YEAR function accepts a date value as a parameter and returns the four-digit year. This will cause no problems unless the returned year is stripped of its century and is utilized in further calculations.

There is one function in particular that will not operate correctly beyond the year 1999. The LUPDATE function, which returns the date of the last update of a table, will not return the correct century after December 31, 1999. The reason this function fails can be attributed to the storage of the last updated date without the century in the table header. When this function retrieves the year 00, it assumes the date is in the 20th century.

Any time dates are converted to or from text, the possibility of incorrect date interpretation exists. For this reason, you should investigate any date functions that perform these operations, verifying that all dates are handled correctly.

WHERE TO LOOK FOR DATE FUNCTIONS

FoxPro, like the other Xbase DBMS products, allows the use of date functions in many areas. Besides their obvious use in programs, functions can be used to build indexes, to set filters on open tables, to set up relationships between open tables, and to retrieve and update data in tables via Standard Query Language commands.

Furthermore, all environment settings at any time can be saved to Views. Views can be thought of as a snapshot of your FoxPro environment. When you save a view, any open tables, how they are related to other tables, and filters set on tables, as well as system settings, are stored in the view file. You can then execute the Set View command to open the saved view. This restores the environment to its state at the time the view file was created. If views are being used, it may not be apparent what functions are being utilized or how they are being utilized. To investigate views, execute the Set View command and check all filters, relationships, and system settings.

IMPORTING AND EXPORTING TEXT DATA

FoxPro, like most database software, supports the import and export of text data. You can import text files by using the import wizard or the Append From command. Either method will allow you to import date data, and, as with most COTS, the rules applied to data entry hold true for importing. That is to say, the date window that is applied to the FoxPro environment is adhered to.

You can export text files by using the Export menu selection off the File menu or the Copy To command. Either method will permit you to export dates. However, unlike the import, the FoxPro settings have no effect on the way dates are output. All dates exported include the full four-digit year.

There are other ways to output text data from FoxPro tables, including use of SQL statements or printing reports. You can still use these methods, as long as the date data is forced to output in the full four-digit year format.

WORD-PROCESSING SOFTWARE

What Is a Word Processor?

A word processor is a computer program that simulates a typewriter. It enables its user to create, edit, save, and print documents. Unlike a typewriter, a word-processing application provides its user with many commands and options to expedite the creation of documents.

The original word processors were fairly simple character-based programs that provided basic editing features. Their successors, which run in GUI environments, are highly complex applications with an extensive collection of commands, functions, and tools. The modern-day word processors, such as Microsoft's Word or Corel's WordPerfect, are so rich in features that they also fit into the category of desktop publishing software.

How Is Data Handled by Word Processors?

Word processors handle and store dates in two ways. In general, dates entered by the user are stored and manipulated as simple text strings. However, with the release of newer, more robust word processors, much date and time information is stored with files and is available for insertion into word-processing documents via fields and macros. This type of date information is generally stored in an application-defined date format.

Pinpointing the Problem Areas

With respect to word processors, there are five problem areas that may affect the date compliance of your product:

- Date entry
- Import and export of text file data
- Table sorting
- Operational date ranges
- Functions and macros

PROBLEM: DATE ENTRY

For the most part, dates entered by the user are stored as text values. These entered dates are not validated; thus, the entry of the invalid date 02/30/1998 would be allowed. Depending on the use of the document, this may or may not be a problem. If the document's sole purpose is to generate a printout, then the invalid date might as well be a typographical error. However, if the date value will be used in table sorts or if the document will be exported to a text file that feeds other applications, this will become a date compliance issue.

PROBLEM: IMPORT AND EXPORT OF TEXT FILE DATA

Importing text file data, specifically date data, will only become a date compliance issue when the imported dates will be sorted in a table. On the other hand, exporting documents with date information that is invalid or that doesn't display the full four-digit year will always cause date compliance problems.

PROBLEM: TABLE SORTING

Most word-processing software provides a means to insert tables into documents and to sort these tables. When tables are sorted by date, several problems could occur. Word-processing products vary on how dates are sorted. Some treat dates as text, and others attempt to interpret the date prior to sorting. In either case, a date value may appear to be valid on entry, yet could sort incorrectly because the entered date was ambiguous or was outside the operational date range of the product.

PROBLEM: OPERATIONAL DATE RANGES

The compliance of a word-processing product, like that of any other COTS, is dependent on its operational date range. Most people who use word processors create documents for printing and don't require any date functionality beyond entering text values. For these users, their word processor's date compliance is unimportant. On the other hand, people who use the word processor's advanced date functionality might not be able to utilize their product when they need to reference dates beyond the software's operational date range.

PROBLEM: FUNCTIONS AND MACROS

Most word processors provide a set of functions to calculate and manipulate dates. Furthermore, some word-processing software lets you automate tasks using a macro programming language. These languages usually provide their own set of date functions.

More often than not, these date functions will allow you to perform text-to-date conversion. This will be a compliance issue if the date does not adhere to the assumed format or if century interpretation is left to the software.

General Word Processor Tips and Techniques

ENTER AND DISPLAY THE EXTRA TWO DIGITS

If you use your word processor to create documents with sorted tables or for exporting data to other applications, it is always a good idea to enter and display the full four-digit year. This ensures that all date data entered will be sorted correctly and interpreted correctly by any application that may receive the exported text files.

KNOW YOUR DATA

If text files are to be imported into word-processing documents, all date data should be investigated. If date data is imported, then you must either interpret the century or go to the source to guarantee that the correct century is assumed.

KNOW YOUR PRODUCT

When you enter two-digit year date formats and perform calculations on or sort by these dates, you should understand whether your word processor is sorting the text date or the interpreted date. Some word-processing software will sort text dates by breaking down the date into year, month, and day. It then sorts by each part as separate keys. Other products interpret the date using their own windowing rules and then sort by the date number just as spreadsheet software would. The latter products, which interpret the date prior to sorting, sometimes have a limited operational range. Thus, when an interpreted date is out of the operational range, the sort will return some confusing and unexpected results.

KNOW YOUR FUNCTIONS AND MACROS

Many date functions allow the use of text date data. As we've already mentioned, this is one of the leading sources of noncompliance in COTS. Thus, it is important to identify these functions, locate them in your documents, and verify that they're being used in a compliant fashion.

If the document is one you created, this should not be a difficult task. However, if someone else created the document, or if it was created from a template file, there might be a problem. These documents may utilize functions in fields or macros in a way that isn't easy for a novice user to detect. In these cases, it is a good idea to seek help from a more experienced user, or to use a third-party tool that will scan your documents and macros for date functions and data.

Summing It Up   Word-processing software is not the ideal platform for handling date data. There are two reasons for this difficulty. First of all, user-entered dates are usually treated as and stored as text data. Second, entered dates are generally not validated or masked on input, thus increasing the chance that invalid date information will be received. If date information is vital for you or your business, it is better to use database or spreadsheet software to collect and manage your date data.

Word

Microsoft Corporation manufactures the Word word-processing software. A recent release in this product line is Word 97, which is also shipped with the Office 97 suite. This section concentrates on this version of Word; however, much of what is covered holds true for older versions.

Figure 7-12 identifies some of the releases in the Word product line and shows the results of Microsoft's year 2000 compliance testing and research. If your version of Word is not identified, Microsoft hasn't addressed its compliance.

HOW DATES ARE HANDLED

Word 97 has many features that handle date and time values. Some of these features include revision control and document information such as the file creation date and the current date, which can be inserted into documents via fields. Date and time values stored by these features are represented by a 32-bit integer, which retains

Manufacturer: Microsoft Corporation			
Version	**Compliant**	**Operational Range**	**Date Window for Two-Digit Years**
97	Yes	1/1/1900 through 12/31/2411	1/1/1930 through 12/31/2029
95	Yes, with minor issues	1/1/1900 through 12/31/2411	1/1/1901 through 12/31/2000
6	Yes, with minor issues	1/1/1900 through 12/31/2411	1/1/1901 through 12/31/2000
5 for DOS	No	1/1/1980 through Unknown	N/A

FIGURE *Compliance table for Microsoft Word products.*
7-12

the full four-digit year. All dates from January 1, 1900, to December 31, 2411, will be handled correctly using this method.

For the most part, all dates entered into Word documents by the user are treated as simple text. The lone exception to this rule is dates entered into tables that are then sorted. The dates are still stored as text, but the sort applies date windowing to determine the sort results. The table sort of dates is discussed more thoroughly later in this section.

DATE ENTRY

The entry of date data into Word documents only becomes an issue in three instances. If the entered dates are used in calculations, in table sorting, or to export to other applications, then it becomes the user's responsibility to enter all dates with the four-digit year.

Unlike spreadsheet and database software, there is no way to mask or validate dates entered directly into documents. However, through macros written in Visual Basic for Applications, you can create forms with text boxes to accept date information. These entered dates can be masked and validated using VBA code.

TABLE SORTING

As mentioned earlier, table sorts handle dates differently than other text values. Prior to sorting, Word attempts to interpret the text strings as date values. If the text string is not a valid date between January 1, 1900, and December 31, 2035, the resulting sort will return erroneous results. When dates have been entered in two-digit year format, Word applies a date window from 1930 to 2029. Thus, the two-digit years 00 to 29 are translated as 2000 to 2029, respectively.

DATE FUNCTIONS AND MACROS

Word itself does not support date functions or calculations. However, date calculations can be carried out via Visual Basic for

Applications function. Using the VBA editor, macros can be viewed and updated. You should scan all macros to locate all code that performs date calculations. This code should then be verified to ensure that it utilizes the full four-digit year.

Dates may be input via text boxes on VBA forms or using the InputBox method. Whenever dates are input via code, the user must be allowed to enter the four-digit year. Any input masking and validation that limits the entry of full dates should be located and modified to do so.

IMPORTING AND EXPORTING DATE DATA

Word does allow you to open and save documents in a text file format. In opening or importing text files, there's only one instance when date compliance becomes an issue: the use of imported text in table sorts. When you save or export documents in a text file format for the purpose of passing data to another application, you should expand any date data to include the correct century.

WordPerfect

The Corel Corporation's WordPerfect product line is, and has been for many years, one of the industry's leading word processors. A recent release, WordPerfect 8, which is also part of the WordPerfect

Manufacturer: Corel Corporation			
Version	Compliant	Operational Range	Date Window for Two-Digit Years
7 and 8	Yes	Unknown through 12/31/9999	1/1/1951 through 12/31/2050

FIGURE *Compliance table for Corel WordPerfect products.*
7-13

8 Office Suite, is covered in this section. Figure 7-13 contains date compliance information about this product line. If your version of WordPerfect is not represented, Corel Corporation either has not tested it, or has not addressed its compliance.

HOW DATES ARE HANDLED

WordPerfect, like most word-processing software, handles dates in two ways, either as text or as codes. Dates entered into documents are generally stored as simple text strings. The one exception is the functionality provided to insert codes into documents. These codes are placeholders for data that may change from one editing session to another. Pertinent date information, such as the current date or the file's creation date, is typically contained in these placeholders. It is important to note that date information retrieved by codes contains century information.

DATE ENTRY AND DISPLAY

WordPerfect users can enter dates into documents in several ways. The most common way is simply to type the date as text. Another method is to use the Date/Time selection from the Insert menu. When you select Date/Time, the Date/Time dialog box is displayed. From this dialog box, you can insert the date and time as text or as a code and select its display format.

The display format of dates entered as text or keyed directly into a document can only be changed by retyping the date. On the other hand, you can change the display of date codes inserted into a document at any time by using the Date/Time dialog box. Additionally, dates inserted using the Date/Time dialog box can be formatted using a list of default formats or custom user-defined formats. You can apply custom formats by pressing the New Format button on the Date/Time dialog box, which opens the Custom Date/Time Format dialog box. Using this dialog box, you can define a custom format.

Dates entered in WordPerfect tables are treated slightly differently. When you update a table, the Table toolbar is displayed. The Number Format pull-down list from this menu can be used to format dates. Additionally, you can format a selected cell or range of cells by right-clicking the selected cell or cells and choosing Numeric Format from the pop-up menu. This opens the Properties for Table Format dialog box, and you can then set the format for the cell, or range of cells.

DATE SORTING IN TABLES

WordPerfect handles date sorting in tables differently than Microsoft Word does. To sort by date, you must set up your date and sort specifications properly. All dates must be entered in a valid short date format with a four-digit year (mm/dd/yyyy). Also, these dates must be separated by a forward slash (/) or a hard hyphen, which can be entered by pressing the Ctrl and – keys simultaneously.

To set up the sort specification and sort the table, position anywhere in the table and choose the Tools|Sort|New menu selection. A dialog box where you can define the values for sorting will be displayed. Several steps are required to sort dates correctly. First, the column containing the date should be separated by words. Second, three keys must be defined, the first for the year, the second for the month, and the third for the day. Third, each key should be set as a numeric sort key instead of an alphanumeric sort key.

FUNCTIONS AND MACROS

WordPerfect supports date functions in two places. First, tables inserted into a document may contain functions used to perform date calculations. The set of functions supported by tables are the same as the Quattro Pro functions. Second, WordPerfect macros can contain date functions. These macros are written in the PerfectScript programming language, which supports its own set of date functions.

All instances where these date functions are utilized should be investigated to ensure that the functions are used in a compliant manner.

IMPORTING/EXPORTING TEXT FILES

Text files can be imported and exported by WordPerfect using the File menu's Open and Save As selections. When importing and exporting text files, WordPerfect functions identically to Microsoft Word. The only areas of concern are the use of imported date data in table sorts and the use of exported date data in other applications. In either case, the full four-digit year should be included with dates to ensure compliance.

GENERAL GROUPWARE

Groupware software, also known as workgroup software, provides the means to enable groups of co-workers attached to a LAN or the Internet to organize their activities and communicate with each other. Some common tasks these types of products perform are e-mailing, scheduling, and sharing of data. Because of the date-sensitive capabilities of this type of software, year 2000 compliance is an extremely critical issue.

Pinpointing the Problem Areas

Groupware products, like spreadsheet, database, and word-processing software, handle user-entered dates, as well as dates supplied by the operating system or server. Generally, these automatically retrieved dates will never cause a problem, unless the date provided is incorrect. The real problem lies with the user-entered dates. The scope of user-entered dates includes dates entered through forms, through an import facility, and through user-generated calculations. Thus, the three problem areas are date entry, date functions, and the import/export of date data.

PROBLEM: DATE ENTRY

Workgroup software, like most COTS, will handle dates well into the 21st century. Despite this fact, date entry using the two-digit year format might cause unexpected results. Inputting dates in this manner forces the software to interpret the century, which may or may not be the one intended.

PROBLEM: IMPORT/EXPORT OF DATE DATA

Some groupware products provide a means of importing or inputting date data via files. For the most part, these files contain a stored date with the century included. A problem might occur when imported files don't provide the full date or an acceptably formatted date.

The most common file type causing problems is the text file. Dates stored in text files are simple text strings that are, one hopes, in a format that will be accepted by the workgroup software. When a text file is imported, date data is interpreted and translated as if it were entered via the product's interface. Thus, any dates input with two-digit years might result in invalid translation.

Although the export of data does not affect a product's successful operation into the 21st century, it may affect other products' compliance. When date data is exported to files, the full date should be output. With some products this might not be an issue. However, date data exported using a text file format usually will be output in the same format in which it is displayed on the software's screen.

PROBLEM: DATE FUNCTIONS

Some workgroup software furnishes a set of date functions to perform calculations that may be used to store dates. For the most part, these functions can handle calculations into and beyond the 21st century. The real problems occur when the functions are used in a noncompliant fashion: for example, date translation to and from text values not containing the century, or calculations using incorrect function parameters.

General Groupware Tips and Techniques

WHAT YOU SEE IS WHAT YOU GET!

It's always best to set up your product to display dates with their century, regardless of the type of software you're operating. Not only does it let you see the stored date, it also might affect the format in which date data is exported.

KNOW YOUR PRODUCT

When you enter or import dates, especially dates in a two-digit year format, you should know how your product applies or assumes the century. It is also a good idea to know what valid date ranges and formats your product can handle.

KNOW YOUR DATA

When you use the import or export functionality of your groupware product, you must know your data. Not only should the date data include the full date, it should contain dates in the operational or valid date range of your product. Furthermore, the date data should be in a format your products or the receiving products can understand.

Know your functions and verify their use

Familiarization with date functions includes knowing what parameters are accepted and what values are returned. Once you understand how these functions work, you should locate and investigate all occurrences. Always verify that they are used in a compliant fashion. Standards of compliance should contain the inclusion of the century in all dates, as well as the valid formatting of all calculated dates.

Summing It Up

Most groupware products are strict when it comes to acceptable input date formats. For this reason, these products are less likely than other types of products to have date compliance problems. However, since one of the major uses of workgroup software is sharing data in and out of an organization, date compliance is still a major issue.

Outlook

The Microsoft Outlook product line is one of the more popular groupware products on the market today. Figure 7-14 identifies

Manufacturer: Microsoft Corporation			
Version	Compliant	Operational Range	Date Window for Two-Digit Years
8.5	Yes	1/1/1601 through 12/31/4500	Current date – 30 years through current date + 70 years
8.0x	Yes	1/1/1601 through 12/31/4500	Current date – 30 years through current date + 70 years

Figure *Compliance table for Microsoft Outlook products.*
7-14

compliance information released by Microsoft and other pertinent information is covered in the remainder of this section.

HOW DATES ARE HANDLED

All dates in Outlook 97 and 98 are stored with the full date. Additionally, the full date is used whenever stored dates are manipulated. The current date, which is widely used, is retrieved from the system clock. Thus, this product's compliance depends upon the clock's compliance.

DATE ENTRY

The entry of the two-digit and four-digit year format is valid. As Figure 7-14 shows, Outlook applies a sliding date window for interpreting the century on entry of dates in the two-digit year format. All of these dates are assumed to be in a window from 30 years before to 70 years beyond the current date.

DATE DISPLAY

The Outlook product line applies the system short date format for displaying dates. Thus, you should adjust the regional settings to display the date in a four-digit year format.

IMPORTING/EXPORTING

There is only one case in which importing or exporting date data to and from Outlook could become a compliance problem. When you import or export comma- or tab-delimited text files, the date data must be converted from text to the stored date format and vice versa. As described earlier, imported text dates follow the same interpretation rules as dates entered directly into Outlook screens. Also, exported dates are output based on the system short date format set in the Control Panel's Regional Settings. You should check all incoming or imported text files to verify that full dates are included in the format expected. Furthermore, the Short Date format in the Regional Settings should be set to a four-digit year format.

OTHER ISSUES

For Outlook 97 versions earlier than 8.5.5104.6, a dynamic link library or DLL must be obtained from Microsoft to achieve compliance. The DLL OUTLLIB.DLL version 8.03.5228 can be acquired through Microsoft Technical Support. To verify the version of this dynamic link library, locate the file using Windows Explorer or the Find utility off of the Start menu. Once the Properties dialog box is displayed, select the Version tab to view the file's version number.

Lotus Notes

The Lotus Notes groupware software was developed to handle 21st century dates from its first release. The remainder of this section discusses other applicable issues.

HOW DATES ARE HANDLED

Lotus Notes, like Outlook, stores dates in its own internal format, which can handle dates into and beyond the 21st century. Furthermore, all date calculations using these stored dates will execute correctly. Lotus Notes has its own server, which retrieves the current date and time from the operating system at startup. If the operating system is not compliant, then the compliance of Lotus Notes may be affected.

DATE ENTRY

All versions of Lotus Notes permit the entry of two-digit and four-digit years. In releases prior to version 4.5, all two-digit years were assumed to be 20th century. The only way to enter 21st century dates was to enter the four-digit year. In releases 4.5 and greater, the date window spans from 1950 to 2049; thus, the two-digit years 00 to 49 are assumed to be 21st-century dates.

DATE FUNCTIONS

Lotus Notes supports date functions in traditional macros and in LotusScript scripts (release 4.0 and greater). You should locate all occurrences of date functions and verify that they are used in a compliant fashion. Carefully check for date-to-text and text-to-date conversion functions.

OTHER COTS: FINANCIAL, PAYROLL, AND MAIL

The year 2000 compliance of all the products discussed in prior sections was dependent on two things:

- First, the product had to be year 2000 ready, meaning it had to be able to handle dates into the year 2000 and beyond.
- Second, all dependent components had to be year 2000 compliant, and the product itself had to be used in a compliant fashion.

The products discussed in this section differ from those previously discussed, because their year 2000 compliance will mainly rely on the manufacturer's ability to provide a compliant version. These types of software are generally very strict in what dates and date formats the user may input. Furthermore, the user setup of the product won't affect its compliance either way.

The three types of COTS often used by home and small business personal computer users are covered in this section. They are financial, payroll, and mail software.

Financial Software

WHAT IS FINANCIAL SOFTWARE?

The first financial software products to hit the market were nothing more than basic checkbook-balancing programs. These products have evolved from these simple applications into robust accounting systems that function in a manner similar to the manual accounting model. Software products of this type enable their users to quickly and easily balance accounts, transfer funds from one account to another, and generate numerous reports and graphs.

The accounting process includes date-sensitive and date-dependent events and information. For this reason, financial software's year 2000 compliance is a critical topic. If your current accounting application can't handle dates beyond December 31, 1999, chances are good it will function either improperly or not at all.

These types of programs are ideal for small businesses that can't afford to hire accountants to manage their books. Some of the better-known products are Quicken, QuickBooks, M.Y.O.B., and Money. These products will be covered in the remainder of this section.

QUICKEN/QUICKBOOKS

Date entry   Regardless of the version or product, you're permitted to input dates in a four-digit year format so that any date in the product's operational range can be referenced. Another method allows you to enter dates outside the two-digit year date window. The forward slash separating the day and year can be replaced with an apostrophe, denoting years above or below the date window, depending on your product.

In Quicken for Windows versions 6 and 98, you can use the apostrophe method to enter dates from 1901 through 1927. Additionally, Quicken for DOS versions 5 through 8, Quicken for Windows versions 1 through 5, and all QuickBooks versions allow the entry of 21st-century dates using this method.

Online banking feature   Currently, only Quicken 98's online banking feature, with the R3 update, supports dates after

Manufacturer: Intuit Corporation			
Version	Compliant	Operational Range	Date Window for Two-Digit Years
6 and Quicken 98	Yes	1/1/1901 through 12/31/2027	1/1/1928 through 12/31/2027
1 – 5 for Windows	Yes	1/1/1901 through 12/31/2027	1/1/1901 through 12/31/1999
5 – 8 for DOS	Yes	1/1/1901 through 12/31/2027	1/1/1901 through 12/31/1999
1 – 4 for DOS	No	1/1/1901 through 12/31/1999	1/1/1901 through 12/31/1999

FIGURE 7-15 *Compliance table for Intuit Quicken products.*

Manufacturer: Intuit Corporation			
Version	Compliant	Operational Range	Date Window for Two-Digit Years
Windows (All)	Yes	1/1/1901 through 12/31/2027	1/1/1901 through 12/31/1999
DOS	Yes	1/1/1901 through 12/31/2025	1/1/1901 through 12/31/1999

FIGURE 7-16 *Compliance table for Intuit QuickBooks products.*

December 31, 1999. If you are using Quicken for Windows version 5 or 6, you can get an update from your financial organization or from Intuit by the second quarter of 1999. Another option is to upgrade to Quicken 98 with the R3 update. If you are using QuickBooks for Windows version 5, Intuit intends to release a free upgrade in October 1998 that will enable the use of dates in 2000 and beyond.

M.Y.O.B.

Best!Ware corporation has reported that its latest releases of the M.Y.O.B. product line are year 2000 compliant. These releases include M.Y.O.B. Plus version 7.5 and M.Y.O.B. Premier. Additionally, Best!Ware suggests that users test these products themselves by using the Widgets Inc. sample data files shipped with these products.

MONEY

Online banking feature   The operational date range for the Money product line differs depending on the online banking service used. Versions 3, 4, and 97 can handle dates from January 1, 1993, through December 31, 2075, for the Checkfree/ISC/NPC specification. Version 98 handles dates from January 1, 1993, through December 31, 2092. Only versions 97 and 98 support the OFX, OFC, and VISA services. When 97 is used with these services, dates from January 1, 1948, through December 31, 2075, can be managed. Money 98 used with these same services can transmit or receive dates between January 1, 1900, and December 31, 2200.

Manufacturer: Microsoft Corporation			
Version	Compliant	Operational Range	Date Window for Two-Digit Years
98	Yes	1/1/1900 through 12/31/2200	Current year – 33 years through current year + 66 years
97, 4, 3, 2, 1	Yes	1/1/1948 through 12/31/2075	1/1/1948 through 12/31/2047

FIGURE 7-17   *Compliance table for Microsoft Money products.*

Payroll Software

WHAT IS PAYROLL SOFTWARE?

For the most part, payroll software is very distinct financial software, focused on electronically processing a company's payroll. Most payroll products provide a means to store employee-specific information, to enter time and attendance from cycle to cycle, to pass data to or from other financial systems, and to generate reports and government forms.

Anyone who has had to perform payroll processing can tell you that date information plays an important role in this type of task. Dates are used to record period end and start dates, as well as an employee's hire date and date of birth. The previously mentioned dates could be used to determine when certain payroll functions are performed or when an employee is eligible for retirement or has passed their working test period. A payroll application that could not handle 21st-century dates would become inoperable on January 1, 2000.

Two of the more popular personal computer based payroll products are QuickPay and Timeslips. The compliance of these product lines is covered in the remainder of this section.

QUICKPAY

Other issues　Date entry of years from 2000 to 2027 while using QuickPay 3 for Windows follows the same rules as the Quicken and QuickBooks products discussed earlier. The user may enter the four-digit year or use the apostrophe method.

QuickPay 2.0, 2.1 for Windows and 2.0 for DOS use either the Quicken or QuickBooks products as a front end. All dates are entered through these parent products; thus, the compliance, operational date range, and date window of these versions of QuickPay depend on the installed version of Quicken or QuickBooks. Refer to the previous section for the date constraints of your Intuit software.

Manufacturer: Intuit Corporation			
Version	Compliant	Operational Range	Date Window for Two-Digit Years
Windows 3	Yes	1/1/1901 through 12/31/2027	1/1/1901 through 12/31/1999
DOS 3	No	1/1/1901 through 12/31/1999	1/1/1901 through 12/31/1999
2.0, 2.1 Windows	See above	See above	See above
2.0 DOS	See above	See above	See above

FIGURE 7-18 *Compliance table for Intuit QuickPay products.*

TIMESLIPS

The Timeslips product line is manufactured by the Sage U.S. Corporation. According to Sage U.S., the following products are certified to work until at least the year 2030: Timeslips 5 for Windows v5.5, Timeslips Remote for Windows v5.5, TAL for Windows v5 and higher, Timeslips Speller for Windows v5 and higher, Timeslips Deluxe for Windows v7.0 and higher, and TSRemote Deluxe for Windows v7.0 and higher. None of the Timeslips DOS versions are year 2000 compliant.

Mail Software

WHAT IS MAIL SOFTWARE?

Mail software can be thought of as an electronic mailbox. This type of product provides the means to create, send, receive, and forward electronic mail. These products usually include an editor to enter text and a facility to attach files for transmission to other mailboxes. To transmit and receive mail, the user's computer must be connected to a local area network or to the Internet.

For the most part, mail software uses dates in only three places. First, the current date is retrieved from the operating system or system clock for date calculations. Second, a timestamp containing the current date and time is attached to outgoing mail. Third, a timestamp is attached to received mail. Non-compliance in mail products would affect date sorting of sent and received messages still in mailboxes, as well as archiving or purging of messages based on the mail's age, which is the current date minus the received or sent date.

The groupware products discussed in a previous section provide the same functionality as e-mail products, but with additional features. Two of the more popular mail titles are cc:Mail and Pegasus Mail. The compliance of these two products is covered next.

cc:Mail

The Lotus Development Corporation manufactures the cc:Mail product line. According to Lotus, all cc:Mail Release 8.x software is year 2000 compliant. Furthermore, Lotus declares that cc:Mail Release 6.03.01 for Windows and Release 6.02 for DOS only are compliant when using cc:Mail Release 8.x post offices (DB8).

PEGASUS MAIL

Pegasus Mail version 2.54 for Windows and version 3.40 for MS-DOS are both stated to be compliant.

Manufacturer: David Harris			
Version	Compliant	Operational Range	Date Window for Two-Digit Years
2.54 for Windows	Yes	1/1/1970 through 12/31/9999	N/A
3.40 for MS-DOS	Yes	1/1/1970 through 12/31/9999	N/A

FIGURE *Compliance table for Pegasus Mail products.*
7-19

CHAPTER

8

Servers and the Year 2000

THIS CHAPTER CONTAINS:

- Servers and Local Area Networks
- Novell Netware
- Windows For Workgroups
- Server Operating System Compliance
- Windows NT
- LANtastic

SERVERS AND LOCAL AREA NETWORKS

A server is a personal computer containing more memory and drive space than your average computer. Servers are typically used to support a local area network (LAN) environment. A LAN connects many different workstations, printers, and other devices within a limited geographic area (such as an office). The server operating system controls this environment. It recognizes and limits access to resources such as applications, files, printers, and other workstations through security and directory services.

The server operating system has a date and time function that affects workstations connected to it as well as applications installed on it. Although the server is really just another personal computer, because the server operating system is responsible for controlling all the resources connected to the network it must be carefully evaluated and tested for year 2000 compliance. All areas of the server should be tested. This includes the BIOS, server operating system, and the applications installed on the server, as well as the workstations connected to the server. This can be a very complex process which could corrupt your production environment resources and data. Therefore, if you have a local area network you should seek outside professional assistance to address this phase of your year 2000 problem identification and correction process.

However, if you feel you have the expertise to undertake this phase of testing, first talk to the manufacturer of your server operating system to obtain all information regarding problems, fixes, and concerns that need to be factored into your test plans.

Caution. Year 2000 ready testing of any network operating system should be done in a test environment only, not in a live production environment.

Reminder. Always back up your server before performing any year 2000 tests or changes.

SERVER OPERATING SYSTEM COMPLIANCE

Popular server operating systems include Novell Netware, Microsoft NT, Microsoft Windows for Workgroups, and LANtastic. The information in the balance of this chapter addresses these four operating system packages and their year 2000 status. This information was obtained from vendor Web sites and may have changed since our research was completed.

NOVELL NETWARE

Current versions of Novell products have been tested for year 2000 readiness. Netware 4.11 and Netware 3.2 are year 2000 ready or Novell will provide fixes that can be downloaded from the Internet.

Certain Netware products are not being tested or are not supported for year 2000 issues. Novell suggests customers who are running Netware versions 2.x, 3.11, 3.12, or 4.10 (or any prior version) migrate to the newer Netware versions.

Go to the Novell Web address *www.novell.com/p2000/patches.html* to locate information and patches for the year 2000.

Following are some of the patches listed at this Web location. Before downloading and applying any of these patches, please review Novell's on-line disclaimers and descriptions of the problem fixes. For a list of available patches, refer to Figure 8-1 on the next page.

MICROSOFT NT SERVER

The Microsoft Windows NT 5.0 server operating system is stated to be year 2000 compliant. If you are running any lower version of the NT server, you might want to consider upgrading.

Server Operating System	Fix File
Year 2000 update for intraNetware (Netware 4.11 Support Pack 5)	lwsp5b.exe
Year 2000 update for Netware 3.12	312y2kp2.exe
Year 2000 update for Novell Clients	C1ty2kp1.exe
Year 2000 update for Novell Administrator for Windows NT vv2.0c	Na4nty2k.exe
Year 2000 update for Netware ConnectView v2.0	ncv20y2k.exe
Year 2000 update for BorderManager v2.1	bm21yk.exe
Year 2000 update for ManageWise v2.5	mwnxp01a.exe
Year 2000 update for LAN WorkGroup 5.0	lwp501.exe
Year 2000 update for LAN WorkPlace 5.0	lwp501.exe
Year 2000 update for LAN WorkPlace Pro	lwp501.exe
Year 2000 Update for Hostprint 1.11	See Web site for update

FIGURE *Novell Netware patches.*
8-1

For servers running Windows NT version 4.0, a patch is needed for year 2000 compliance. To obtain this patch, complete the following:

STEPS

1. Go to Microsoft's Web address:
   http://www.microsoft.com/year2000.

2. Click on Product Guide.

3. Click the down arrow on "Choose a Product".

Server Operating System	Fix File
Microsoft Windows NT 4.0 Service pack 3:	http://backoffice.microsoft.com/ downtrial/moreinfo/nt4sp3.asp

FIGURE *Microsoft NT patches.*
8-2

4. Scroll down to "Operating Systems".

5. Choose "Windows NT Server Standard and Enterprise Edition 4.0" and click on "GO".

6. Click on "Microsoft Windows NT 4.0 Service Pack 3".

7. Download the fix file indicated in the chart below.

Windows NT Server version 4.0 is stated to have the following problems. You can contact Microsoft and provide them with the appropriate "Qxxxxx" numbers to obtain articles containing more information regarding these problems and their fixes. The "Qxxxxxx" is the article ID number.

User Manager Does Not Recognize February 2000 as a Leap Year	(Q175093) User Manager and User Manager for Domains will not accept Feb. 29, 2000, as a valid date to expire an account.
Control Panel Date/Time Applet	(Q183123) The Control Panel Date/Time applet's displayed date may jump ahead one more day than expected. The system date is correct; only the displayed date is wrong.

Custom Date Properties on Office Files	(Q183125) When the properties of Office files are modified from the Shell, only two-digit years are allowed and they are assumed to be in the 20th century.

Find File Entry Fields	(Q183124) There are two date entry fields in the Start Menu, Find Files or Folders, Date Modified tab that will show nonnumeric data if the year is greater than 1999.

WINDOWS FOR WORKGROUPS 3.11

Windows for Workgroups version 3.11 is stated to be compliant, with minor issues.

Microsoft requires that you run MS-DOS version 6.22 with Windows for Workgroups. If you are not, then you will need to purchase an update version from a local software retailer.

You also need to obtain the updated version of WINFILE.EXE from the Web address *http://www.microsoft.com/year2000* product information area.

STEPS

1. Go to Microsoft's Web address: *http://www.microsoft.com/year2000.*

2. Click on Product Guide.

3. Click the down arrow on "Choose a Product".

4. Scroll down to "Operating Systems".

5. Choose "Windows for Workgroups 3.11" and click on "GO".

6. A Prerequisite area will display: "Updated version of WIN-FILE.EXE. For more information see Knowledge Base article Q85557." Click on the word WINFILE.EXE and this will start to download the file for you.

LANTASTIC

All recent Artisoft LANtastic software releases have been tested. The results are listed at Artisoft's Web address, *www.artisoft.com/y2000.html*. They state that any product not listed has been discontinued and will not be tested for year 2000 compliance. They recommend that customers complete their own testing to determine if they have year 2000 problems. If you experience problems, then consider upgrading to a compliant version. You can contact the sales department at Artisoft (1-800-846-9726) to inquire about compliant version prices.

A compliance summary for Artisoft software products can be found at *www.artisoft.com/y2000.html*.

As noted earlier, you may want to seek professional assistance to complete this server operating system compliance testing. The next chapter, "Hiring Consultants and Contractors," discusses what to look for in a consultant.

Server Operating System	Compliance Status	Fix File
LANtastic for Windows NT	Year 2000 compliant	
LANtastic 8.0	Year 2000 compliant	
LANtastic 7.0	Is compliant with applied fixes	NOS700.EXE
LANtastic Dedicated Server 1.1	Not compliant	• Server is based upon Netware 4.02 which is not year 2000 compliant. • Will continue to function, but will not process dates correctly after 12- 31-1999. • Problem cannot be fixed. • Vendor recommends replacement of software prior to year 2000.

FIGURE *LANtastic patches.*
8-3

9

Hiring Consultants and Contractors

THIS CHAPTER CONTAINS:

- Availability of Resources
- Methodology and Approach
- What Will It Cost?
- Quality and Credentials
- Getting What You Pay For

This book was designed to provide a process by which personal computer and small business owners can identify and resolve their year 2000 date handling problems. Some individuals and business owners may not feel qualified or willing to undertake this work. They may decide to seek outside professional assistance. If this is your position, then there are a number of factors you need to consider before you march out and hire contractors or consultants. This is a high-priority project whose outcome could affect the fate of your company.

Where can you find qualified resources, and how do you know if the person or company you are contracting is capable of getting the job done? Do they have a well-defined and reasonably sound methodology for performing the work? How do you ensure that you get what you pay for, and what is a fair price for the work? These are some of the questions addressed in this chapter. We hope this information will help you make your hiring decisions and secure work agreements that give you the control you need to ensure your needs will be met.

AVAILABILITY OF RESOURCES

A major issue for large and small businesses alike is the current shortage of technology resources. Actually, this shouldn't be news to anyone. Numerous articles and broadcasts have focused on this issue. Starting salaries for recent college graduates with technology-related majors have soared. Savvy technologists who recognize their worth are changing jobs to gain significant pay increases. Many are joining or starting their own contracting and consulting firms. Companies that have downsized and outsourced their technology operations are now feeling the backlash of these resource shortages. Prices for technology services are increasing and many are paying more for less. Even foreign/off-shore labor sources (such as India, Ireland, and Russia) are drying up because of the demands being imposed by the year 2000 crisis as well as demands in Europe for technology changes needed to support Euro Dollar conversion work.

Companies who have opted to maintain in-house technology support organizations are struggling to retain their highly qualified staff. Some are experiencing turnover rates in the 30%+ range and can't find adequate replacements. Many firms have instituted retention programs that offer flexible work arrangements and regular bonuses to staff with needed technology skills. A number of companies are offering to pay programmers who volunteer to do year 2000 repair work after hours on a piecework, flat fee, or hourly rate basis. State and federal government agencies are being particularly hard hit, because they can't compete with salaries being offered in the private sector. Instead, these agencies are turning to outside technology firms who are charging going rates for necessary services.

It really boils down to simple economics. Demand far exceeds supply, and the price curve is veering straight up. One negative side effect for the small business owner is that the larger or more established consulting firms are in huge demand and therefore are not bidding on smaller contract assignments. They are focused on the high-revenue end of the market. Another negative repercussion is that some less-than-qualified individuals are jumping on the Year 2000 Computer Crisis bandwagon and offering their services at markup rates. As a private consumer, you need to recognize this fact and do everything possible to ensure that you are dealing with a reputable company or individual.

There are a variety of ways to identify contractors and consulting firms who may be able to suitably perform your year 2000 problem assessment and repair work:

- If you have used a contracting or consulting firm in the past and have been satisfied with their services, contact them and ask about their experience and interest in performing year 2000 assessment or repair work.

- Contact a nearby trade association, such as the Better Business Bureau, or a state-level consumer affairs group and request information about area companies who are selling year 2000 problem resolution services.

- Contact one of the Year 2000 User Groups identified in Appendix J. Attend a meeting and request information about vendors who are marketing their year 2000 services to that group. Talk to other members who may be willing to refer you to outside resources they have used and were satisfied with.

- Visit the Year 2000 Information Center Web site location noted in our chapter on sources for year 2000 information, to access lists of vendors who are offering year 2000 related services.

- Check the Yellow Pages for computer software service company listings and make cold calls to determine whether some of these companies have an interest in bidding on your work.

- If you are willing to have someone perform the work on weekends or after normal business hours, run a local newspaper ad seeking an experienced professional who may be interested in doing the work on this basis. There are many capable full-time employees who are more than willing to do this to earn extra dollars.

QUALITY AND CREDENTIALS

Research the background and credentials of anyone you think about hiring. Many business professionals choose vendors based on referrals and advice from peers. However, given the critical nature of the year 2000 problem and its potential adverse impact on your business, you need to take extra measures to ensure that you make the right hiring decisions. Ask the prospective contractor pertinent questions to help you determine whether they can meet your needs.

- *Experience and References* — Find out if potential resources are familiar with the software you are running. If they aren't, that will affect work quality as well as the amount of time needed to complete the work. Also, find out what year 2000 work they've completed. If they have confidence in that work, they'll be happy to share this and provide you with references. Check those references. Find out what specific work the contractor performed, in what time frames, and what resources were assigned. Was the reference satisfied with how the work was completed? Were the results what they expected? Were there any extra costs, delays, or problems?

- *How Long* — How long has the consultant been in the year 2000 business? A consulting firm may have been around for some time, but what type of work have they specialized in? Find out if they have done any real year 2000 assessment or repair work. Ask them to describe the date-handling problem and its potential impact on hardware, operating software, business software, and data files. If you don't feel satisfied with how well they understand the problem, then rule them out.

- *Staff Size and Availability* — Are available resources qualified to perform the necessary work? Can they start and complete the work when you need it done? Request a summary of the credentials and experience of each person who will be assigned to your project. This is particularly important if the work is to be subcontracted. If you're not satisfied with the resources the consultants plan to assign, talk to them about your concerns and see how they respond. Ultimately it may come down to an issue of trust. However, this shouldn't deter you from seeking a level of comfort and confidence in the people who will be doing the work.

- *Methods and Tools* — Do the consultants have a documented methodology that will be followed to ensure the quality and consistency of work results? Can they describe their assessment or repair processes and testing techniques? What software tools will they use to accomplish the work, and will you be expected to pay for these tools?

- *Guarantees* — Findout if the consultants offer work guarantees and whether they will put their guarantees in writing. Given that it is a seller's market, most contractors are not going to agree to anything more than the standard terms of work delivery and acceptance. If they provide a written guarantee, it's a plus, but don't count on it.

Bear in mind that reputable contractors and consulting firms will provide enough information to assure you they have the know-how, techniques, tools, and resources available to deliver the results you need. However, it's your responsibility to ask the right questions and to confirm the answers you receive so you feel confident you're selecting the right company or person for the job.

METHODOLOGY AND APPROACH

It is very important that you make sure the company or individual you hire has a well-thought-through methodology for completing the work you need done. If they will follow a documented step-by-step process, there's a better chance that the project will be well executed and that you will be able to effectively audit their progress. Have work bidders provide a documented summary of the methods, techniques, tools, and work approach they plan to use if you hire them. Whether you're working with an independent contractor or a large consulting firm, if they won't describe their methodology, it's likely they haven't given it a lot of thought and are basically intending to "wing it."

What constitutes a sound methodology for identifying and resolving year 2000 problems? This book outlines one that anyone can successfully apply. It includes the following phases and steps, and describes how to complete each one.

I. Inventory and Impact Assessment Phase
- Inventory your assets
- Test and assess which products and files have problems
- Audit manufacturer/vendor contracts and legal agreements
- Contact vendors and outside service providers

II. Solution Planning Phase
- Identify problem resolution options and costs
- Assess risks
- Formulate a solution plan

III. Implement Solutions
- Acquire upgrades or fixes
- Retest

Any sound year 2000 problem resolution methodology should include similar phases and steps. It should also describe the process, tools, and techniques that will be employed to accomplish each piece of the project.

SAMPLE VENDOR PROPOSAL FOR YEAR 2000 COMPLIANCE EVALUATION

Following is a sample Year 2000 Work Proposal. It responds to a request made by a Service Agency who wants a Year 2000 Impact Assessment performed for its PC and Local Area Network hardware and software. The agency has roughly 100 PCs and one LAN. Part of their request is for the vendor to tag each of their hardware assets and load the inventory information and assessment findings into a database that will be turned over to the agency at the conclusion of the project. The vendor is also required to create reports detailing compliance upgrade needs and costs for each PC. The proposal does the following:

- Confirms the requirements and project scope.
- Defines what will be delivered, including sample reports.
- Identifies the vendor resources plus service agency support needed during project execution.
- Outlines the project plan.
- Provides a summary of project costs.
- Includes a Vendor Profile to certify qualification to perform the work.
- Provides a detailed description of the methodology that will be followed to complete the project.

I. PROPOSAL COVER LETTER

April 1, 1998

Daniel Smith, Director of Operations
XXX Service Agency
100 Main Street
Any City, MA. 99999

Dear Mr. Smith:

We are interested in being the Year 2000 Service Provider to accomplish your information Technology Evaluation. We will determine personal computer and network upgrade/replacement requirements and provide information to help you select solution alternatives to achieve year 2000 compliance. We will utilize the services, methodology, and software developed by our staff, and third-party vendors, to accomplish this work.

We will inventory all desktops and peripherals, as well as your network operating system, server hardware, and other network components. We will test and research compliance status and will load all inventory results and compliance information into an Inventory Repository Database. This database will be accessible for your on-line viewing, maintenance, planning, and reporting purposes at the conclusion of this engagement. In addition to delivering the database, we will also produce reports outlining overall inventory and compliance findings as well as assessment results for each network node device.

The attached proposal package includes a profile of our company and qualifications for performing this work. It details the scope of work to be performed, describes the format and proposed content of each deliverable, describes agency support needs, and outlines the project plan and delivery time frames. It also provides a detailed explanation of the methodology we will use and the price and terms of payment for work completion.

We appreciate being given the opportunity to bid on this work and are confident you will be fully satisfied with our work results.

Sincerely,

Susan Jones
Consultant Specialist
Millennium Services Group

II. MILLENNIUM SERVICES GROUP COMPANY PROFILE

Millennium Services Group is a local consulting firm which was formed in 1996 by a small group of independently successful computer technology professionals who average more than 15 years of development and support experience in various areas of mainframe, client server, database, and network/desktop computing disciplines. In addition, we all have extensive hands-on project leadership and management experience and have worked on various Year 2000 Compliance Initiatives.

Our work force includes a core group of 25 professionals supplemented by access to a pool of 20 part-time resources who are all highly experienced in performing various aspects of Year 2000 Assessment and Remediation work. Our company is focused on providing solutions for year 2000 problems. We have developed a variety of tools, techniques, and methodologies that have been practically applied to assist businesses in addressing their year 2000 date issues. We have successfully completed more than a dozen year 2000 projects to date and would be happy to provide references who can attest to our ability to deliver promised results.

The founders of the Millennium Services Group have their roots in the New England area and have solid reputations with prior corporate and state government employers for delivering high-quality work results. We are continually seeking business engagement opportunities requiring our high standards of performance and commitment to quality and customer satisfaction. Our goal is to maintain our position as an established year 2000 solution provider and also become recognized for our ability to develop and implement technology solutions that will enable our customers to make a successful transition into and well beyond the next millennium.

III. PROJECT SCOPE AND REQUIREMENTS

The scope of work includes 100 service agency PCs, two file servers, a backup device, archive/restore drives, 25 modems, 10 printers, two fax machines, and all other LAN-connected hardware that might be affected by year 2000 date-handling problems.

All equipment and software is located at the XXX Service Agency building, 100 Main Street, Any Town, Massachusetts.

Work effort will include:

- Completing an inventory of and tagging all hardware assets.
- Testing each PC for BIOS compliance.
- Identifying all operating system and business software running on each piece of hardware.
- Researching operating system and software product compliance.
- Creating a user data file inventory for each PC.
- Scanning user data files to identify those containing fields with two-digit years.
- Researching BIOS and software upgrade or fix options and costs.
- Creating and entering all inventory, test, and research results into a relational inventory database.
- Generating reports identifying all hardware and software assessment findings along with upgrade or replacement options.

At a minimum the Database Inventory Repository will include:

- Name of hardware user or owner
- Physical floor location of the hardware
- Type of hardware
- Hardware manufacturer, make, model, serial number
- Asset identification number (sequentially assigned)
- Installed RAM
- Size of hard drive
- Available drive space
- CPU speed
- Installed peripherals
- Results of BIOS check for year 2000 compliance
- Application data files containing fields with two-digit years stored on each hardware node

- Operating system and package software products installed on each hardware node
- Any compliance findings and assessment results separately listed for each software and hardware product

IV. DELIVERABLES

We will customize and install our Database Inventory Repository to provide the following deliverables:

1. A maintainable database containing all PCs and assorted network hardware and software with associated Y2K compliance information as listed in your specification. It will include the ability to print:
   - The entire database
   - Selected PC or other component records
   - Reports detailing all hardware/software and if it needs upgrading or replacing

   Delivery of the database will include on-site installation and a half-day training session for up to four people.

2. Asset stickers, which will be affixed to all equipment and will indicate BIOS compliance test results.

3. Reports, which will contain hardware and software component assessment results for each network node, with upgrade/replacement recommendations. Pricing of available BIOS upgrades will be included. These reports will be delivered in a 3-ring binder with attached diskettes containing the soft-copy formats. Sample report formats are attached.

4. A high-level summary report outlining overall agency inventory findings, compliance impacts, and standard PC/server platform recommendations. This report will be delivered in hard-copy format and will be accompanied by a formal presentation to Service Agency officials.

V. SAMPLE OUTPUT REPORT FORMATS

Asset ID: Owner Name:

Location:

Make: Model: Serial #:

Processor Specifications (if applicable)

RAM: CPU Speed:

HD Size: Available HD:

BIOS Compliant: {Y,N}

Information for Non Compliant BIOS

Version:

Manufacturer:

Date Produced:

Upgrade Source:

Upgrade Cost:

BIOS Upgrade Recommendation:

Operating System

Vendor: Product: Version:

Compliance Need: [if needed to what version]

Software

Product /Version	Vendor Name	Compliant (y/n)	Upgrade Recommendation

Noncompliant User Data Files: (contain two-digit years)

File Type	File Name	File Type	File Name

FORM   *Node level compliance report (One report will be generated for each PC and Server Node)*

9-1

Agency Name:		Agency Location:		

Software Summary

Product Name	Version	# Copies Installed	Compliant (y/n)	Compliant Version # (If Available)

Hardware Summary

Product	Model	Manufacturer	# Installed	Upgrade Option/s

Form *AGENCY HARDWARE AND SOFTWARE COMPLIANCE*
9-2 *(One report will provide a summary of each unique hardware and software type and upgrade option)*

VI. Resources and Department Support Requirements

A total of two consulting resources and a full-time technical coordinator will be provided to perform this inventory assessment. The physical inventory gathering and assessment testing work will be performed on-site at your offices at 100 Main Street, Any City, MA 99999.

Inventory Repository customization, data imports to the repository, product compliance research, and final report preparation work will be carried out at the vendor's business offices.

It is anticipated that the equivalent of one full-time resource will be required from your company throughout the duration of the project to do the following:

- Identify equipment location and ownership
- Issue User IDs and grant network access rights to MSG project staff
- Provide an overview of LAN and PC setup configurations and directory structures
- Perform server backups and schedule network outages prior to server BIOS testing
- Provide access to any needed hardware or software documentation and to secured network hardware components that must be inventoried
- Schedule time with users to gather the inventory and to test desktop hardware
- Provide server environment setup for implementation of the Inventory Repository
- Coordinate the Inventory Repository training session

VII. INVENTORY/ASSESSMENT METHODOLOGY

This methodology provides a comprehensive approach to completing a PC workstation/LAN based inventory and Year 2000 Compliance Assessment. It is not designed for a specific environment, nor is it dependent on the utilization of unique assessment tools. It includes:

- Identifying and tagging all hardware components with a sequentially assigned asset number that will be cross-referenced to the delivered inventory database and final reports
- Executing thorough and reliable BIOS compliance tests
- Performing the research necessary to reliably evaluate all other hardware, operating system, standard software, and data file compliance readiness

The methodology is divided into the following five-step process:

STEP 1— Preparation for Data File Analysis	This first step is necessary to ensure that locally stored data files can be subsequently identified and evaluated for the use of two-digit years. It involves executing standard operating system commands or a utility that will globally scan each PC and server directory to identify commercial off-the-shelf software packages that are locally resident. This is supplemented with a user survey to request identification of the software applications that each user runs.

Both the scan results and survey information are reviewed to identify the data file name extensions associated with the list of software. This information is subsequently used to update the scanning utility that will be run during the physical asset inventory step.

We will use Check 2000 PC (Greenwich Meantime-UGA) and OnMark 2000 (Assess) tools, plus customized scan commands and a survey form containing commonly grouped software application products to carry out this first phase of activity.

STEP 2—Physical Asset Inventory	This next step accomplishes the physical inventory data collection process. For each PC and server, the asset owner name and identifying information is gathered and recorded on a data collection sheet. At the same time we will sequentially assign an asset number to each piece of hardware and affix a bar-coded asset tag containing the asset

ID number to each hardware device. A combination of operating system commands and a scanning utility, updated with the data file extensions determined during step 1, will then executed to obtain memory, speed, hard drive, peripheral, local software, and local data file names. This information is later imported to the Inventory Repository Database which will be cross-referenced by the assigned asset number.

For hardware components other than PCs and servers (e.g., routers, hubs, maus, bridges/gateways, backup units), the asset owner and physical identification information is gathered and recorded on an inventory sheet along with a sequentially assigned asset number. A bar-coded asset tag is produced and attached to the device and the manually gathered inventory data is later input to the Inventory Repository.

| STEP 3— Compliance Tests and Data File Evaluation | This step involves testing each PC/server BIOS component to verify its ability to correctly handle dates beyond the year 2000. It also includes identification of any local data files containing two-digit rather than four-digit years. |

We use a strict definition of Y2K compliance for x86-based personal computers. The hardware clock must be compatible with the Motorola MC146818RTC, and the BIOS must report the occurrence of the year 2000 in real time. A stricter definition may be imposed on compatibility, and interpretations that are more liberal may cause Y2K failures. It is our opinion that the strict definition is easy and inexpensive for PC vendors to implement. The strict definition also maintains complete compatibility with industry standards.

For BIOS testing we will utilize a tool that verifies MC146818 RTC compatibility.

We will verify real-time progression from December 31, 1999, to January 1, 2000, and verify recognition and support of leap years from 2000 through 2004. We will also test the ability to manually set and retain the operating system date during a power-down and power-up situation. This will include validating that the date stamps on files are correctly retained.

Prior to testing a server's BIOS, we will require that a full backup of the server be performed. Server testing must be performed while the network is down, either during non-business hours or during a scheduled work outage. Also, we will not perform operating system date change tests at the server level because of the adverse impact this would have on LAN environment operation and stability. For example, the system would start to purge file server data files exceeding retention date limits, scheduled jobs that should not be run would automatically kick off, and some system IDs would be locked out.

If the BIOS test fails, we will determine the BIOS manufacturer, date of manufacture, and version level through execution of the system setup. This information will be needed for subsequent research of vendor compliance upgrade requirements and costs and will be retained in the Inventory Repository. If, at the end of the test, the system does not fail for year 2000, we will certify it as being year 2000 compliant from a BIOS perspective and note this on the asset identification tag as well as in the Inventory Repository.

Various automated and manual scanning techniques can be employed to identify data files containing two-digit years. We may employ DateSpy and Date*find*-db (AMS Group International Distributors Inc.) and custom-developed scanning utilities, as well as some manual review methods.

Results of the BIOS tests and the data file date analysis will be imported to the Repository based on the associated PC or Server asset identification number.

STEP 4— Compliance Research

This step involves performing compliance research on BIOS versions that fail the MC146818RTC tests, as well as on all operating-system versions, commercial off-the-shelf software product versions, and network hardware and software components (e.g., routers, hubs, dial in software, virus scanners, NLMs).

Research includes locating and obtaining information regarding compliance claims or compliant product availability time lines. Information sources may include direct vendor interaction, accessing vendor Web sites, or utilizing documents that have been published by reliable industry sources. We already have a comprehensive database of most national vendors hardware and support software and their year 2000 direction.

Any out-of-compliance issues will be input by product in the Inventory Repository.

STEP 5—
Recommendations

The previous four steps will ensure that each PC and server has a comprehensive node profile inventory of the software components and the operating system running on each physical platform. Recommendations will then be formulated based on availability of compliant upgrades and BIOS upgrade costs, as well as an overall node-level view of software upgrade interdependence on the operating system version and in turn on the hardware platform computing capacity requirements of that node.

Additional considerations such as longer-term application development direction and future computing strategies and plans will not be identified and therefore cannot be factored into the overall compliance recommendation.

VIII. PROJECT PLAN

A high-level project plan outlining major tasks/milestones and estimated completion targets is documented on the following page (see

Phase/Task	Start Date	Completion Date
I. Preparation Phase:	5/18/98	5/25/98
Obtain System ID's and Security Access		
Overview of System Environment		
Establish Inventory/Test Schedules		
Install/Modify Inventory Database		
Prepare for Data File Analysis		
II. Physical Asset Inventory Phase:	5/25/98	5/29/98
Conduct Inventory		
Load Results to Database		
III. Compliance Test and Evaluation Phase:	6/1/98	6/12/98
Test PCs		
Perform Server Backups		
Test Servers		
Load Results to Database		
IV. Compliance Research Phase	6/12/98	6/24/98
V. Recommendation and Report Preparation	6/25/98	7/1/98
VI. Present Findings and Recommendations	7/2/98	7/2/98
VII. Conduct Repository Training	7/2/98	7/3/98

TABLE *Project Schedule*
9-1

Tables 9-1 and 9-2). It assumes timely coordination of and access to needed Agency information, resources, and assets during the initial preparation, physical asset inventory, and compliance testing phases of the project.

A 7-week time frame is estimated to complete the project , including report preparation, repository delivery, and training. At the conclusion of the work effort, a formal presentation of the overall inventory and assessment findings will be made to the Agency executive staff.

IX. PROJECT COSTS

Millennium Service Group Resource Daily Rates	
Technical Coordinator	$500
Technical Specialist	$400
(Daily rates are based on an 8-hour work day)	
Resource Costs	
1 Technical Coordinator for 34 Days	$17,000
1 Technical Specialist for 34 Days	$13,600
1 Technical Specialist for 20 Days	$ 8,000
Total MSG Resource Charges	**$38,600**

TABLE *Project Costs*
9-2

Other Expenses

Agency will be responsible for licensing of software tools which will be used to perform the automated analysis. Estimated cost for purchase of software licenses is between $500 and $1,000.

Agency will also be responsible for all federal, state, and local taxes related to this agreement as well as any out-of-pocket expenses, mailing, and long-distance phone charges incurred in connection with the services provided.

Terms of Payment

Customer will be invoiced on a bi-weekly basis for both time and materials. Payment will be due within 30 days of invoice date.

End Sample Proposal

GETTING WHAT YOU PAY FOR

The best way to ensure that you get what you pay for is to clearly define the scope of work you want performed. Document your expectations in terms of the information and results that need to be delivered. Build interim performance checks, status reviews, and work acceptance approvals into your contracts. The clearer you are in describing your needs, the better your chances are of securing the services and results you want.

For example, if you want someone to perform a Year 2000 Impact Assessment and then present you with findings, options, and cost estimates to fix the identified problems, clearly state this. Your scope statement should quantify and identify what needs to be evaluated. Include the numbers and types of personal computers, local area networks, operating system software, and installed business software. Indicate that you want detailed reports identifying specific technology versions you are running, what pieces of hardware and software have problems, and what those problems are. Ask the consultants to identify repair or upgrade options, whether any data file conversions will be required, and the estimated time and costs to acquire or implement needed solutions. Tell them you want documented information from vendors about whether your products are compliant. Indicate how frequently you want to meet to discuss and review progress.

Suppose you have already evaluated your hardware and software problems and are seeking outside help to repair a specific business application found to be noncompliant. Once again, you need to specifically state the extent of the work and the work completion measurements. For example, identify the size of the system, including number of programs and data files, and what you want corrected. Make sure you are clear about whether you want all date fields expanded or whether the vendor may use some type of sliding window calculation to derive the century value when needed. Identify the test criteria you want them to use to validate results.

Indicate that you want documented test results. Stipulate that a portion of the payment for services will be withheld until you have tested or reviewed these results.

An important note about technology contractor and consultant work guarantees is that if they are willing to warrant the work you contract them to perform, they will usually limit the damages and liability they are willing to assume. Generally, they will agree to repay a portion of the fees they collected, or they will correct the errors/faulty work at no cost. Therefore, if you incur business revenue losses because of their failure to perform the work they promised, you won't be in a position to sue them for these losses. The bottom line is, you need to stay involved to ensure that your needs are understood and satisfied.

WHAT WILL IT COST?

How much will these assessment and repair projects cost? Your ability to successful negotiate contract terms and price will depend largely on your ability to find more than one person or company who is qualified and willing to do the work. Given the existing technology resource market conditions, most contractors are not willing to work on anything other than a time and materials basis. Basically, they want you to pay them for the hours they work.

Companies or individuals offering fixed prices either are very stringent about defining the exact scope of work they will perform or will quote a cost that is inflated to allow for possible work overruns. A usual practice is to estimate the actual work effort and then tack on another 30% for the risk factor. It's difficult to say whether you are better off to seek a fixed-price bid, or simply pay on an hourly rate basis. Either way you need to regularly monitor and review work results to ensure appropriate progress and quality. Otherwise, you are going to be operating on sheer blind trust.

Regardless of the payment method agreed to, there are a couple of provisions you should consider including in your work agreements that provide some payment liability protection. The first is a "cancellation for no cause" provision. This gives you the right to terminate the contract without justification, and with no obligation to pay for any work other than what was completed prior to cancellation. If it's a fixed-price contract, this provision should stipulate what portion of the payment you would owe. The second provision is to indicate that you will not pay for unsatisfactory work performance.

> **SAMPLE CANCELLATION PROVISION LANGUAGE**
>
> This Agreement may be canceled upon 5 business days' advance written notice, with no liability to the client, except for work previously completed under this contract. Fixed price work will be paid on a pro-rata basis through the date of work cancellation.

> **SAMPLE SATISFACTORY WORK PERFORMANCE PROVISION LANGUAGE:**
>
> The <Client> will pay the <Contractor> for satisfactory performance of the work at the rates described in the attached schedule. Failure to deliver interim and final work results as outlined in the contract work schedule will constitute unsatisfactory performance.

Rates for services vary by skill/experience level, specialization, geographic area, and whether the resource is independently contracting or subcontracting through another consulting firm. Bigger software services firms typically charge from 25 to 35% more than they pay to their subcontractors. Most of them also charge a premium for highly sought-after skills.

- Independent contractors or systems professionals with full-time jobs who offer their services on a part-time basis typically charge the most reasonable rates. In the Northeastern and Southeastern United States, we have seen rates ranging from $30 to $60 an hour.

- Smaller technology services firms in the same region are generally charging anywhere from $45 to $75 an hour for programmers or technology specialists, and anywhere from $65 to $100 an hour for technical project coordinators or managers. Again, skill and expertise demands are what primarily drive the rate.

A Sample Small Business Year 2000 Impact Assessment Cost Model

What might it cost to hire contractors or consultants to perform a year 2000 impact assessment for a small business operation? As already noted, many variables could affect the time and effort involved. Let's assume you wanted the following Year 2000 Impact Assessment work performed and you had a company that was going to base its bid for this work on an average rate of $50 per hour.

WORK SPECIFICATION

1. Perform and create a documented inventory of all hardware, operating systems, business software, and data files.

2. Test all PC hardware and operating systems for year 2000 compliance.

3. Contact the hardware and software vendors to obtain documented information about product compliance and upgrade requirements and costs.

4. Scan the custom-developed programs, macros, input screens, output reports, and user files to identify all date usage and calculation problems.

5. Create reports documenting all assessment findings and problem correction options and costs.

6. Develop a plan for problem correction.

SCOPE OF EVALUATION

Ten personal computers running DOS and Windows operating systems. One file server running Novell Netware. The shrink-wrapped software running on the PCs includes WordPerfect and Lotus 1-2-3. QuickBooks plus two custom-developed Visual Basic applications (an inventory tracking and an order processing system) are running from the server.

We can't stress enough that the time, effort, and cost associated with any year 2000 assessment or repair project is going to vary depending on the scope and complexity of the technology involved. Of course, the rate the vendor must pay to attract and retain qualified resources has a direct bearing on what they ultimately will charge. In the scenario just outlined, if the bidder's hourly rate was $40 instead of $50, then the cost would drop from a $5,200–6,000 range to a $4,160–4,700 range. Or, if it were $60

ESTIMATED COST

	Estimated Work
Complete Hardware and Software Inventory	1 day
Test PC/Server BIOS and Operating Systems	2 day
Scan and Evaluate Custom-Developed Applications	3-4 days
Review User Spreadsheets and Data Files	1-2 days
Research Product Compliance and Upgrade Options	2 days
Formulate Repair/Replacement Cost Estimates	1 day
Create Assessment Reports and Develop Repair Plan	2 days
Project Coordination and Administration	1 day
Total Work Effort	13–15 days
Average Daily Rate (assuming 8 hours per day at $50 an hour) =	$400
Total Estimated Cost:	$5,200–6,000

an hour, the cost would be roughly $6,240 to $7,200. The vendor may also add a 20–30% risk factor.

It's difficult to speculate what a fair average cost might be. If you wanted to hire someone to simply conduct an inventory and test BIOS and operating system compliance, a reasonable time estimate would probably be 1–2 hours per PC and 2–4 hours per server. Assuming you can find a qualified resource who is willing to do this work for $50 an hour, you would end up paying $50–100 per PC and $100–200 per server. You would then still need to test and research software and data file compliance in order to fully understand the scope of your repair effort.

The bottom line is, costs may vary significantly. What you pay will depend on many factors, not the least of which is availability of resources. One certainty is that costs will continue to go up as the millennium deadline gets closer. If you have a small business operation, consider a small local contracting firm, or a qualified part-time professional who has good credentials and a well-thought-through approach for addressing your year 2000 needs. This is probably where you will find your best value.

In summary, there are a number of critical factors you need to consider if you decide to secure outside help. You need to feel confident that whomever you hire has the required resources, skills, and experience to get the job done. Check references. Determine whether the contractor has a well-defined methodology for performing the work. Make sure you are clear about the results you expect. Try to obtain proposals from more than one contractor. Determine whether their costs seem reasonable. Bear in mind that costs will not necessarily guarantee the results you need. The "Millennium Bug" could affect your company's ability to operate beyond this decade. Even if you hire outside resources, you must manage and monitor compliance initiatives as if your business depended on it — because it well may.

CHAPTER 10

Legal Concerns

THIS CHAPTER CONTAINS:

- The Need for Diligence

- Software Licensing Rights
- Insurance Coverage

- Product and Service Guarantees and Warranties
- Auditing Your Contracts
- Don't Procrastinate

THE NEED FOR DILIGENCE

If you are a small business owner, it is important for you to understand the legal implications and possible consequences of not dealing with your year 2000 problems in a diligent manner. If a critical piece of software or hardware fails, or if one or more of your suppliers' services are disrupted or terminated because they failed to address their year 2000 problems, your business revenues are going to be affected. Imagine arriving at work on January 2, 2000, eager and ready to start the New Year. By noon you're wondering why the shipping company has not arrived to pick up your normal shipments. Why? Because the shipping company's computers are down and they have no way to track their customer account information.

Suppose your ability to operate your company is disrupted for an extended period, and you lose customers and business to competitors. If that happens, will you be able to sue the manufacturer of the software that failed or generated inaccurate information? As for the suppliers who failed to deliver the products and services contracted to you, which you were relying on to generate your products and services — could you hold those suppliers financially responsible for your business income losses?

Given that the year 2000 issue is now a widely publicized and recognized problem, chances are it will be very difficult to prove someone else is responsible for your business failure, particularly if you didn't take steps to avoid that failure. Furthermore, if you lose your business, can you afford to hire a lawyer to litigate your case? It's not likely a lawyer would take this type of case on a contingency basis unless you can prove you did everything possible to avoid the problems.

It's probably safe to assume you want to avoid litigation if at all possible. However, if you make every effort to ensure that you and your vendors are compliant, and the problem still has a serious impact on your business, then you'll want to be sure you've taken the necessary steps to position yourself for successful legal action. The old sports adage that "the best defense is a strong offense" really applies in this instance. Be proactive and diligent about protecting your legal position. The following four action steps can help you achieve this goal.

> Document your compliance efforts and maintain a written record of all communications.

We have already discussed the need to contact your hardware and software suppliers to determine if the products you acquired from them are year 2000 compliant. Not only is it important to do this, but you should keep a written record of both the requests you make and responses you receive. This documentation will prove useful if you are forced to sue at a later date.

It would also be wise to maintain a written record of whatever actions you take to fix, or to ensure that your business partners and suppliers fix, their year 2000 problems. If your business operation is interrupted, and one of your customers or business partners decides to sue you for failure to live up to your service or contract agreements, then your ability to prove you made every effort to deal with this problem may be critical to your defense.

> Request written compliance information from your suppliers and business partners.

The second thing you should do is identify all external business suppliers or partners you rely on or interface with and request written information about their state of year 2000 readiness. Chapters 12 and 13 deal more extensively with how to identify and contact business organizations and agencies that affect your personal or business well-being. The chapters also cover the types of information to request from those organizations to assess whether they are appropriately dealing with their year 2000 problems. If your suppliers or business partners are not aware or are not dealing with the year 2000 problem, you need to know and take action now. The fact that you may be able to sue these companies later on will be irrelevant if your business is lost. It could take years to obtain any type of settlement.

> Perform an audit of your technology and business contracts.

A third and equally critical step is to perform a thorough review of all your contracts and license agreements to understand their terms, conditions, and guarantees. Certain clauses may allow you to obtain vendor support to fix faulty products at no cost or hold the manufacturer liable for payment of losses.

Determine if your technology vendors are obligated to fix year 2000 failures. If not, it's better to find out now, so you can take steps to replace the products or fix them yourself before your business is affected. Some contracts may contain conditions requiring you to provide written notification of your intention to take action to remedy a problem the manufacturer refuses to address. If you fail to provide this notification, you may not be permitted to pursue any type of legal action against them in the future. In fact, the vendor may be able to successfully sue you because you violated the terms of your contract.

You also need to determine what your responsibilities are to your customers if your problems affect them. Will they be able to hold you financially responsible for breaking contract agreements or selling them faulty products or services?

It is equally important that you review and understand what losses your insurance contracts will cover. Does your liability insurance exclude coverage of year 2000 related losses? If so, determine what your options are. Maybe you can renegotiate agreements, or limit your liability by implementing a well-documented correction plan.

> Negotiate year 2000 compliance guarantees into all future
> contracts.

From this point forward, make sure any new vendor or service-provider contracts or agreements you sign contain a year 2000 compliance guarantee. Try to be specific about the terms and conditions related to liquidation damages, and repair obligations if the product or service fails. Do this with renewal contracts as well. This includes all of your service or support agreements, not just technology-related contracts.

If you are a business owner, consider seeking legal help to draft and negotiate contract compliance language and terms. This is particularly important if you are making a significant financial investment or will be relying heavily on the product/service you are purchasing to support a critical piece of your business operation. We've seen a number of different year 2000 compliance warranties. Some vendors use very brief statements that don't provide much in the way of buyer protection. Obviously, it's important to ensure that your contracts provide as much protection as possible, but a lot will depend on how much leverage you can exert in the contract negotiation process.

PRODUCT AND SERVICE GUARANTEES AND WARRANTIES

Guarantees and warranties provided with commercial off-the-shelf (COTS) products are very limited. None of them we reviewed included any specific warranties or guarantees that stated the product was "year 2000 compliant." Most of them included language indicating the product would generally perform according to the features and functions described in the product documentation. Product warranty periods varied, with some major COTS manufacturers limiting their warranty period to just a few months. During this period, if the buyer feels the product is not performing as claimed, the only remedy is to return it with a receipt for a refund of the purchase price.

COTS vendors rely on the fact that most people who buy their products aren't making a significant financial investment, aren't going to take the time to review the contract guarantees, and basically recognize they must accept the product "as is" if they want to use it. In fact most people simply bypass the standard contract agreement statement that is usually displayed on the screen when they install a new piece of software on their personal computer. These statement says something like, "Proceeding with installation of this software indicates you have read and agree to the terms of the software license agreement as stipulated by the vendor." Clearly, you as an individual consumer really have no ability or opportunity to negotiate any type of year 2000 compliance guarantees with COTS manufacturers. Basically, it's a "buyer beware" situation.

On the other hand, if you have any signed license or service agreements, they may contain provisions requiring the other parties to fix known problems and product defects. These provisions may require you to submit a written notification about the problem by a particular date, or the vendor won't be under any legal obligation to make the corrections. Some contracts have terms that obligate the vendor to fix reported problems, but only if you agree to pay for the work. Also, many contracts place limits on the warranty time periods.

As far as new contracts and service agreements are concerned, this is where you have the ability to negotiate specific warranties against year 2000 failures. As a buyer, if you don't include specific year 2000 Warranty language in your contracts, it will be harder for you to take successful legal action if year 2000 product failures or service disruptions occur later on. In addition, most general product warranties limit or exclude vendor liability for any indirect losses you may sustain from use of their product, such as loss of business revenues. It is therefore important to include a specific year 2000 warranty provision. Make sure the contract language specifically warrants year 2000 compliance and includes a precise definition of what year 2000 compliance means. This will ensure your right to seek and recover financial damages, should the vendor breach this agreement.

For example, suppose you were offered a contract that states,

"Seller guarantees this software will not falter at the approach of January 1, 2000, and beyond." This statement offers no guarantee that you, the buyer, will be able to rely on the system to *accurately process and represent date information* before, during, and after the year 2000, to consistently input and output four-digit years, or to properly handle and follow the quad-centennial leap year rule.

Figure 10-1 shows some sample contract language that could be used with any type of product or service provider. It clearly defines the scope of compliance expected and the period of time a product or service will be guaranteed by the seller.

Again, it is important that your Year 2000 Warranty language be precise. Consider seeking professional assistance from a contract specialist. There are literally hundreds of thousands of companies worldwide, and probably as many different views and opinions of what product compliance claims they should include in their contracts. Ideally, some of these companies are starting to conform to the common definitions of year 2000 compliance that have been formulated by recognized standards institutes. Figure 10-2 shows the definition of year 2000 conformity, which was published by the British Standards Institute in Document Reference DISC PD2000-1. This definition has attained fairly broad use.

The British Standards Institute allows this definition to be freely copied, provided that the text is reproduced in full and the source and reference number of the document is quoted. If you choose to use this exact definition in your contracts, be sure to comply with this stipulation.

Another definition, which is included in the United States Federal Acquisition Regulations, is documented in Figure 10.3. It is used by federal agencies who are purchasing or renewing technology product and service contracts to help them develop their contract requirements.

1. Company XYZ specifically represents and warrants that:

   1.1 Products/Services are designed to be used prior to, during, and after the calendar year 2000 A.D.

   1.2 Products/Services will operate in any of these time periods without error or interruption relating to date data, including date data that represents or references different centuries or more than one century.

   1.3 Products/Services will not abnormally end or provide invalid or incorrect results because of date data, including date data that represents or references different centuries or more than one century.

   1.4 Products/Services are designed to correctly recognize and calculate century date data values, including same-century and multicentury formulas and date values.

   1.5 Products/Services base includes support software and databases which will correctly manage and manipulate all data involving dates, including single-century and multicentury dates, and will not cause any abnormal process termination, or generate incorrect values, or invalid results involving such dates.

   1.6 Products/Services support software and databases will provide that all date-related user interface functionality and date fields will specify an explicit indication of century.

   1.7 Products/Services support software and databases will provide that all date-related data interface functionality and date fields will specify an explicit indication of century.

   1.8 Products/Services support software and databases will provide that February 29, 2000, will be correctly recognized as a leap-year date.

2. The term of the Year 2000 Compliance Warranty set forth in section 1 will begin as of the date of contract acceptance by both parties and end after the Product/Services have operated without a breach of the warranty for a period of 24 months, or no sooner than January 2, 2002, whichever is later.

FIGURE *Year 2000 Compliance Provisions*
10.1

Year 2000 Conformity shall mean neither performance nor functionality is affected by dates prior to, during and after year 2000.

In Particular:

Rule 1   No value for current date will cause any interruption in operation.

Rule 2   Date-based functionality must behave consistently for dates prior to, during and after year 2000.

Rule 3   In all interfaces and data storage, the century in any date must be specified either explicitly or by unambiguous algorithms or inferencing rules.

Rule 4   Year 2000 must be recognized as a leap year.

FIGURE *Year 2000 Conformity*
10.2

39.002 Definitions.

Year 2000 compliant means, with respect to information technology, that the information technology accurately processes date/time data (including, but not limited to, calculating, comparing, and sequencing) from, into, and between the twentieth and twenty-first centuries, and the years 1999 and 2000 and leap year calculations, to the extent that other information technology, used in combination with the information technology being acquired, properly exchanges date/time data with it.

39.106 Year 2000 compliance.

(a) When acquiring information technology that will be required to perform date/time processing involving dates subsequent to December 31, 1999, agencies shall ensure that solicitations and contracts:

(1) Require the information technology to be Year 2000 compliant; or

(2) Require that non-compliant information technology be upgraded to be Year 2000 compliant prior to the earlier of (i) the earlier date on which the information technology may be required to perform date/time processing involving dates later than December 31, 1999, or (ii) December 31, 1999; and

(b) As appropriate, describe existing information technology that will be used with the information technology to be acquired and identify whether the existing information technology is Year 2000 compliant.

FIGURE *Federal Acquisition Regulations (FAR)—Section 39—Final*
10.3

SOFTWARE LICENSING RIGHTS

If a software vendor has no contractual obligation to fix recognized year 2000 problems, whether or not you can correct those problems yourself depends on whether you have access to the software source code. Source code is the logic statements that were written by the programmer who created the software. The only way to fix the software is to change this code. The version of the software that is loaded onto your personal computer is the run-time code, not the source code.

Unfortunately, with most COTS products as well as with industry-specific or custom software applications developed by an outside vendor, you have typically only purchased a license giving you the right to use the product. You are not given access to the source code. Furthermore, you cannot modify the source code without the vendor's express permission. However, your software contract may contain provisions or terms that give you the right to access and modify the source code under specified conditions. For example, you may have the right to fix the software if the vendor refuses to live up to an agreement to fix a major problem that is seriously affecting your use of the software for its intended business purpose. Such a right may also be specified if the vendor is no longer in business.

Some laws grant you similar rights if a vendor refuses to fix a product failure that could significantly disrupt your business operation or revenue flows. In these situations you would first have to provide appropriate written notification of your intent to modify the code. Otherwise, the vendor could successfully sue you. It's best to seek legal advice before pursuing this course of action.

A key thing to note here is, you must have access to the source code in order to modify it. Some contracts contain Source Code Escrow agreements that require the seller to give a copy of the source to some independent third party at the time they sign the contract. Later, the buyer can request access to that source code, if the seller refuses to live up to specified contract conditions. Obviously, if you don't have a source code escrow agreement, then you will need to obtain a copy of the source from the seller. As you conduct your software contract audit, make note of those contracts containing escrow agreements and the conditions governing access to the source. Later, if you find you need to fix the software, you'll know what steps you need to take to obtain a copy of the source code.

AUDITING YOUR CONTRACTS

The types of documents requiring your review include:

- Technology license and software purchase agreements
- Product, support and service contracts
- All subsequent contract addenda that you have signed
- Vendor marketing materials
- Public company reports
- Insurance policies

Your objective in performing this audit is to determine your rights and obligations as they relate to year 2000 problem resolution and damage recovery. You need to know the following:

1. If you have product warranties and whether they cover correction of date handling problems or service disruptions.
2. If or when your warranties will expire.
3. If the vendor has the right to charge you for correcting these problems.
4. Whether you have a source escrow account, and who is holding the source.

5. What terms and conditions must be met for you to access the escrowed source code.

6. What damage limits have been agreed upon.

7. What provisions are included that would limit your rights if you don't do what they stipulate, such as sending written notification of problems to the vendor.

8. Whether the vendor has made product or service representations in the contract or product marketing materials leading you or anyone else to believe they will not be affected by century date-handling problems.

9. If the vendor company is publicly traded, whether the quarterly or annual reports make any statement about known problems.

10. Whether your property or liability insurance contracts cover losses related to year 2000 failures.

You want to make sure that you don't unintentionally do something that could limit your ability to recover losses or allow the vendor to shirk responsibility for fixing these problems. You also want to be in a good defensive legal position if you end up in court. Make note of any implied or specific warranties. Be thorough in your review and place particular focus on your critical vendor contracts. Finally, don't hesitate to seek legal or professional assistance if you're not confident about reviewing all this legal language yourself.

INSURANCE COVERAGE

Many insurance companies who write Director and Officer (D&O) liability insurance coverage for business owners and corporate directors are now excluding or limiting their liability for losses related to the year 2000 problem. Since the year 2000 date-handling problem has been known for quite some time, insurance companies are taking the position that executives have had enough time to correct it. Therefore, business owners will be directly responsible for paying settlements arising out of customer or stockholder lawsuits specifically related to losses or damages suffered because of year 2000 product or service failures. For those business owners and executives who are relying on this type of insurance as a safety net, this is a serious issue. If they opt to ignore this problem, they may be placing their personal financial security at risk.

Commercial insurance companies are also choosing not to cover year 2000 related property or business disruption losses. The Insurance Services Offices, an organization which many commercial insurance companies belong to, recently adopted new general liability and property damage exclusion language for year 2000 in their standard contract forms. Companies who write commercial insurance are starting to use these contracts on both new and renewal policies. So it wouldn't be wise to count on this type of insurance coverage to recoup your investment or business income losses. Review your liability insurance contracts in detail and formulate your action plan to identify and remedy your year 2000 problem risks accordingly.

You may be wondering if any insurance companies are actually selling year 2000 loss protection insurance. In early 1997 a couple of major insurance companies designed and began offering this type of coverage to indemnify companies for losses sustained if they failed to correct all their year 2000 system problems. However the cost, underwriting, and ongoing year 2000 correction plan audit requirements required to obtain one of these policies was so extensive that they weren't able to sell the insurance. Potential customers decided they would be better off spending the premium dollars to ensure that their date problems were fixed in time. Another major drawback with these policies was the limit on the amount of liability the insurers would assume. Basically, they were willing to pay up to the limit of the total cost to repair the problems, but they excluded business revenue losses, which could end up being more substantial than the cost of repairing the problems.

DON'T PROCRASTINATE

In the final analysis the best course of action is to work diligently to do the following:

- Identify your critical products and services and determine which ones have or are likely to have year 2000 problems.
- Audit your contracts and legal agreements to understand what your rights and loss/liability exposures are.
- Write your vendors and request certification that their products and services are or will be made compliant.
- Correct your problems, with professional assistance if necessary.
- Negotiate future contracts that guarantee year 2000 compliance and include financial remedies for year 2000 product and service failures.
- Keep a documented record of what you have done to correct your problems and any vendor or business partner communications related to your problem identification and resolution efforts to ensure a strong defensive position if you eventually end up in court.

If you hope to gain any type of advantage in beating the year 2000 challenge, you've got to start immediately. The steps you need to take to protect yourself are clear. The calendar is not going to stop, and the longer you wait, the slimmer your chances of adequately protecting your assets and ability to successfully run your business after December 31, 1999.

CHAPTER

11

Sources for Year 2000 Information

THIS CHAPTER CONTAINS:

- Additional Information Sources
- User Group
- Web Sites

ADDITIONAL INFORMATION SOURCES

The year 2000 problem has gained worldwide recognition. Information is now being regularly shared in newspapers and magazines, on television, and on the radio about the problem's potential impact on various industries and government agencies. As the year 2000 approaches, many individuals are seeking information and assistance to better understand and address its impact. Many business organizations, individuals, vendors, and government entities are finding two resource categories to be highly beneficial to their year 2000 identification and resolution process. These are web sites and dedicated year 2000 user groups.

This chapter identifies some of the most popular year 2000 web sites and describes their area of specialization in relation to the year 2000 problem.

WEB SITES

Web sites are a valuable source of year 2000 information. Most web sites include knowledge bases with search engines. This means you can enter search words and find information in their knowledge databases that matches the entered criteria. Search for phrases such as "year 2000" or "Millennium Bug". Today's web sites tend to include many pages of information pertaining to this topic. You are sure to find an overwhelming number of Web locations dedicated to it.

The Appendix section of this book includes web locations for the following topics:

- Appendix B.— Hardware Manufacturers
- Appendix C — Operating System Manufacturers
- Appendix D — Software Application Titles
- Appendix E — Software Manufacturer Demographics
- Appendix F — Government Agencies
- Appendix J — User Group Listing and Contacts

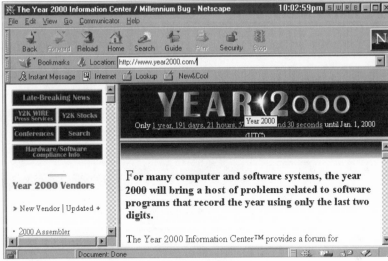

FIGURE
11.1
http://www.year2000.com/ Copyright 1998 by Year2000.com Partnership, http://year2000.com/. Used with permission.

Web sites can be accessed by anyone. Web locations that we recommend visiting are listed on the following pages.

1. The Year 2000 Information Center: *http://www.year2000.com* (see Figure 11-1).

   This web site is one of the greatest resources of information on the year 2000 problems. The site is provided by de Jager & Company Limited and The Tenagra Corporation. Peter de Jager is a world-recognized leader in raising year 2000 awareness. This web site is visited by more than 230,000 people each month.

   The site provides access to a tremendous amount of information:

   • Lists of vendors that offer year 2000 related products and services

   • Lists of year 2000 user groups

   • Schedules of upcoming year 2000 related conferences

   • An archive of current and past articles and press releases

   • Links to other year 2000 sites

2. *www.y2k.com* (see Figures 11-2 and 11-3). This site explores the multitude of legal issues related to identifying, controlling, and remediating the year 2000 problem, in addition to the litigation that will arise if and when the malfunctions

FIGURE *www.y2k.com* Copyright 1997, Y2K, l.l.c.. Used with permission.
11.2

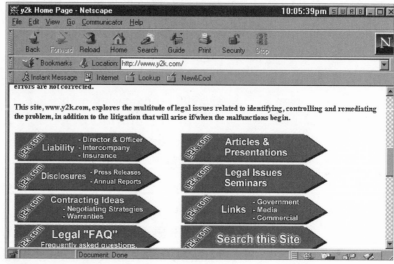

FIGURE *www.y2k.com* Copyright 1997, Y2K, l.l.c.. Used with permission.
11.3

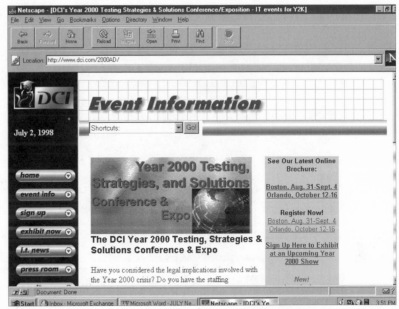

FIGURE *http://www.dciexpo.com/2000ad/* Copyright 1998 by DCI (978) 470-3880.

11.4 All event names are trademarks of DCI or its clients. Used with permission.

begin. It also provides links to other government, media, and commercial sites containing relevant year 2000 information.

3. *www.dciexpocom/2000ad/* (see Figure 11-4). This web site lists upcoming year 2000 conferences. These conferences can be costly, but very helpful for the small business owner. You can acquire information about solutions being offered. You can also talk to experienced consultants, industry experts, keynote presenters, and solution providers. Unlike other conferences and seminars, this new conference program includes in-depth seminars, addresses the "nuts and bolts," and provides you with the strategies and solutions you need to bring your year 2000 project to a successful completion.

4. *http://rightime.com/* (see Figure 11-5). The RighTime web site offers free downloadable programs to help you test and validate your computer hardware's ability to correctly store and process year 2000 dates. It also offers a free program that can be downloaded and installed to fix the problem if the test

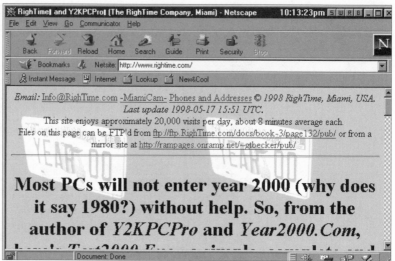

FIGURE **11.5** *Screen prints from http://rightime.com* Copyright 1991-97, The RighTime Co., Miami. All Rights Reserved. Used with Permission.

indicates the fix can be applied. This site also provides links to several other key information sites containing valuable vendor information and frequently asked questions regarding resolution of the year 2000 problem.

5. *http://www.computerworld.com.* This is the Computer World web site. It contains articles and information on all aspects of computer hardware and software. Year 2000 related topics constantly appear in this weekly industry newspaper. There is a "Year 2000" section that you can click on from their main web page that will bring you to year 2000 related topics.

6. *http://www.monmouth.army.mil/y2k/comply.htm.* This site lists the compliance status of numerous software products. It identifies each product's classification, whether it is compliant, and sources of the compliance information being reported, plus any known upgrades or associated costs. This information was compiled by the U.S. Army Material Command and is updated as new information becomes available.

7. *http://www.mitre.org/research/COTS/COMPLIANCE_CAT.html*
   This web site provides information and links to other vendor
   sites to speed research regarding compliance information and
   upgrade or repair options for a variety of commercial off-the-
   shelf products. The site is sponsored by DISA.

8. *http://y2k.policyworks.gov.* This web site is sponsored by the
   U.S. government. It is designed to assist federal agencies in
   accessing product compliance information for many commercial off-the-shelf software products by providing links to
   vendor sites. It also provides access to information from
   agencies and private industry sources regarding actual product experience.

USER GROUPS

Joining a year 2000 user group is an excellent idea for the small business owner as well as for individual computer users. These groups
meet on a regular basis to share pertinent information and experi-
ences. They provide contact with other business owners and users
who are willing to help those pursuing year 2000 problem resolution.
Participants in these user groups recognize that the year 2000 problem can be overwhelming for all levels of computer users. Refer to
Appendix J for a list of user groups in the United States along with
contact and regular meeting schedule information. E-mail or call the
contact person in your area to attend an upcoming meeting.

User group meetings can provide the following:

• Guest speakers who share valuable information
• Question-and-answer sessions
• Networking with other area business contacts and vendors

CHAPTER

12

Other Companies and Government Agencies

THIS CHAPTER CONTAINS:

- Overview
- Review Your Inventory Worksheet
- Who Is Important to Me?
- How to Contact Them

OVERVIEW

Other companies as well as government agencies play an important role in determining your year 2000 compliance. If your system interacts with an outside source, passing data back and forth through EDI (electronic data interchange) or other electronic exchange of data, it may fail while inputting this information. If your personal or business information relies on a system run by an outside source, your computer system or personal life may be adversely affected by their noncompliant system.

We will not attempt to provide a year 2000 status of government or business organizations' computer systems. We will not list facts regarding what agencies are compliant, are in the process of becoming compliant, or have not addressed the problem. We will, however, explain how to determine which organizations are important to you and how to contact them. In the next chapter, we provide more detailed guidance about the information you need to request and how to evaluate whatever responses you get.

Sending a letter and asking for information is an important step in guarding against and minimizing the impact of possible service failures. You need to do this with your critical suppliers, as well as government agencies you interact with on a regular basis. Don't be intimidated about asking for year 2000 status from any company or organization. It is their responsibility to provide you with the information you need.

WHO IS IMPORTANT TO ME?

You should consider any business organization, government agency, employer, religious organization, charitable organization, or other institution that has you or your company listed as a customer, supplier, partner, employee, or member. If you belong to something, chances are you are a record in a database. This means the computer sees you as one element in its vast array of elements. How it responds to you (your element) depends on the nature of the system and how reliant it is on date information to accurately process your records. If a system uses date functionality to process claims, award dividends, compute finance charges, award interest, compute a payment, mail documentation, or other activities, there is a chance it could fail. Will you be receiving scheduled benefits or payments? Do you have an outstanding loan? Consider these issues and list on your inventory worksheet all agencies and companies who might pose a problem if their systems failed to accurately process dates.

Don't dismiss an agency or institution because you owe them money. If their systems fail, chances are they will fail in their favor. You don't want to be billed any more than you already owe. Credit card companies are highly driven by date functions. It is very important their systems be year 2000 compliant. How would a 99-year finance charge look on your bill? You'll probably be over your limit, thus making your card useless until the problem is straightened out. Not good if you regularly rely on your card for essential needs.

A good approach to compiling your list of companies is to identify everyone you are making regular payments to for any of the following:

- Services
- Loan payments
- Parts
- Insurance
- Savings
- Financial investments

Take a look at your canceled checks for the past 6 months and also write down everyone from whom you're receiving regular payment checks. If you operate a business, review your accounts receivable and payable information. As you review those to whom you make regular payments, ask yourself how critical each company's products or services are to your personal well-being or to the ongoing operating ability of your business. If the products or services are important, then make sure you include the source company on the inventory worksheet.

Naturally, each person or company will have a different assessment of what is critical. The following questions might help you to decide whether it is important to include a company on your inventory worksheet.

- Do I need this company's services to support cash flow (make payments or cash checks)?

- Have I borrowed money from the company or organization, and do I have a written record of what I borrowed, the terms of the loan, and payments I have made?

- Have I invested money in this company, or is this company managing my savings or investments for me?

- Is this company or agency managing my pension or retirement income plan?

- Am I relying on this company or agency for a benefit payment (e.g., Social Security, veteran's disability, unemployment)?

- Do I have accrued cash values in the insurance policies that I've purchased from this company?

- Am I relying on this company to provide parts or services that allow me to manufacture my products, and could I survive without them (for how long)?

- If I couldn't rely on this company to provide its product or service, could I perform or provide it myself?

- Would loss of this company's product or service affect my health (e.g., a pharmacy that couldn't fill my prescription)?

- Would loss of this companies service affect my ability to distribute my products (e.g., shipping companies, airlines, bus services, mail services)?
- Do I rely on this provider to perform a state or federally mandated function (e.g., prepare income tax returns, file quarterly or annual reports, perform audits)?

REVIEW YOUR INVENTORY WORKSHEET

The following list gives you an idea of some of the agencies and the types of service providers who might end up on your Inventory Worksheet.

- Banks
- Credit card companies
- Social Security Administration
- Pension plan administrators
- Investment managers and brokerage firms
- Medicare and Medicaid
- Insurance companies (life, health, property, auto, etc.)
- Utility companies
- Distributors
- Regulatory boards
- IRS
- Airlines
- Freight companies
- Mail delivery service companies
- Parts suppliers
- Phone services
- Hospital/emergency services
- Security services

Obviously, this is not a complete list, and the various items' importance to each individual will vary. However, if you have nothing but hardware and software suppliers on your inventory worksheet, you have more work to do. You need to create a list that includes every agency and company with whom you have a critical relationship or that you depend on.

HOW TO CONTACT THEM?

You need to find out who to direct your information requests to. Appendixes B, E, and F provide mail and web site addresses for contacting some of the major personal computer hardware and software suppliers as well as U.S. federal government agencies. If you don't find the information there, consult your most recent bill or other piece of documentation listing the organization's phone number or address. Then call or write them to request the name of the person who can provide you with information about how the company is handling their year 2000 date problem. Ask them for the name of their "Year 2000 Coordinator." If they don't have a coordinator or have no idea what you are talking about, you probably have cause for concern. At this point, any people or companies who aren't aware of this problem and aren't actively addressing it either have their heads in the sand or are in total denial. If you're critically dependent on such a company, you can be sure you are at risk.

Web Sites

If you don't have a phone number or postal address, try the Internet. As noted in the previous chapter, the World Wide Web is a growing source of information and may provide you with the answers you need. See if the company has a web address. If so, connect to the web site and browse for necessary information. Most companies list the Year 2000 Coordinator's name and e-mail address.

E-Mail

If you have the address, send an e-mail to the Year 2000 Coordinator requesting any information that may be available as well as responses to your specific list of questions and concerns. How thoroughly and quickly a company responds will indicate how seriously and diligently they're dealing with this problem.

Information Request Letter

If the company doesn't have a web site, then you should send your request via mail. Be thoughtful about the questions you ask and information you request. Chapter 13 is designed to help you to think through the types of information you need, and Appendix H provides some sample letters. Use these letters as templates, or write your own tailored requests to find out how your vendors are dealing with the year 2000 issue. Don't dismiss this as an unnecessary step.

13 Information Request Letters

THIS CHAPTER CONTAINS:

- Information Request Letters

- What Questions Should You Ask?

- How Will Information Request Letters Help Me?

- What's Next—What Are the Options?

OVERVIEW

A crucial step in determining whether the hardware or software products you have purchased will correctly handle dates beyond the year 2000 is to send a letter to each supplier, requesting documentation or a warranty of their products' compliance.

You also need to determine whether other companies and government agencies you rely on are technologically ready for the year 2000. What steps have they have taken to ensure that their systems will accurately maintain and process your record of transactions, payments, orders, etc., both during and after the transition into the next century?

Obviously, the more you depend on a product or service supplier, the more critical it is for you to have this information. The year 2000 is foreseeable, and you want to be sure you are relying on companies who are carefully dealing with this issue.

This chapter provides you with some detailed guidance about the types of information you need to request. For example, in the case of software suppliers, it's not important to ask for the name of the author of the software application, or how much time was spent designing it, or when it was written. This information will not help you. You need to know specifics pertaining to how their products handle year 2000 dates and whether they will handle these dates correctly 100% of the time in all situations. As for agencies or other businesses, inquire about how they have evaluated their system date problems, how they've corrected or plan to correct the problems, and by when. Ask them to give you an assurance they will not be adversely affected by failure of their systems. Also ask what measures their business partners are taking to ensure compliance.

Remember, it is important to request and obtain written responses. Get and keep any documentation that is provided for your own legal protection. Ask if the company has a formal letter or "white paper" explaining their year 2000 position and how this problem will affect you. Request that they send this to you or tell you where and how to obtain a copy.

This chapter explains the benefits of sending the letters and what you need to know in order to determine whether a company's products or services are at risk of failure. It identifies specific questions and talks about how to use and evaluate company responses. Sample request letter templates are also included in Appendix H as well as on the CD-ROM.

HOW WILL INFORMATION REQUEST LETTERS HELP ME?

Let's review how the information you request will help you to effectively deal with your year 2000 date problem risks.

Hardware and Software Suppliers

These requests are a straightforward way of determining whether your hardware or software has date-handling problems, and whether the vendors plan to fix any acknowledged problems. Of course, the requests also let vendors know that their customers expect them to address this issue. You need to know your suppliers' positions so you can determine the best course of action for your situation.

Some vendors will acknowledge that particular versions of their product do indeed have the date "bug." However, if they have a compliant version, they will likely recommend that you purchase an upgrade. There are a number of issues involved in deciding whether to purchase an upgrade; we will discuss these issues later. You should wait until you've gathered and evaluated all of your hardware and software information before deciding whether it's the best option for you.

Other suppliers may offer free upgrades or the needed support to fix noncompliant products, but expect this to be more the exception than the rule. Finally, you may find some vendors who will suggest ways for you to work around known problems. This could spare you the added expense of purchasing a replacement product.

If you own a small business and have made a significant invest-ment in a technology product, another benefit of contacting the vendor is to have a documented record of correspondence. This will be important if the vendor refuses to stand behind the product. A written record of communication will prove useful if it becomes necessary for you to recover your losses through legal channels at a later date.

Other Companies	

Other Companies

As for companies you depend on for banking or investment serv-ices, accounting support, payroll processing, parts supply, pension plan administration, insurance, etc., you need enough information to assess their risk of operational failure. You can determine this based on their willingness to explain the specific steps they have taken or to share their plans for evaluating and addressing their date problems. Here are some other indicators of how serious and diligent they are being about addressing this problem:

- Their willingness to provide a guarantee that their products and services will not fail because of year 2000 date-handling problems
- The time and resources the company has spent or will spend to research and resolve their date issues
- Whether they are willing to give you a specific contact who is involved in their year 2000 project and who can give you more detailed information and assurances
- Whether they are taking proactive steps to alert their cus-tomers about the problem and about any anticipated service changes
- Whether their definition of "year 2000 compliance" seems rea-sonable and consistent with your understanding of the term
- Their ability and willingness to share how they have addressed the problem with their business partners

If an organization refuses to give you any information, or ignores your request, you will need to send them a follow-up letter. Also, begin to think about finding alternative sources for the products or services they provide. If you receive no response to your follow-up request, let the supplier know you plan to take your business to a company that is being proactive about the year 2000 issue. Then do the leg work and find such a company. Don't make idle threats. Push for the information you need, and take action.

The bottom line is, you need enough information from each company to figure out how vulnerable they or their products are to failure. You need to determine whether you will experience any serious disruption of services because they are not diligently addressing the year 2000 problem. Remember — if they're at risk, then you're at risk. And there are some risks you simply can't afford to take.

Government Agencies

Now what about those government agencies? You're probably thinking, "It's just a waste of time to request any type of information from them." Regardless of how skeptical you are, please send them a letter. At the very least it will make them aware that people are seriously concerned. Ultimately, with rising broad-based public pressure, the agencies will need to step up corrective actions or at least formulate alternatives to deal with anticipated problems.

There is another practical reason for contacting certain government agencies: those with whom you have accrued current or future benefits, such as the Social Security Administration or the Department of Veterans Affairs. You need to obtain a documented record of the benefits to which you are entitled. Also ask that they send you a record summarizing the years of service or contributions you have made entitling you to those benefits. You need to obtain these records now, because you may not be able to get them later if the agency's computer systems fail because of year 2000 date-handling problems. You will have documentation (provided by them) to expedite settlement of disputes. These records will be invaluable. This is where an ounce of prevention will be worth a pound of cure.

WHAT QUESTIONS SHOULD YOU ASK?

The specific questions you ask might vary depending on your relationship with the company or agency and whether you have purchased or leased the use of their products. In all cases you need to be direct. Identify which of their products and services you are using, request the information you think you need, and set a date by which you expect them to respond. Also note the date when you send each request letter. If you don't get a response by the deadline indicated, follow up or start researching the availability of alternative products or companies. You must be proactive.

Hardware/ Software Suppliers

If you are sending the request to a hardware or software supplier, consider requesting the following information for the specific versions of the products that you have purchased or licensed:

- Request a guarantee that the products accept, store and correctly process a full four-digit year date.

- Request a guarantee the products recognize and correctly process February 29, 2000, as a leap year.

- Ask if the products are using some formula-based method to recognize the correct century and to execute date-dependent logic instead of allowing for the input or output of a full four-digit year.

- If the product uses a formula method, ask the vendor to send you information explaining what the method is and if it guarantees correct calculation of all possible dates 100% of the time.

- If the products are not currently capable of accurately handling year 2000 dates in all situations, ask the vendor what plans there are to make them compliant, and by when.

- Ask if you'll be charged for a compliant version of the product when it becomes available, or if they will send you a free upgrade.

- Ask if you will need to convert the data files created with the noncompliant version of the products in order to access your existing data files with the newer product versions.

- If you need to convert your data files, ask if the vendor provides any tools or can recommend methods to help you with the conversion.

- Ask what hardware or other software requirements are associated with upgrading to their compliant versions (e.g., operating system, hard disk space, and memory requirements).

- Ask if they are offering any specific type of year 2000 problem correction assistance or if they will provide "white papers" explaining their position on the problem.

If the supplier responds that the product is not compliant and the vendor has no intention of correcting it, then check your software license agreement. See if it contains any type of guarantee that requires the vendor to correct the problem. In some situations (e.g., where you may be facing a significant investment loss) you may want to consider involving a lawyer in the contract review. You need to judge for yourself whether this is necessary.

Suppose the noncompliant product is a critical application. If it's clear that the vendor isn't obligated to correct the problem, then you could request that the vendor permit you to either fix or hire someone to fix the software code for you. Bear in mind that in addition to the vendor's permission, you will also need a copy of the software source code. Unless you have a source code escrow agreement and have met the conditions of your contract granting you access to the source code, you will also need to request this from the vendor. If you're not sure whether you have a source code escrow agreement, check your contract or have a lawyer review it for you.

Other Companies	If you are sending the request to a company or business organization you rely on for your personal financial security or to satisfy other essential personal or business operation needs, your questions will be different. You need to find out what steps these companies and their business partners have taken to minimize the chances of their business operation being halted or disrupted because they did not deal with their year 2000 problems.

In your request letters, be sure to list the products and services you have purchased. Ask the company to provide information and assurances about these specific items. Following are some questions you should consider including in your request letters:

- Ask them if any of these products involve date handling or rely on the accurate passing and manipulation of dates by or between computer systems to ensure their reliability.

- Request disclosures about whether these products or services are affected by any known or suspected date-handling problems. If they are, when does the company plan to have the problems corrected?

- Ask them to send you a guarantee their products or services will not malfunction or become unavailable because of year 2000 date problems.

- Ask them how they tested or are planning to test to ensure that the systems used to deliver these products are year 2000 compliant.

- Ask them to explain the steps they have taken to ensure they will not be adversely affected by business partners' date problems.
- Request their definition of "year 2000 compliance."
- Request that they tell you how much time and resources they have spent or will spend to identify and correct year 2000 problems.
- If they are a public company, ask them to provide an independent auditor's report about the state of their compliance efforts.
- Ask them if they will provide you with the name of someone you can talk to at their company to obtain more detailed information.
- Ask them what proactive steps they are taking to inform their customers about this issue.
- Find out at what level of the company the resolution of the problem is being managed. This will be an indicator of how committed senior management is to solving the problem.

Also, if these products or services involve any type of electronic data interchange between you and the company, you need to ask if the information format of that interchange will need to be modified to accommodate expanded date fields on files you send or receive. Ask the company to let you know if and when the formats will change and when you need to be ready to test the changes. This is also true for any paper material that is exchanged.

Government Agencies

The kinds of information and responses you will receive from government agencies will vary depending on your circumstances. In your request letter, explain why you have a vested interest in determining a particular agency's state of "year 2000 readiness." Ask them to share whatever information is available about the status of their efforts to correct their date problems. Once again, remember that even if they don't respond, the flood of information requests is certain to draw their attention to the problem.

Obtain a copy of your personal information records. Make sure you get a documented summary of the information that establishes your present or future benefit entitlement. These agencies will probably have standard request forms for this type of information. Ask the agency to explain the process you need to follow and where to obtain copies of the forms.

WHAT'S NEXT—WHAT ARE THE OPTIONS?

Once you decide that certain products are not going to work or that a company you rely on is at risk, you need to figure out what your options are. There are really only three. We refer to them as the three "R's":

- Repair
- Replace
- Retire

Let's consider a situation where one of your software vendors acknowledges that the product you licensed from them has known date-handling problems. They tell you they don't plan to fix these problems. What are you going to do?

1. Should you fix or hire someone to fix the software for you?

   As noted in the chapter dealing with legal concerns, the main issue here is that you may not have the legal right to do this. In most cases the vendor owns the code that was used to create the version of the software running on your computer. Unless the vendor gives you the code and the permission to change it, your only alternatives are to replace the software or stop using it.

Suppose, however, that you discover you do own the source code, or you have a source-code escrow account and a contract condition that gives you the right to change the code in this situation. What does this mean? It means you have to find a resource who is willing and able to make the necessary changes. This could be an expensive alternative and raises another level of risk management that you will need to deal with. Refer to our chapter on hiring consultants and contractors for more specific guidance on what to consider when hiring resources.

2. Should you purchase a comparable product that is "year 2000 compliant"?

In many cases the vendor will suggest that you purchase an upgraded version of their product. Remember, don't make any quick decisions. Find out what other products are available and determine which of these products will run with your hardware and operating system. Ask the supplier. You don't want to buy a piece of software and then find out that it requires more memory or a different operating system. The best approach is to wait until you have a complete picture of all your hardware and software date-handling problems. There may be several products that have problems and need to be replaced. Typically, your software needs dictate what kind of operating system you need, as well as your minimum hardware requirements. Also, you need to consider whether data file conversions will be involved and the availability of tools to help you convert critical files. These issues are covered in more detail in Chapter 6.

3. Should you simply stop using the software?

Obviously, this will depend on how critical the application is to your personal or business needs. If it's a product you use very infrequently, the decision will probably be an easy one.

Whether you're evaluating options for your software products or for other companies whose products and services are at risk of failure, you need to follow the same thought process. Will they be able to repair their problems in time? If the information they've provided leads you to believe they will, you may want to stick with them and closely monitor their progress. Are there other companies, offering the same products and services, that you think are better prepared? Will they guarantee there will be no date-related service failures? Have they provided enough information for you to be confident in their claims? Perhaps eliminating use of the product or service is also a reasonable option. That is a choice only you can make.

Sadly, despite all the media attention that has been given to the year 2000 problem in the past several years, many companies and agencies have only started to address this critical issue with a real sense of urgency during the past 12 months. Some will fail to root out and fix all their date-handling problems before service failures occur. Others will flat out fail. Your objective is to minimize any impact these failures will have on your economic security and your business's continued survival. We hope the information in this chapter, together with the sample letters included in Appendix H, will help you to achieve that objective.

14 Tools and Testers

OVERVIEW

Hardware and software tools and testers are automated ways to define, plan, test, and implement solutions to your year 2000 problem, and to convert files as necessary. By definition, a tool is something used to help an individual carry out a specific task. However, tools require human intervention. Your lawn mower can't mow the lawn by itself. It's a tool designed to simplify the task and get it done in a more efficient manner. It requires a user to gas it up, start it up, and push or drive it around the yard. The same applies to tools and testers designed for the year 2000 problem. You are the key element.

UNDERSTANDING THEIR PURPOSE

"At last, the part of the book I've been looking for. An automated way to solve everything. I'll just install this software, kick it off, come back in the morning and the Millennium Bug will be gone." Wrong!

It's a common misconception that there is a cure-all tool that will solve every year 2000 problem. In fact, many software developers claim they've developed such a tool. This is absolutely not true. It takes a lot more than a single tool to solve all your problems. As you've learned from this book, there are so many different areas of your computer to be concerned with that no one piece of software could fix them all.

Year 2000 tools are actually designed to conduct specific tasks. Some test your BIOS and RTC/CMOS. Some conduct date rollovers in the operating system. Some scan spreadsheets and databases, while others inventory all the software executables on your hard drive. It would be foolish to believe one tool can do all this.

In an effort to provide an integrated solution approach, some companies offer suite packages. These are many different software applications bundled into one product that performs various tasks. Examples of these type of packages include OnMark 2000,

Eon2000, and Tally Systems. These are definitely more complete solutions. However, they still rely on human intervention and knowledge of when to use what tools.

To make the most out of tools and testers you must properly define the individual year 2000 tasks at hand, then find a tool or suite of tools to match each task. For example, one step in your year 2000 compliance project may be to properly evaluate your spreadsheet software and scan all saved worksheets. Suppose that you determine your spreadsheet software is noncompliant. Through vendor follow-up, you obtain a compliant version of the software. You now need to evaluate 85 worksheet files for date sensitivity. Do you manually open and check each file? No — you look for a tool specifically designed to scan spreadsheets. You find one that meets your needs and run it against your files, getting a nice clear report. You now need to evaluate how you will deal with the date issues found within these files.

Most manufacturers of year 2000 tools and testers understand that there is no cure-all. Many offer consulting services along with their methodologies and tool sets to provide a more complete solution. In fact, some manufacturers were reluctant to include their applications in our book because we didn't include their methodology. This is because they realize that the use of tools alone does not guarantee a successful outcome. If you are a business owner with a substantial amount of software and hardware, use this book as a guideline, but also consider consulting a team of professionals. See Chapter 9, "Hiring Consultants and Contractors."

PURCHASING CONSIDERATIONS

If you're thinking about buying a tool or tester, ask the vendor to send you a demonstration copy. In addition, ask for references. Specifically request them to identify contacts who have used their products. Call the references and determine what experience and results they've had with the tool. Evaluate the tool to ensure that it meets your needs. Let's face it: it's your money. Don't throw it away on a tool that won't do exactly what you expect.

Appendix G and the CD-ROM in this book contain many different tools and testers. We did not vigorously examine each application, nor are we going to make any specific recommendations. However, feel free to install and evaluate each tool on the CD to determine whether it meets one of your needs. If you find a tool you like, contact the vendor for more information.

Software applications contained on the CD-ROM are owned by their manufacturers and/or resellers. Each has its own licensing agreement with which you must comply.

Make sure you validate the results of each tool or tester by running a manual test. After all, you are relying on the expertise of the tool developer. Remember, the definition of compliance — what is and what isn't — differs from company to company. One company may claim an issue need not be addressed, while another insists it should. Tools and testers are designed based on a company's definition and interpretation of compliance.

We loaded the applications contained on the CD-ROM and got mixed results. All applications did what they claimed to do; however, some were more thorough than others. For example, we evaluated some of the BIOS testers on a 100-MHz Pentium machine with a BIOS manufactured in 1996 (the manufacturer's name is purposely withheld). This machine was barely two years old. One tester claimed that the machine was partially compliant, while another claimed it needed a BIOS update. The reason for the difference is that one tool was merely a tester, offering no fix, while the other was a "test-and-fix" product.

Through our research we came across a real-life example of what can happen if too much faith is put into a tool or tester. We removed the names and simplified the story.

> One relatively small firm, which needed to inventory and evaluate all of their computer systems, both hardware and software, chose to purchase a suite of tools and testers to accomplish the task. A vendor claimed they had an all-in-one package, which was a fail-safe

tool that would evaluate all their PC system components, test the hardware and software, and automatically resolve all date problems. The cost for the suite was roughly $200,000. Only after buying this rather costly package did the company discover that it addressed less than 50% of their problems. In the end, they spent an additional $200,000 to use their own staff, create their own plan, gather specific tools and utilities, and conduct the conversion internally.

This book outlines a manual methodology for achieving year 2000 compliance. Use tools and testers to supplement or simplifying some of the individual tasks outlined in this book. Tools aren't a necessity for fixing the year 2000 problem, but the right tool for the right task will greatly minimize the time and money you spend.

DIFFERENT TYPES OF TOOLS

There are several categories of tools and testers at your disposal. They are described in Table 14-1.

Category	Description
Project management	Tools to help you plan and manage year 2000 assessment and conversion projects
Inventory	Tools that gather, track, and report what hardware or software products are running on your system
Analysis	Tools that scan and analyze programs or data files to locate date sensitive code or data
Testing	Tools that help perform hardware and software year 2000 compliance testing
Fix	Tools that repair hardware and software to handle dates into the year 2000
Conversion	Tools that translate software and data from one format or platform to another

TABLE *Table of tool categories.*
14.1

Project Management	These tools help you to develop a plan to evaluate and resolve your year 2000 problems. They are useful for establishing a list of tasks, assigning resources and accountabilities, setting schedules, estimating costs, and recording results. This is your bible for monitoring, tracking and measuring results.
Inventory	These tools are used to scan your system and gather a complete record of your hardware and software portfolio. These tools are single-user or network enabled and search a LAN/WAN or single PC. They gather characteristics of the system. A user name, node number, or asset number is assigned to each component and a list of its software and hardware is attached. Some provide a status and recommendations for each component, or allow a user to maintain a status on the component once the inventory is complete.
Analysis	These are tools that help you locate and evaluate potential problem areas. They allow you to scan and search for specific data values or text strings. This type of tool is used in the evaluation phase of the project to help you determine the scope of your problems. Analyzers may be specific to one product type or capable of analyzing multiple applications and/or data files.
Testing	These tools can help you automatically set up, execute, and control various aspects of your year 2000 testing process. Some perform a particular task, such as a BIOS test or date rollovers. Others allow you to enter user-definable test scenarios and collect or compare results.

Fix	Fixing tools are used to assist in bringing a noncompliant hardware or software component into compliance. A fixing tool may be combined with a testing tool. It provides the actual patch or overlay that accommodates compliance, assuming complete replacement is not required.
Conversion	Conversion tools are used to migrate noncompliant data and code. They find and replace user-definable date formats and values within data files and program source code.
What Do I Use?	The types of tools that will be useful to you depend on the scope of your year 2000 problem. If you are managing a year 2000 assessment and conversion project, any or all of these types of tools would prove valuable. For a personal computer user or a small business owner, the analysis, test, fix and conversion tools might best serve your purposes.
Overview of CD Tools	The CD-ROM software included with this book contains evaluation versions of several tools and testers. The name, type, and description of each of these products are listed in Table 14-2. In addition, Appendix G contains manufacturer product pages that summarize each tool's purpose and features.
Obtaining Other Tools	During our research we came across hundreds of different tools and testers. Why did we only include the ones we did? They pertain to individual users and small business owners. We discovered that most year 2000 information, including tools and testers, was

Name	Type	Description
Centennial 2000	Hardware test, fix	RTC and BIOS test and fix tool with a facility to collect the results
Check 2000 PC	Hardware, software, inventory, test, fix, analysis	Suite of tools that tests and fixes BIOS problems, inventories hardware and software, and tests applications; single or multi user
Date*find*-db	Software analysis	Customizable database and spreadsheet analyzer
DateSpy	Software analysis	Microsoft Excel spreadsheet analyzer
Fix2000	Hardware and software test and fix	Scans PC software applications and fixes problems; also contains RTC repair utility
Killer	Hardware test	RTC and BIOS tester
Millennium Bug Toolkit	Hardware and operating system tester	Hardware and operating system tester
Millennium Bug Compliance Kit	Hardware test and fix	RTC and BIOS test and fix
NetKeeper	Hardware Tester	RTC and BIOS tester
OnMark 2000 Assess 16-Bit Assess 32-bit Bios Test and Fix	Hardware, software, inventory, test, fix, and analysis	Suite of tools that tests and fixes BIOS problems, inventories hardware and software, analyzes spreadsheets and databases, and tests applications
Prove It 2000	Hardware and operating system test and fix	RTC and BIOS test and fix, operating system test.
Yes2K	Hardware test and fix	Tests RTC and BIOS on single PC or Network

TABLE *Description of supplied tools.*

14.2

designed for large corporations. There wasn't a lot of information designed to help the individual user and small business owner who is primarily concerned with desktop PCs and small local area networks.

We recognize that more tools and testers will become available as the millennium approaches. To find more information on tools and testers, try using the Internet. Go to any of the following search engines:

- www.altavista.com
- www.excite.com
- www.hotbot.com
- www.infoseek.com
- www.lycos.com
- www.yahoo.com

Enter any of the following search criteria:

- "Y2K"
- "YEAR 2000"
- "Y2K TOOLS"
- "YEAR 2000 TOOLS"
- "Y2K TESTERS"
- "YEAR 2000 TESTERS"

For more information on search engines, go to one of the web addresses just listed and search for the following:

- "SEARCH ENGINES"
- "SEARCHING THE WEB"
- "SEARCHING THE INTERNET"

CONCLUSION

It is important to know the pros and cons of tools and testers. There is no silver bullet. You must have a detailed plan to identify the tasks to be accomplished and to determine where a tool may prove useful. Remember to look before you leap. Evaluate available tools, talk to others who have used them, and make your purchase decisions carefully. Use this book as a methodology and complement it with a tool or tester when appropriate.

15 Determining and Implementing Solutions

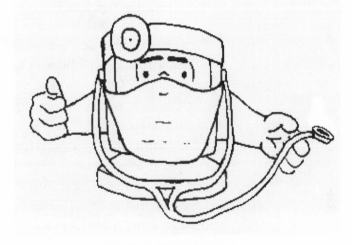

THIS CHAPTER CONTAINS:

- Overview
- Option Tables
- Implementing the Pieces
- Applying the Three R's
- Case Scenario

OVERVIEW

Decisions, decisions, decisions! You have finally reached the point where you need to make some decisions about the path you will follow to bring your computer system to year 2000 compliance. By now you should have done all this:

- Created your inventory
- Tested or researched the individual components
- Reviewed your product guarantees and liabilities
- Obtained manufacturer repair or upgrade information

Remember, while each component of a system is different and was designed to perform different functions, they are still all highly interdependent. This means you must look at each piece individually and also understand the impact one has on another, as well as on the whole system.

This chapter has two objectives. The first is to outline an approach for selecting an appropriate solution path for each component found to be noncompliant. This approach involves assessing the importance of each failed component and identifying its reliance on other system components and products. This will allow you to see the "big picture" and ensure that you understand the impacts of companion product upgrade or conversion work. The second objective is to describe the steps involved in implementing solutions and to highlight key considerations that should be factored into their implementation.

APPLYING THE THREE R'S

In Chapter 13 we talked about identifying solution options and introduced the "three R's":

- Repair the failure
- Replace it with a compliant product
- Retire or eliminate product use

If you've followed the steps outlined in this book, you now have a complete inventory of all your system components and know which ones have year 2000 problems. If they do have problems and were purchased from a second party, you should also know whether the manufacturer will repair it or is offering a compliant upgrade, or whether a replacement product is available through another source. If you haven't yet gathered or researched this information, you need to do this before you proceed any further.

Once you have completed all of the preliminary inventory, testing, and research work it will be time to proceed with assessing your solution options. Do you repair, replace, or retire? The following steps are involved in making this determination:

- Reviewing the inventory and determining which noncompliant pieces are most important to you and worth upgrading or replacing.
- Identifying what fix or replacement options are available.
- Evaluating system requirements associated with each solution option.
- Building case scenarios that take into account product interdependencies.
- Selecting the most reasonable solution to satisfy your needs.

Take out all of your inventory worksheets: Hardware, Operating System, Software, and Data Files. Develop a list of noncompliant products and files, identifying those that failed year 2000 testing. As you review these worksheets, ask yourself whether each item is critical to your needs. If it's a product you use very infrequently, you may decide to simply get rid of it. If so, cross it off the list. If it's a data file you no longer need, mark it for deletion.

If the product or component is one you wish to keep, then review your inventory worksheet to see whether the manufacturer offers a fix or replacement. Also review your research findings and any information obtained from the vendor about the other system requirements needed to support the fix or upgrade. You need to compare these requirements to your existing system setup to determine what the ripple effect will be.

For example, suppose the spreadsheet package you use is not compliant, but the manufacturer offers a newer version that is. The new version requires a Windows 95 operating system with 16 megabytes of memory and 120 megabytes of available hard drive space. After reviewing the inventory worksheet, you see you do not meet the operating system or hardware requirements. Before you decide to select this product as your year 2000 solution path, you must first assess whether you want to upgrade your operating system to Windows 95. However, you also need to determine whether other compliant software products you are using will be able to run with Windows 95. If not, you will need to replace them as well.

Once you have thought through all the ripple effects, you'll have a case scenario that clearly defines the implications of this particular solution path. If you've identified other possible replacement products, once again assess their system requirements, chase the ripple impacts, and build your case scenarios. Then it's up to you to decide which solution path best suits your needs and pocketbook.

For software that isn't a commercial off-the-shelf product, repair is only an option if the developer agrees to make the necessary changes, or if you have access to the application source code. In that case, you need to decide whether you can make the changes yourself or hire someone to make the changes for you. Either way, you will need to formulate a plan that involves thoroughly testing the repair work to ensure that compliance has been achieved.

OPTION TABLES

Building an option table will help you compare system requirements associated with various solution options and match them against your existing system setup. Create an option table for each component you wish to repair or replace. Then scan these tables to make sure your decisions consistently follow a compatible thread of operating system, hardware, and memory requirements. The following examples present option tables for four noncompliant product components: a BIOS, an operating system, a spreadsheet, and a database.

We later use these tables to build a sample case scenario. Please note that the information used in these tables does not represent actual component requirement or pricing data. It is purely hypothetical. Our objective is to demonstrate the use and benefit of building option tables to formulate solution case scenarios.

Noncompliant Product	Product:	BIOS
	Manufacturer:	American Megatrends Inc.
	Version:	2.3
	Date:	1994
	Description:	Computer's Basic Input/Output System

Product	MFG	Processor	HD Space	OS	RAM	Conversion Tools	Cost
AMI BIOS Version 3.5	AMI	486 XX MHz	None	Any	Any	N/A	$100
OnMark BIOS Fix	Viasoft	386 XX MHz	2 MB	ANY DOS	4 MB	N/A	$75
YEAR2000. COM	RighTime	386 XX MHz	2 MB	Any DOS	4 MB	N/A	$100
Option 4							
Option 5							

TABLE *Replacement Options*
15.1

Noncompliant Product

Product:		DOS and Windows
Manufacturer:		Microsoft Corp.
Version:		5.0 and 3.1x
Description:		Operating system

Product	MFG	Processor	HD Space	OS	RAM	Conversion Tools	Cost
DOS Version 6.22	Microsoft	486 XX MHz	5 MB	Earlier DOS	4 MB	Yes	$300
WINFILE.EXE	Microsoft	486 XX MHz	15 MB	Windows 3.1x	4 MB	Yes	None
Option 3							

TABLE *Replacement Options*
15.2

Noncompliant Product

Product:	Lotus 1-2-3
Manufacturer:	Lotus Development Corp.
Version:	x.x
Description:	Spreadsheet application
Number of Data Files:	125
Interfaces:	None

Product	MFG	Processor	HD Space	OS	RAM	Conversion Tools	Cost
Lotus 1-2-3 Version x.x	Lotus	486 XX MHz	15 MB	WIN 3.11	16 MB	No	$300
Excel Version x.x	Microsoft	486 XX MHz	15 MB	WIN 3.11	16 MB	Yes	$400
Quattro-Pro Version x.x	Corel	486 XX MHz	23 MB	WIN 95	16 MB	Yes	$450
Application 4							
Application 5							

TABLE *Replacement Options*
15.3

Noncompliant Product

Product:	Paradox
Manufacturer:	Inprise
Version:	x.x
Description:	Database application
Number of Data Files:	30
Interfaces:	Marketing SQL Database

Product	MFG	Processor	HD Space	OS	RAM	Conversion Tools	Cost
FoxPro Version x.x	Microsoft	486 XX MHz	15 MB	WIN 3.11	16 MB	No	$400
Access Version x.x	Microsoft	486 XX MHz	15 MB	WIN 95	16 MB	Yes	$400
Approach Version x.x	Lotus	486 XX MHz	23 MB	WIN 95	16 MB	Yes	$350
Application 4							
Application 5							

TABLE *Replacement Options*
15.4

CASE SCENARIO

Table 15.5 on the following page shows a sample case scenario situation. See how we used the 3 R's, built our decision tables (as shown earlier), and formulated a solution path that we feel will best meet our requirements.

Our Options

Through research we found one BIOS replacement and two different BIOS fix programs. For our operating system we found two fix options provided by the manufacturer. The spreadsheet and database

Our Computer		Compliant
Hardware/Firmware		
Computer:	IBM-compatible clone	N/A
Processor:	80486 DX2 66 MHz	N/A
BIOS:	AMI-BIOS V2.3 1994	Failed
RAM:	16 MB	N/A
Operating System		
OS: DOS 5.0 WIN 3.11	Failed	
Peripherals		
Printer:	Epson dot matrix	Yes
Fax Modem:	Hayes compatible 14,400	Yes
Software		
Spreadsheet:	Lotus 1-2-3 Version x.x	Failed
Database:	Paradox Version x.x	Failed
Faxing:	Delrina WinFax Pro Version x.x	Yes

TABLE *Transition date table.*

15.4

applications offered three possible replacements, one by the manufacturer and two from other manufacturers. (See the Option Tables.)

Deciding to Repair, Replace, or Retire

While applying the 3 R's, we looked for a lowest common denominator in our option tables. We noticed that all our compliance fixes could be done using our existing 80486 processor running Windows 3.1x. We decided to use the OnMark 2000 BIOS Test and Fix to repair our BIOS, since it has the lowest cost. We will update our operating systems with DOS 6.22 and apply a new WINFILE.EXE, since the only other option would be to select a new operating system. We decide to upgrade our spreadsheet application to a compliant version of Excel because it offers conversion tools for migrating our spreadsheet files. For our

Database product we select Visual Foxpro 3.0, which is compliant with minor issues because it does run under Windows 3.1X with the DOS 6.22 upgrade.

Applying the Solutions

To repair our BIOS we used the free OnMark 2000 BIOS Test and Fix program included on our CD-ROM. Next we contacted a local software store and purchased and installed a copy of Microsoft DOS 6.22. We then went to the Microsoft web page and downloaded and installed the latest copy of WINFILE.EXE for Windows 3.1x. Then we contacted the local software store again and purchased and installed Microsoft Excel and Visual Foxpro 3.0. Finally, we ran data conversions for our spreadsheet files and database files by following the documentation and utilizing the tools provided by Microsoft.

IMPLEMENTING THE PIECES

We realize that the case scenario we've just discussed is quite simple, and that the situations you face could be much more complex. However, the scenario does show how to systematically solve your year 2000 problems by comparing and evaluating first the individual problem pieces, and then the total solution in context. Once you've identified your solution path, you must either implement the solution yourself or seek professional assistance.

Most vendors will offer some type of solution implementation support or at least assistance advice. If you're going to implement the solution yourself, visit the vendor's web site or call to obtain more detailed information on how to perform the upgrade. The following sections outline what's involved in implementing fixes for common computer components.

BIOS

The work involved in implementing a BIOS fix varies depending on whether it is a BIOS patch, a BIOS board or extension, or a software workaround. To install a physical board, you'll have to open your computer system case and plug a component into the motherboard. For a logic extension or software workaround, you'll need to load the software into your computer.

- A firmware BIOS patch is a tiny program you can load into your computer that will overlay the original BIOS each time the system is powered up. The overlay is year 2000 compliant and controls any date functionality that was previously deficient. You can either have the manufacturer mail it to you or download it from their Internet web site.

- A Millennium BIOS Board works at the lowest level of your computer. It creates a BIOS extension that allows any PC to change the date correctly from December 31, 1999, to January 1, 2000. It plugs into an available expansion slot inside your computer. These boards come with instructions for installation.

- Replacing the BIOS board requires removal of the existing board and replacing it with one that is compliant.

- Many software developers have designed patch or fix programs that bypass the BIOS logic. Carefully follow the installation instructions to install the fix exactly as stated in the documentation. If you encounter a problem, contact the manufacturer or consult a professional.

Operating System

An operating system upgrade consists of documentation and a set of floppy disks or CD-ROMs. Instructions for installation are included. Most upgrades include a boot disk or an executable program on disk 1. If the upgrade includes a boot disk, simply insert the disk into your drive and restart the computer. The boot disk will take over and load a program that will install the upgrade. Follow the instructions on the screen and in the manual. An executable upgrade will require you to execute a program from disk. Simply insert the disk into the drive and type the name of the command. The documentation will list the name of the command. These are most commonly known as SETUP or INSTALL. Follow the instructions on the screen and in the manual. See Appendix C for information pertaining to operating systems and Appendix E for their manufacturers.

Software Applications	For commercial off-the-shelf software, contact the manufacturer, reseller, or computer store for advice on upgrading to a compliant version. Again, use the Internet or e-mail to obtain this information. See Appendix D for software titles and Appendix E for manufacturer information. Migrations usually involve installing an upgrade and converting data, code, or macros.

Installing an upgrade means physically updating the software program files to a newer version. These files reside on your computer's hard disk, floppy disk, CD-ROM, or some other medium. These are the actual executable files and supporting files that run the application, sometimes known as object code, binaries, or libraries. The update should include installation instructions and a program such as SETUP or INSTALL, which you will have to run to complete the migration.

Once the updated version of the software application is in place, you may or may not have to convert data, code, or macros. This is the actual data or custom instructions that you've entered into the application. Data is your information — it did not come with the application, you entered it. Macros are lists of one or more instructions that perform a task. For example, in a particular spreadsheet you may have added a due-date macro that adds 30 days to the invoice date entered into one of the spreadsheet cells.

The vendor may provide conversion or migration tools that automatically convert or help you to quickly pinpoint and correct these types of incompatibilities. The tools should come with instructions for converting data, code, or macros. It will be up to you to decide whether you need professional assistance with completing your upgrade or file conversion.

Wrap-up

Selecting and implementing the appropriate solutions requires careful thought. It requires looking at the big picture and understanding the ripple effect of individual component impacts. You must consider the ease of transferring your existing data into a new application, or whether you will need to upgrade your hardware and operating system to support migration to a new software product version. You must apply the three R's, build decision tables, and formulate your solution scenarios to ensure that your decisions and their implications are clearly laid out. Once you've determined your path to compliance, formulate your implementation plans. Contact the vendors for upgrade or conversion implementation advice and follow their instructions carefully. In most cases you can achieve compliance without seeking professional help, but don't hesitate to do so if you feel it's needed.

In the final analysis, the goal is to achieve year 2000 compliance before the clock strikes midnight on the last day of this decade. We hope the guidance provided in this book helps you toward that end. If not, seek assistance elsewhere — but please, please don't ignore this critical problem. The start of the next century should be a new beginning, not the end for you and your business.

APPENDIX

A Inventory Worksheet

HARDWARE INVENTORY

COMPUTER HARDWARE INVENTORY

Computer Manufacturer: _____

Computer Serial Number: _____

Computer Model Number: _____

CPU (Central Processing Unit) Type: _____ Speed: _____

RAM (Random Access Memory): _____

Total Hard Disk Space: Available Hard Disk Space:

C: _____   C: _____

D: _____   D: _____

E: _____   E: _____

BIOS Manufacturer: _____

BIOS Version Number: _____

PERIPHERALS

1. Peripheral Type/Name: _____

   Model Number: _____

   Serial Number: _____

   Version Number: _____

2. Peripheral Type/Name: _____
   Model Number: _____
   Serial Number: _____
   Version Number: _____

3. Peripheral Type/Name: _____
   Model Number: _____
   Serial Number: _____
   Version Number: _____

4. Peripheral Type/Name: _____
   Model Number: _____
   Serial Number: _____
   Version Number: _____

5. Peripheral Type/Name: _____
   Model Number: _____
   Serial Number: _____
   Version Number: _____

6. Peripheral Type/Name: _____
   Model Number: _____
   Serial Number: _____
   Version Number: _____

7. Peripheral Type/Name: _____
   Model Number: _____
   Serial Number: _____
   Version Number: _____

8. Peripheral Type/Name: _____
   Model Number: _____
   Serial Number: _____
   Version Number: _____

COMPUTER HARDWARE TEST RESULTS/INFORMATION

Hardware Component	Year 2000 Rollover Test Pass/Fail	Leap Year Roll Over Test Pass/Fail	Manufacturer Contact Information	Possible Fix Options

OPERATING SYSTEM AND SOFTWARE APPLICATION INVENTORY AND TEST RESULTS/INFORMATION

Software/Operating System Title: _____

Version Information: _____

Manufacturer: _____

Year 2000 Rollover Test Pass/Fail: _____

Leap Year Rollover Test Pass/Fail: _____

Manufacturer Contact Information: _____

Possible Fix Options:

_____

_____

_____

_____

Software/Operating System Title: _____

Version Information: _____

Manufacturer: _____

Year 2000 Rollover Test Pass/Fail: _____

Leap Year Rollover Test Pass/Fail: _____

Manufacturer Contact Information: _____

Possible Fix Options:

_____

_____

_____

_____

OPERATING SYSTEM AND SOFTWARE APPLICATION INVENTORY AND TEST RESULTS/INFORMATION

Software/Operating System Title: _____

Version Information: _____

Manufacturer: _____

Year 2000 Rollover Test Pass/Fail: _____

Leap Year Rollover Test Pass/Fail: _____

Manufacturer Contact Information: _____

Possible Fix Options:

_____

_____

_____

_____

Software/Operating System Title: _____

Version Information: _____

Manufacturer: _____

Year 2000 Rollover Test Pass/Fail: _____

Leap Year Rollover Test Pass/Fail: _____

Manufacturer Contact Information: _____

Possible Fix Options:

_____

_____

_____

_____

OPERATING SYSTEM AND SOFTWARE APPLICATION INVENTORY AND TEST RESULTS/INFORMATION

Software/Operating System Title: _____

Version Information: _____

Manufacturer: _____

Year 2000 Rollover Test Pass/Fail: _____

Leap Year Rollover Test Pass/Fail: _____

Manufacturer Contact Information: _____

Possible Fix Options:

_____

_____

_____

_____

Software/Operating System Title: _____

Version Information: _____

Manufacturer: _____

Year 2000 Rollover Test Pass/Fail: _____

Leap Year Rollover Test Pass/Fail: _____

Manufacturer Contact Information: _____

Possible Fix Options:

_____

_____

_____

_____

SOFTWARE FILES INVENTORY

Application Name: _____

File Name	File Format Type	Date Field, Macro or Function Problem	Migration/ Expansion Needs	Other Application References

SOFTWARE FILES INVENTORY

Application Name: _____

File Name	File Format Type	Date Field, Macro or Function Problem	Migration/ Expansion Needs	Other Application References

SOFTWARE FILES INVENTORY

Application Name: _____

File Name	File Format Type	Date Field, Macro or Function Problem	Migration/ Expansion Needs	Other Application References

SOFTWARE FILES INVENTORY

Application Name: _____

File Name	File Format Type	Date Field, Macro or Function Problem	Migration/ Expansion Needs	Other Application References

SERVICE PROVIDER/GOVERNMENT AGENCY/OTHER ORGANIZATION INVENTORY

Name: _____　　Name: _____

Contact Information: _____　　Contact Information: _____

Contact Notes: _____　　Contact Notes: _____

_____　　_____

_____　　_____

_____　　_____

Date Disclosure Letter Was Sent: _____　　Date Disclosure Letter Was Sent: _____

Received a Response Y/N: _____　　Received a Response Y/N: _____

Year 2000 Compliant Status: _____　　Year 2000 Compliant Status: _____

_____　　_____

_____　　_____

_____　　_____

Name: _____　　Name: _____

Contact Information: _____　　Contact Information: _____

Contact Notes: _____　　Contact Notes: _____

_____　　_____

_____　　_____

_____　　_____

Date Disclosure Letter Was Sent: _____　　Date Disclosure Letter Was Sent: _____

Received a Response Y/N: _____　　Received a Response Y/N: _____

Year 2000 Compliant Status: _____　　Year 2000 Compliant Status: _____

_____　　_____

_____　　_____

_____　　_____

SERVICE PROVIDER/GOVERNMENT AGENCY/OTHER ORGANIZATION INVENTORY

Name: _____   Name: _____

Contact Information: _____   Contact Information: _____

Contact Notes: _____   Contact Notes: _____

_____   _____

_____   _____

_____   _____

Date Disclosure Letter Was Sent: _____   Date Disclosure Letter Was Sent: _____

Received a Response Y/N: _____   Received a Response Y/N: _____

Year 2000 Compliant Status: _____   Year 2000 Compliant Status: _____

_____   _____

_____   _____

_____   _____

Name: _____   Name: _____

Contact Information: _____   Contact Information: _____

Contact Notes: _____   Contact Notes: _____

_____   _____

_____   _____

_____   _____

Date Disclosure Letter Was Sent: _____   Date Disclosure Letter Was Sent: _____

Received a Response Y/N: _____   Received a Response Y/N: _____

Year 2000 Compliant Status: _____   Year 2000 Compliant Status: _____

_____   _____

_____   _____

_____   _____

B Hardware Manufacturers

ALR CORPORATION

Address	Advanced Logic Research, Inc.
	9401 Jeronimo
	Irvine, CA 92618
Internet	*www.alr.com*

Web Site for Year 2000

        www.alr.com/alr_corporate_information/year2000.htm

Phone	1-800-257-1230
Fax	(714) 458-0532

Web address *www.arl.com* is the location to go to inquire information regarding ALR computer products and their year 2000 compliance status.

Steps

1. Type in the net address *http://www.alr.com*
2. On the main web page, scroll down and click on Year 2000.
3. Search for your product information.

AST CORPORATION

Address	AST Corporation
	16215 Alton Parkway
	P.O. Box 57005
	Irvine, CA 92619-7005
Internet	*www.ast.com*
Phone	(714) 727-4141
	1-800-876-4278
Fax	(714) 727-9355

The web address *www.ast.com* is the location for information regarding AST computer products and their year 2000 compliance status.

Steps

1. Type in the net address *http://www.ast.com*

2. On the main web page, scroll down to the Year 2000 field and click on it.

3. Search for your product information.

APPLE COMPUTER INC.

Address 1 Infinite Loop
Cupertino, CA 95014

Internet *www.apple.com*

WebSite for Year 2000
www.apple.com\macos\info\2000html

Phone 1-800-500-7078

The web address *www.apple.com* is the place for information regarding Apple computer products and their year 2000 compliance status.

Steps

1. Type in the net address *http://www.apple.com*

2. On the main web page, scroll down, and in the Search field type in YEAR 2000 [ENTER]

   This presently calls up the web location:

   www.apple.com\macos\info\2000html

3. Search for your product information.

COMPAQ COMPUTER CORPORATION

Address   P.O. Box 692000
            Houston, TX 77269

Internet   *www.compaq.com*

WebSite for Year 2000

            www.compaq.com/year2000

Phone   1-800-888-5858

The web address www.compaq.com is the location for information regarding Compaq computer products and their year 2000 compliance status.

Steps

1. Type in the net address of *http://www.compaq.com*

2. On the main web page, click on "Year 2000".

3. Search for your product information.

DELL CORPORATION

Address   Dell Computer Corporation
One Dell Way
Round Rock, TX 78682

Internet *www.dell.com*

Phone   1-800-247-9362

Fax   1-800-950-1329

The web address *www.dell.com* is the location for information regarding Dell computer products and their year 2000 compliance status.

Steps

1. Type in the net address *http://www.dell.com*

2. On the main web page, click on the Search field and type in
   `YEAR 2000 [CLICK ON SEARCH]`

3. Search for your product information.

FIGURE *www.dell.com*

GATEWAY CORPORATION

Address   Gateway 2000 Sioux Falls
700 E 54th Street North
Sioux Falls, SD 57104

Internet   *www.gateway.com*

Phone   1-800-846-2000

The web address www.gateway.com is the location for information regarding Gateway computer products and their year 2000 compliance status.

Steps

1. Type in the net address *http://www.gateway.com*

2. On the main web page, scroll down and click on the Year 2000 Compliance field.

3. Search for your product information.

HEWLETT PACKARD CORPORATION

Address   HP requests phone and Internet contacts only

Internet   *www.hp.com*

Phone   1-800-633-3600

The web address *www.hp.com* is the place for information regarding Hewlett Packard computer products and their year 2000 compliance status.

Steps

1. Type in the net address *http://www.hp.com*

2. On the main web page, scroll down to the field "Visit HP's Year 2000 Program site: Find out how HP is addressing the Year 2000 challenge."

3. Search for your product information.

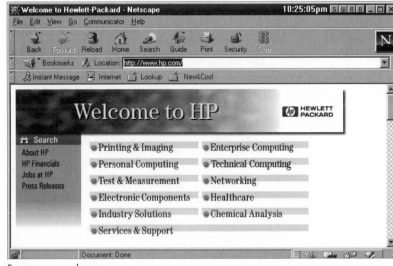

FIGURE   *www.hp.com*

B-2   Copyright © 1994-1998 by Hewlett-Packard Company. Used with permission.

IBM CORPORATION

Address   500 Columbus Avenue
Thornwood, NY 10594

Internet   *www.ibm.com*

WebSite for Year 2000
www.ibm.com/IBM/year2000

Phone   1-800-772-2227

The web address www.ibm.com is the location for information on IBM computer products and their year 2000 compliance status.

Steps

1. Type in the net address *http://www.ibm.com*

2. On the main web page there is a Search field. Type in YEAR 2000 [GO]

3. Search for your product information.

APPENDIX

C

Operating System Manufacturers

Operating System	Manufacturer
Character Based	
Compaq DOS	Compaq Computer Corporation
DR. DOS	Novell Corporation
MS-DOS	Microsoft Corporation
OS/2	IBM Corporation
PC-DOS	IBM Corporation
Graphical User Interfaces	
Windows 3.x	Microsoft Corporation
Windows 95	Microsoft Corporation
Mac OS	Apple Corporation
OS/2 Warp	IBM Corporation
Networking	
LANtastic	Artisoft
LINUX	Red Hat Software Inc.
Novell NetWare	Novell Corporation
UNIX	Santa Cruz Operation
Windows for Workgroups	Microsoft Corporation
Windows NT	Microsoft Corporation

APPLE COMPUTER INC.

Address 1 Infinite Loop
Cupertino, CA 95014

Internet *www.apple.com*

Web Site for Year 2000
www.apple.com\macos\info\2000html

Phone 1-800-500-7078

The web address *www.apple.com* is the location for information regarding Apple computer products and their year 2000 compliance status.

Steps

1. Type in the net address *http://www.apple.com*

2. On the main web page, scroll down and, in the Search field, type YEAR 2000 [ENTER]

   This presently calls up the web location:

   www.apple.com\macos\info\2000html

3. Search for your product information.

ARTISOFT

Address	One South Church Avenue
	Suite 2200
	Tucson, AZ 85701
Internet	*www.artisoft.com*
Web Site for Year 2000	
	www.artisoft.com/y2000.html
Phone	(520) 670-7100

The web address *www.artisoft.com* is the location for information on Artisoft computer products and their year 2000 compliance status.

Steps

1. Type in the net address *http://artisoft.com/y2000.html*
2. Search for your product information.

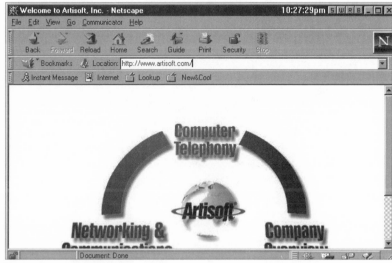

FIGURE *www.artisoft.com*
C-1 Copyright © Artisoft, Inc. All Rights Reserved. Used with permission.

COMPAQ COMPUTER CORPORATION

Address	P.O.Box 692000
	Houston, TX 77269

Internet *www.compaq.com*

Web Site for Year 2000

          www.compaq.com/year2000

Phone 1-800-888-5858

The web address *www.compaq.com* is the place to go for information regarding Compaq computer products and their year 2000 compliance status.

Steps

1. Type in the net address *http://www.compaq.com*

2. On the main web page, click on "Year 2000."

3. Search for your product information.

IBM CORPORATION

Address   500 Columbus Avenue
Thornwood, NY 10594

Internet   *www.ibm.com*

Web Site for Year 2000
www.ibm.com/IBM/year2000

Phone   1-800-772-2227

The web address *www.ibm.com* is the location for information regarding IBM computer products and their year 2000 compliance status.

Steps

1. Type in the net address *http://www.ibm.com*

2. On the main web page there is a Search field. Type in YEAR 2000 [GO]

3. Search for your product information.

MICROSOFT CORPORATION®

Address

One Microsoft Way
Redmond, WA 98052

Internet

www.microsoft.com

Phone

1-800-936-5700

The web address *www.microsoft.com* is the location for information regarding Microsoft® computer products and their year 2000 compliance status.

Steps

1. Type in the net address *http://www.microsoft.com/year2000*

2. Click on the Product Information box, select your product, and continue on.

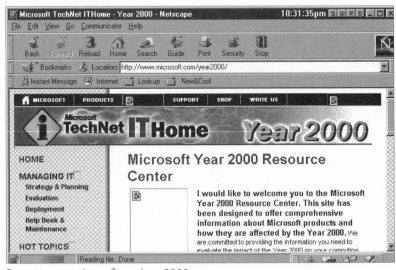

FIGURE   *www.microsoft.com/year2000*

C-2   Box shot is reprinted with permission from Microsoft Corporation ©.

NOVELL CORPORATION®

Address   2180 Fortune Drive
             San Jose, CA 95131

Internet   *www.novell.com*

Phone   1-800-858-4000

The web address *www.novell.com* is the place to go for information on Novell® computer products and their year 2000 compliance status.

Steps

1. Type in the net address *http://www.novell.com*

2. On the main web page, click on the Search field and type
   ```
   YEAR 2000 [CLICK ON SEARCH TERM]
   ```

3. Search for your product information.

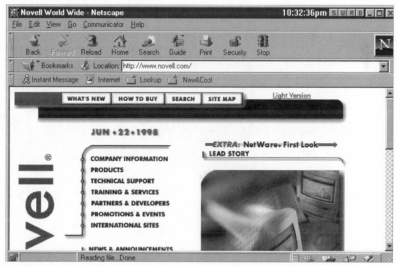

FIGURE *www.novell.com (search result).*

C-3 Screen shot of Novell's web site at *www.novell.com* © 1998 Novell, Inc. All Rights Reserved. Reprinted and used with permission.

RED HAT SOFTWARE INC.

Address   P.O. Box 13588
79 TW Alexander Drive
4201 Research Commons, S100
Research Triangle, NC 22709

Internet   *www.redhat.com*

Phone   1-888-REDHATI

The *www.redhat.com* web address presently does not provide information regarding year 2000 product information, and it is not found through a search option. You can send the company an e-mail, but their support requires that you register with the company online. I suggest you contact their telephone support number as a first step.

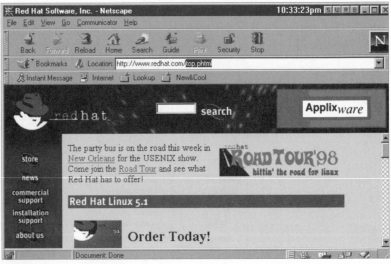

FIGURE   *www.redhat.com*

C-4   Copyright © 1995-1998 Red Hat Software. Used with permission.

THE SANTA CRUZ OPERATIONS, INC.

Address   400 Encinal Street
P.O. Box 1900
Santa Cruz, CA 95061

Internet   *www.sco.com*

Phone   1-800-SCO-UNIX

The web address *www.sco.com* is the location for information regarding The Santa Cruz Operations computer products and their year 2000 compliance status.

Steps

1. Type in the net address of *http://www.sco.com*

2. On the main web page click on the Search field and type in
`YEAR 2000 [ENTER]`

3. Search for your product information.

D Software Application Titles

SOFTWARE APPLICATION TITLES

Software Title	Manufacturer
CAD/CAM Applications	
AutoDesk / AutoCAD	AutoCAD Corporation
CAD Key	Baystate Technologies
TurboCAD	IMSI Corporation
Database Applications	
Access	Microsoft Corporation
Approach	Lotus Development Corporation
DBASE	Borland International Inc./Inprise Corporation
File Maker Pro	Claris Corporation
FoxPro	Microsoft Corporation
Sybase	Sybase Inc.
Works	Microsoft Corporation
Desktop Organizer Applications	
Dataviz Desktop	Dataviz Inc.
Norton Desktop	Symantec Corporation
Starfish Dashboard	Starfish Software

Software Title	Manufacturer
Faxing Applications	
Castelle Faxpress	Castelle Corporation
Winfax	Symantec Corporation
Winfax Pro	Symantec Corporation
Financial Planning & Banking Apps	
Bestware M.Y.O.B.	BEST!WARE Incorporated
Peachtree Accounting	Peachtree Corporation
Quick Books and Quicken	Intuit Corporation
Forms Applications	
CAERE OmniForms	Caere Corporation
JetForms	Jetforms Corporation
Lotus Forms	Lotus Development Corporation
Label Applications	
Expert Labels	Expert Software
LabelPro	Avery Dennison Consumer Services
MyLabels	MySoftware Inc.
Mail Applications	
CC-Mail	Lotus Development Corporation
MS-Mail	Microsoft Corporation
Pegasus Mail	Pegasus Mail
Payroll Applications	
ADP	Automatic Data Processing Inc.
Intuit QuickPay	Intuit Corporation
M.Y.O.B. Accounting w/ Payroll	BEST!WARE Corporation
Timesheet Professional	Timeslips Corporation
Presentation Applications	
Corel Draw	Corel Corporation
Freelance Graphics	Lotus Development Corporation
PowerPoint	Microsoft Corporation

Software Title	Manufacturer
Project Management Applications	
ACT!	Symantec Corporation
Claris Project Pro	Claris Corporation
Microsoft Project	Microsoft Corporation
Remote Access Applications	
Cross Talk	Attachmate Inc.
PcANYWHERE	Symantec Corporation
Procomm Plus	Quaterdeck Corporation
Remote Access Client	Claris Corporation
Select Pro	Attachmate Inc.
Scheduling Applications	
Claris Organizer	Claris Corporation
Lotus Organizer	Lotus Development Corporation
Microsoft Scheduler	Microsoft Corporation
Ontime Calendar	Ontime Corporation
Spreadsheet Applications	
Claris Works	Claris Corporation
Excel	Microsoft Corporation
Lotus 1-2-3	Lotus Development Corporation
Quattro Pro	Corel Corporation
Works	Microsoft Corporation
Virus Applications	
Cheyenne Innoculan	Computer Associates International Inc.
Dr. Solomon's	Dr. Solomon's Software Inc.
McAfee	McAfee Associates
Norton Antivirus	Symantec Corporation
Word Processing Applications	
Claris WritePro	Claris Corporation
Word	Microsoft Corporation
WordPerfect	Corel Corporation
WordPro / AmiPro	Lotus Development Corporation
Works	Microsoft Corporation

APPENDIX

E

Software Manufacturer Demographics

ATTACHMATE

Address	3617 131st Avenue S.E. Bellevue, WA 98006
Internet	*www.attachmate.com*
Web Site for Year 2000	*www.attachmate.com/y2k*
Phone	1-800-426-6283

The web address *www.attachmate.com* is the location to go to inquire information regarding Attachmate computer products and their Year 2000 compliance status.

Steps

1. Type in the net address of *http://attachmate.com*

2. On the main web page, click on "FIND OUT". This presently calls up the web location: *www.attachmate.com/y2k*.

3. Search for your product information.

ARTISOFT

Address   One South Church Avenue
             Suite 2200
             Tucson, AZ 85701

Internet   *www.artisoft.com*

Web Site for Year 2000
             www.artisoft.com/y2000.html

Phone   (520) 670-7100

The web address *www.artisoft.com* is the location for information regarding Artisoft computer products and their year 2000 compliance status.

Steps
1. Type in the net address of *http://artisoft.com/y2000.html*
2. Search for your product information.

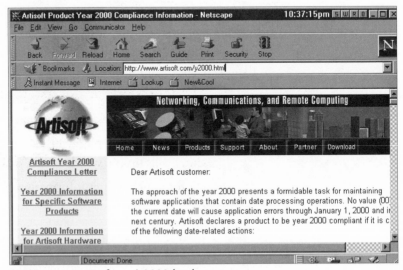

FIGURE *www.artisoft.com/y2000.html*
E-1   Copyright © Artisoft, Inc.. All Rights Reserved. Used with permission.

AUTOCAD

Address   111 McInnis Parkway
San Rafael, CA 094903

Internet   *www.autodesk.com*

Phone   1-800-225-6531

The web address *www.autodesk.com* is the location for information regarding AutoCAD computer products and their year 2000 compliance status.

Steps

1. Type in the net address *http://www.autodesk.com*

2. On the main web page, click on "Quick Search" and type in
   YEAR 2000 [CLICK ON SEARCH]

3. Search for your product information.[end tutorial]

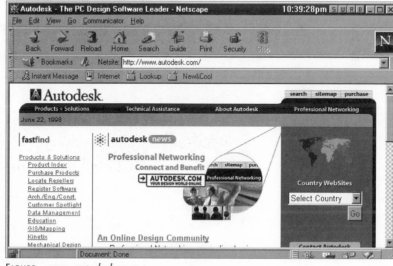

FIGURE   *www.autodesk.com*

E-2   © Copyright 1998 Autodesk™, Inc. This material has been reprinted with the permission from and under the copyright of Autodesk™, Inc.

AVERY DENNISON CONSUMER SERVICE CENTER

Address   20955 Pathfinder Road
             Diamond Bar, CA 91765

Internet   *www.avery.com*

Phone   (972) 389-3699

The Avery web address presently does not provide year 2000 compliance information. You do have the option to send them an electronic mail message.

Steps

1. Type in *http://www.avery.com*

2. On the main web page, scroll down and click on "Contact Us".

3. On the next screen, click on "Contact Us in the United States".

4. Scroll down and click on "productinfo@averydennison.com".

5. Submit your question and send the message.

BAYSTATE TECHNOLOGIES

Addres   33 Boston Post Road West
              Marlborough, MA 01752

Internet   *www.cadkey.com*

Phone   (508) 229-2020

The Baystate web address presently does not provide year 2000 compliance information. You do have the option to send them an electronic mail message.

Steps

1. Send your support questions via e-mail to *support@baystate.com*.

BEST!WARE INC.™

Address	300 Roundhill Drive
	Rockaway, NJ 07866
Internet	*www.bestware.com*

IWeb Site for Year 2000

                 www.bestware.com/year2000.html

Phone	1-800-322-6962

The web address *www.bestware.com* is the location for information regarding Best!Ware™ computer products and their year 2000 compliance status.

Steps

1. Type in the net address *http://www.bestware.com*

2. On the main web page, click on "Year 2000"

3. This site does describe how to test their products for year 2000 compliance.

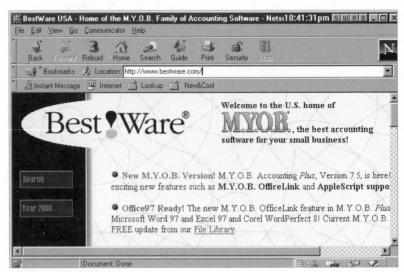

FIGURE *www.bestware.com*

E-3 Copyright M.Y.O.B. and Best!Ware™ are registered trademarks of BW-VA, inc., used with permission.

BORLAND INTERNATIONAL INC.—INPRISE CORPORATION

World Wide Headquarters

Borland has become Inprise Corporation.

Address   100 Inprise Way
Scotts Valley, CA 95066

Internet   *www.inprise.com*

Web Site for Year 2000
www.inprise.com/devsupport/y2000

Phone   (408) 431-1000

The web address *www.inprise.com* is the location to go to inquire information regarding Borland/Inprise computer products and their year 2000 compliance status.

Steps

1. Type in the net address *http://www.inprise.com*

2. On the main web page, click on "Year 2000".

3. Search for your product information.

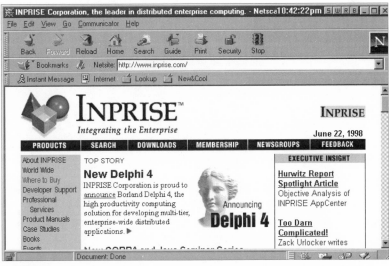

FIGURE   *www.inprise.com*

E-4   Trademarks & Copyright © 1998 INPRISE Corporation. Used with permission.

CAERE CORPORATION

Address	100 Cooper Court
	Los Gatos, CA 95030
Internet	*www.caere.com*
WebSite for Year 2000	
	www.caere.com/y2k
Phone	(408) 395-8319

Caere Corporation states that all Caere products contain no date-specific functionality and are 100% year 2000 compliant. You should always double-check and contact the company to ensure that your product is year 2000 compliant. They also offer Faxback support at (408) 354-4871.

Steps

1. Type in the net address *http://www.caere.com*

2. On the main web page click on "E-MAIL".

3. Click on e-mail support.

4. Click on U.S. and Canada E-mail Support Form.

5. Fill out the form and then click on Submit.

CASTELLE CORPORATION

Address	3255-3 Scott Blvd. Santa Clara, CA 95054
Internet	*www.castelle.com*
Web Site for Year 2000	*www.castelle.com/faq1001-w.html*
Phone	1-800-289-7555

The web address *www.castelle.com* is the location to go to acquire information regarding Castelle computer products and their year 2000 compliance status.

Steps

1. Type in the net address *http://www.castelle.com*

2. On the main web page, click on "Year 2000 Compliance".

3. Search for your product information.

CLARIS CORPORATION

Address   5201 Patrick Henry Drive
              P.O. Box 59168
              Santa Clara, CA 05052

Internet   *www.claris.com*

Web Site for Year 2000
              www.claris.com/about/about/year2000.html

Phone   1-800-965-9090

The web address *www.claris.com* is the location for information about Claris computer products and their year 2000 compliance status.

Steps

1. Type in the net address *http://www.claris.com*

2. On the main web page click on "Products Year 2000".

3. Search for your product information.

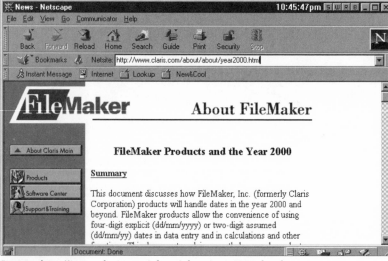

FIGURE   *http://www.claris.com/about/about/year2000.html*

E-5   Copyright © 1994-1997, FileMaker, Inc., formerly Claris Corporation. All rights reserved. Used with permission.

COMPUTER ASSOCIATES INT'L, INC.

Address   One Computer Associates Plaza
                Islandia, NY 11788

Internet   *www.cai.com*

Web Site for Year 2000
                www.cai.com/products/ca2000/y2000cl.htm

Phone   (516) 342-5224

The web address *www.cai.com* is the place to go to acquire information about Computer Associates International computer products and their year 2000 compliance status.

Steps

1. Type in the net address *http://www.cai.com*

2. On the main web page, click on "Year 2000".

3. Search for your product information.

COREL CORPORATION

Address   1600 Carling Ontario K1Z8R7

Internet   *www.corel.com*

WebSite for Year 2000
             www.corel.com/2000.htm

Phone   1-800-772-2227

The web address *www.corel.com* is the place to go for information about Corel computer products and their year 2000 compliance status.

Steps

1. Type in the net address *http://www.corel.com*

2. On the main web page, click on "Search" and type in YEAR 2000 [CLICK ON GO!]

3. Search for your product information.

DATAVIZ INC.

Address   55 Corporate Drive
              Trumbull, CT 06611

Internet   *www.dataviz.com*

WebSite for Year 2000
              www.dataviz.com/Company/y2kcompliancy.html

Phone   (203) 268-0030

At DataViz, they are in the process of investigating and testing the year 2000 compliance of each of their products.

Steps

1. Type in the net address

   http://www.dataviz.com/Company/y2kcompliancy.html

2. Click on "y2k-announce@list.dataviz.com" with "Subscribe" as the subject of the message.

3. They will notify you of any year 2000 product information.

DR. SOLOMON'S SOFTWARE INC.

Address   1 New England Executive Park
Burlington, MA 01803

Internet   *www.drsolomon.com*

WebSite for Year 2000
     www.drsolomon.com/products/suppsoft/y2000.html

Phone   (617) 273-7400

The web address *www.drsolomon.com* is the location for information regarding Dr. Solomon computer products and their year 2000 compliance status.

Steps

1. Type in the net address *http://www.drsolomon.com*

2. On the main web page scroll down to the Search field and type in YEAR 2000 [CLICK ON SEARCH]

3. Search for your product information.

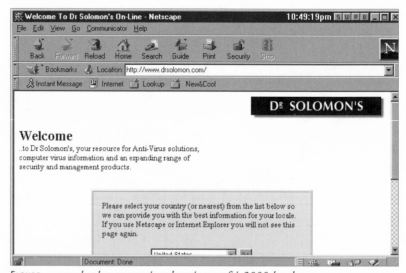

FIGURE *www.drsolomon.com/products/suppsoft/y2000.html*

E-6   Copyright © 1998 Dr Solomon's Software Inc. All rights reserved. Used with permission. Disclaimer: Viewers who need up-to-date information must visit.

EXPERT SOFTWARE

Address	800 Douglas Road
	Executive Tower
	Coral Gables, FL 33134
Internet	*www.expertsoftware.com*
Phone	(305) 567-9990

The Expert Software Web address presently does not provide year 2000 compliance information. You do have the option to send them an electronic mail message.

Steps

1. Send your support questions via e-mail to *support@expertsoftware.com*

IBM CORPORATION

Address 500 Columbus Avenue
Thornwood, NY 10594

Internet *www.ibm.com*

Web Site for Year 2000
www.ibm.com/IBM/year2000

Phone 1-800-772-2227

The web address *www.ibm.com* is the location for information regarding IBM computer products and their year 2000 compliance status.

Steps

1. Type in the net address *http://www.ibm.com*

2. On the main web page, there is a Search field. Type in
   YEAR 2000 [GO]

3. Search for your product information.

IMSI CORPORATION

Address   1895 Francisco Blvd. East
             San Rafael, CA 94901

Internet   *www.imsisoft.com*

Web Site for Year 2000
             www.imsisoft.com/wcp/2000.htm

Phone   (415) 257-3565

The web address *www.imsisoft.com* is the place to go to acquire information on IMSI computer products and their year 2000 compliance status.

Steps

1. Type in the net address *http://www.imsisoft.com*

2. On the main web page, scroll down and click on the Search field. Type in `YEAR 2000` [CLICK ON SEARCH]

3. Search for your product information.

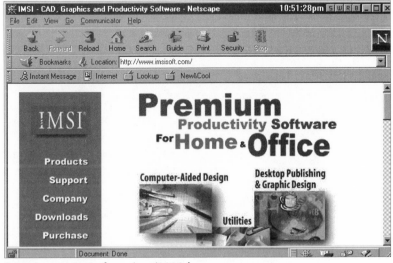

FIGURE   *www.imsisoft.com/wcp/2000.htm*

E-7   Copyright©1998 IMSI . All rights reserved. Used with permission.

INTUIT CORPORATION

Address   2535 Garcia Avenue
            Mountain View, CA 94043

Internet   *www.intuit.com*

WebSite for Year 2000
            www.intuit.com/support/year2000.html

Phone   1-800-446-8848

The web address *www.intuit.com* is the place to go for information about Intuit computer products and their year 2000 compliance status.

Steps

1. Type in the net address *http://www.intuit.com*

2. On the main web page, scroll down and click on the "Support and Updates".

3. Scroll down the Support and Updates screen and select "How do Intuit products address the year 2000?".

4. Search for your product information.

JETFORM CORPORATION

Address	7600 Leesburg Pike
	East Building, Suite 430
	Falls Church, VA 22043
Internet	*www.jetform.com*
Phone	1-800-538-3676

The web address *www.jetform.com* is the location for information regarding Jetform computer products and their year 2000 compliance status.

Steps

1. Type in the net address *http://www.jetform.com*

2. On the main web page, click on the option called "Y2K".

3. Search for your product information.

LOTUS DEVELOPMENT CORPORATION

Address   55 Cambridge Parkway
             Cambridge, MA 02142

Internet   *www.lotus.com*

Phone   1-800-343-5414

The web address *www.lotus.com* is the place to go for information about Lotus computer products and their year 2000 compliance status.

Steps

1. Type in the net address *http://www.lotus.com*

2. On the main web page, scroll down to the Search field and type YEAR 2000 [CLICK ON SEARCH]

3. Search for your product information.

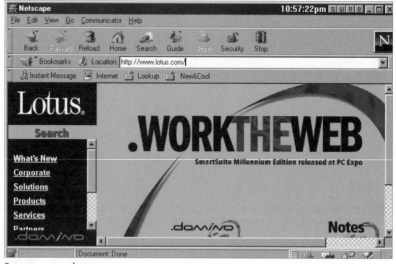

FIGURE   *www.lotus.com*

E-8   Copyright © 1995, 1996, 1997, 1998 Lotus Development Corporation, 55 Cambridge Parkway, Cambridge, Massachusetts 02142 U.S.A. All rights reserved. Used with permission.

MCAFEE ASSOCIATES

Address   2805 Bowers Avenue
Santa Clara, CA 95051

Internet   *www.mcafee.com*

Phone   (408) 988-3832

The web address *www.mcafee.com* is the location for information about McAfee computer products and their year 2000 compliance status.

Steps

1. Type in the net address *http://www.mcafee.com*

2. On the main web page, click on the Search option and type
   `YEAR 2000 [CLICK ON SUBMIT]`

3. Search for your product information.

MICROSOFT CORPORATION®

Address   One Microsoft Way
            Redmond, WA 98052

Internet   *www.microsoft.com*

Phone   1-800-936-5700

The web address *www.microsoft.com* is the location for information about Microsoft® computer products and their year 2000 compliance status

Steps

1. Type in the net address *http://www.microsoft.com/year2000*

2. Click on "Product information" and then select your product.

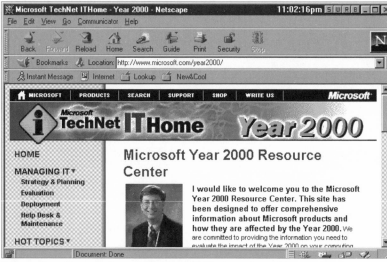

FIGURE *http://www.microsoft.com/year2000 (search result).*
E-9   Box Shot reprinted with permission from Microsoft Corporation ©.

MYSOFTWARE INC.

Address   2197 East Bayshore Road
          Palo Alto, CA 94303

Internet   *www.mysoftware.com*

Phone   1-800-622-2788

The web address *www.mysoftware.com* is the location for information about MySoftware computer products and their year 2000 compliance status. They do not have year 2000 compliance information online, so you must send them an electronic message requesting the information.

Steps

1. Type in the net address *http://www.mysoftware.com*

2. On the main web page, scroll down and click on "Support".

3. Click on "Contacting Technical Support/Support Policies".

4. Send them an electronic message inquiring about your products.

NOVELL CORPORATION®

Address   2180 Fortune Drive
             San Jose, CA 95131

Internet   *www.novell.com*

Phone   1-800-858-4000

The web address *www.novell.com* is the location for information about Novell® computer products and their year 2000 compliance status.

Steps

1. Type in the net address *http://www.novell.com*

2. On the main web page, click on the Search field and type
   YEAR 2000 [CLICK ON SEARCH TERM]

3. Search for your product information.

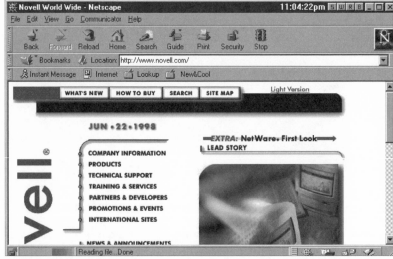

FIGURE   *www.novell.com (search result).*

E-10   Screen shot of Novell's® web site at *www.novell.com* © 1998 Novell, Inc. All Rights Reserved. Reprinted and used with permission.

OPEN TEXT CORPORATION

Address   21700 Northwestern Highway
10th Floor
Southfield, MI 48075

Internet   *www.ontime.com*

Web Site for Year 2000

www.ontime.com/community/brief2000.html

Phone   1-800-559-5955

The web address *www.ontime.com* is the location for information about Ontime computer products and their year 2000 compliance status.

Steps

1. Type in the net address *http://www.ontime.com*

2. On the main web page, click on the Search field and type
   ```
   YEAR 2000 [to the right of "this exact phrase"]
   YEAR 2000 [underneath the Search box, and click on
   SEARCH]
   ```

3. Search for your product information.

PEACHTREE CORPORATION

Address   1505 Pavilion Place
             Norcross, GA 30093

Internet   *www.peachtree.com*

Phone   1-800-247-3224

The web address *www.peachtree.com* is the location for information about Peachtree computer products and their year 2000 compliance status. They presently do not provide information about year 2000 product information, but you can request this information via electronic mail.

Steps

1. Type in the net address *http://www.peachtree.com*

2. On the main web page, scroll down to "How to Contact Us".

3. Through this option, you can send them an electronic message requesting information, but they do charge you a fee. You also have the option to contact their technical support number above.

PEGASUS MAIL

Address Not available at publication

Internet *www.pegasus.usa.com*

Phone See Internet site

The *www.pegasus.usa.com* web address presently does not provide year 2000 product information. They do not provide a technical support number, so the only way to contact them about year 2000 issues is to send them an e-mail at *support@pmail.gen.nz*.

Steps

1. Send an electronic mail message to *support@pmail.gen.nz*

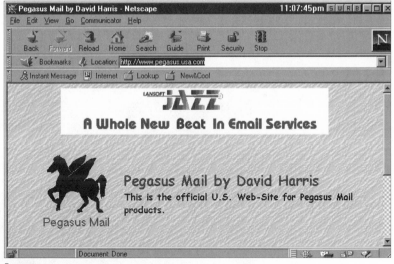

FIGURE *www.pegasus.usa.com*

E-11 Content © Copyright 1990-98 David Harris—All Rights Reserved. Used with permission.

QUARTERDECK CORPORATION®

Address   13160 Mindanao Way Suite 300
              Marina Del Rey, CA 90292

Internet   *www.qdeck.com*

Phone   1-800-678-3600

The web address *www.qdeck.com* is the location for information about Quarterdeck® computer products and their year 2000 compliance status.

Steps

1. Type in the net address *http://www.qdeck.com*

2. On the main web page, scroll down to the column "INFORMATION" and select the option called "Year 2000 Info".

3. Search for your product information.

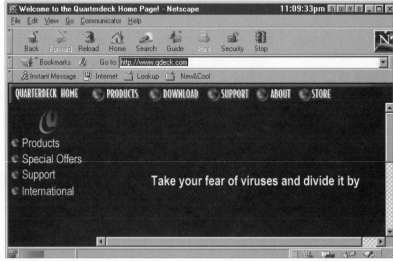

FIGURE *www.qdeck.com*

E-12   © 1998 Quarterdeck Corporation®. All products mentioned are trademarks or registered trademarks of their respective owners. Used with permission.

RED HAT SOFTWARE INC.

Address   P.O. Box 13588
79 TW Alexander Drive
4201 Research Commons, S100
Research Triangle, NC 22709

Internet   *www.redhat.com*

Phone   1-888-REDHATI

The *www.redhat.com* web address presently does not provide information about year 2000 product information, and it is not found through a search option. You can send them an e-mail, but their support requires that you register with the company online. I would suggest you contact their telephone support number as a first step.

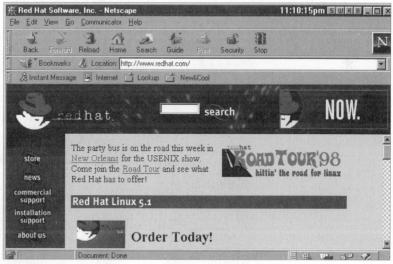

FIGURE   *www.redhat.com*

E-13   Copyright © 1995-1998 Red Hat Software. Used with permission.

SAGE U.S. INC.—TIMESLIPS

Address 239 Western Avenue
          Essex, MA 01929

Internet *www.timeslips.com*

Web Site for Year 2000
          www.timeslips.com/2000.htm

Phone 1-900-680-8463

The web address *www.timeslips.com* is the location for information about Sage U.S. Inc. computer products and their year 2000 compliance status.

Steps

1. Type in the net address *http://www.timeslips.com*

2. On the main web page, click "Year 2000"

3. Search for your product information.

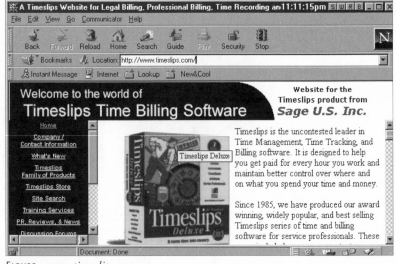

FIGURE *www.timeslips.com*

E-14 Copyright © 1994-1998 Sage U.S. Inc. All rights reserved. Last updated April 16, 1998. Used with permission.

STARFISH SOFTWARE

Address	1700 Green Hills Road Scotts Valley, CA 95066
Internet	*www.starfish.com*
Phone	(408) 461-5800

The web address *www.starfish.com* is the location for information about Starfish computer products and their year 2000 compliance status.

Steps

1. Type in the net address

   http://www.starfishsoftware.com/service/sk_y2k.html

2. Research the area for product information.

SYBASE INC.

Address   6475 Christie Avenue
             Emeryville, CA 95608

Internet   *www.sybase.com*

Phone   1-800-8-SYBASE

The web address *www.sybase.com* is the location for information about Sybase computer products and their year 2000 compliance status.

Steps

1. Type in the net address *http://www.sybase.com*

2. On the main web page, in the Search field, type YEAR 2000 [ENTER]

3. Search for your product information.

THE SANTA CRUZ OPERATIONS, INC.

Address 400 Encinal Street
P.O. Box 1900
Santa Cruz, CA 95061

Internet *www.sco.com*

Phone 1-800-SCO-UNIX

The web address *www.sco.com* is the location for information about The Santa Cruz Operations computer products and their year 2000 compliance status.

Steps

1. Type in the net address *http://www.sco.com*

2. On the main web page, click on the Search field and type
   ```
   YEAR 2000 [ENTER]
   ```

3. Search for your product information.

APPENDIX F

Government Agencies

DEPARTMENT OF VETERAN AFFAIRS

Internet   *www.va.gov*

Phone   1-800-827-1000

The web address *www.va.gov* is the location for information about the Veteran Affairs year 2000 compliance status.

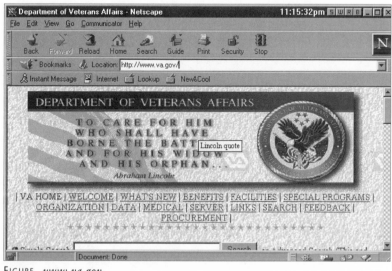

FIGURE *www.va.gov*

F-1   Copyright © 1998 Department of Veterans Affairs. All rights reserved. Used with permission.

Steps

1. Type in the net address *http://www.va.gov*

2. On the main web page, click on the Search field and type
   `YEAR 2000 [ENTER]`

3. Search for your topic information.

FEDERAL DEPOSIT INSURANCE CORPORATION

Internet   *www.fdic.gov*

Phone   1-800-934-FDIC

The web address *www.fdic.gov* is the location for information
about the FDIC-related year 2000 compliance status.

Steps

1. Type in the net address *http://www.fdic.gov*

2. On the main web page, scroll down and click on "Year 2000".

3. Search for your topic information.

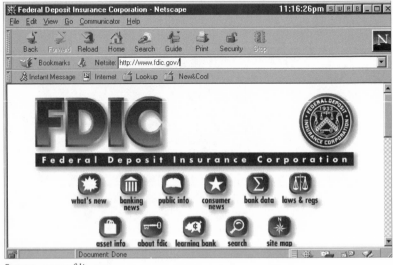

FIGURE *www.fdic.gov*

F-2 Copyright © 1998 FDIC. All rights reserved. Used with permission.

HEALTH CARE FINANCING ADMINISTRATION— MEDICARE/MEDICAID

Internet   *www.hcfa.gov*

Phone   Phone numbers vary by state; see web page

The web address *www.hfca.gov* is the location for information about the Health Care Financing Administration's year 2000 compliance status.

Steps

1. Type in the net address *http://www.hfca.gov*

2. On the main web page, scroll down and click on ``HFCA Special Projects and Initiatives includes: Year - 2000 Compliance``.

3. Search for your topic information.

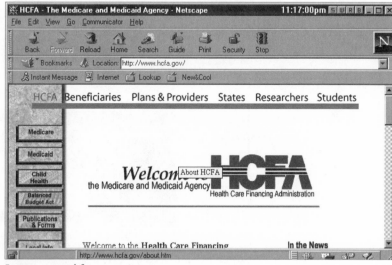

FIGURE   *www.hfca.gov*

F-3   Copyright © 1998 HFCA. All rights reserved. Used with permission.

INTERNAL REVENUE SERVICE

Internet   *www.irs.ustreas.gov*

Phone   1-800-772-1213

The web address *www.irs.ustreas.gov* is the location for information about the Internal Revenue Service related year 2000 compliance status.

Steps

1. Type in the net address *http://www.irs.ustreas.gov*

2. Click on the field "Open here for exciting news".

3. Scroll down to the second screen and click on "Search".

4. In the Search box, type in Year 2000 [ENTER]

5. Search for your topic information.

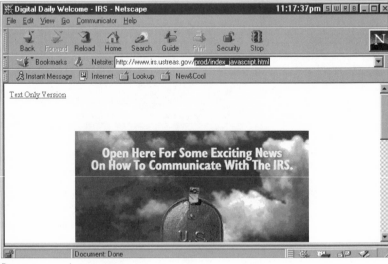

FIGURE   *www.irs.ustreas.gov*

F-4   Copyright © 1998 IRS. All rights reserved. Used with permission.

SOCIAL SECURITY ADMINISTRATION

Internet *www.ssa.gov*

Phone 1-800-772-1213

The web address *www.ssa.gov* is the location for information about the Social Security Administration related year 2000 compliance status.

Steps

1. Type in the net address *http://www.ssa.gov*

2. On the main web page, click on "Social Security Meeting The Year 2000 Challenge".

3. Search for your topic information.

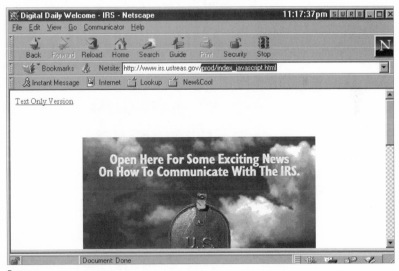

FIGURE *www.ssa.gov*

F-5 Copyright © 1998 SSA. All rights reserved. Used with permission. Disclaimer: Web site information is subject to change.

U.S. FEDERAL GOVERNMENT AGENCIES WEB PAGE

LOUISIANA STATE UNIVERSITY LIBRARY

Internet Site   www.lib.lsu.edu/gov/fedgov.html

Through a search option, no information about year 2000 could be found, but this web site is a great reference area for government information.

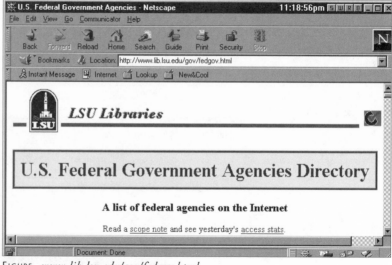

FIGURE *www.lib.lsu.edu/gov/fedgov.html*
F-5   Copyright © 1995 LSU Libraries, Louisiana State University and A&M College, Baton Rouge. Used with permission.

APPENDIX
G

Tools and Testers

Included in this appendix are many different tools and testers we felt would help you to solve your year 2000 problems. These are all third-party tools and can be purchased from their respective manufacturers.

Most tools rely on the individual manufacturer's methodologies. This means the tool is designed to follow a step-by-step procedure to solving your year 2000 problem. Unfortunately, there is no single tool that allows you to click a button and instantly solve all your year 2000 problems. However there are tools specifically targeted to solving certain problems. Please see the individual documentation for descriptions of each tool.

The documentation contained herein was published by each manufacturer. We did not write an editorial for each product. Most information was obtained from Internet web sites or product sheets provided by the manufacturers. Please visit the manufacturers' web sites for updated information.

Included in the back of the book is a CD-ROM, which contains evaluation versions of most software seen here. If you are interested in a tool, please visit the CD-ROM for a demonstration of the actual product. If you are still interested, contact the manufacturer to purchase a copy.

Most of the evaluation applications come with their own copyright and license. So be sure to read them before using the product. You are responsible for following the restrictions stated therein. Remember that software piracy is illegal.

TOOL: DATESPY

Purpose   Scans Microsoft Excel spreadsheets for dates

To Order AMS Group International Distributors, Inc.

Phone   (414) 352-4896

Fax   (414) 228-0487

Internet   *sales@amsgrp.com*

DateSpy will search on selected disk drives, directories or on a LAN for date specific items in worksheets, formulas, formats and macros.

FIGURE *DateSpy*
G-1 Copyright 1998, AMS Group International Distributors Inc.

DateSpy Standard Edition is designed for general computer users and small businesses.

DateSpy Professional is designed for professionals such as IT Managers and Accountants who develop and depend on large complex spreadsheets.

DateSpy Professional provides a template facility. *DateSpy Pro Enterprise* works in conjunction with *DateSpy Professional*. It consolidates all the reports generated by *DateSpy Professional* into a customized enterprise-wide summary of all Excel Spreadsheets.

Features

- Designed for Microsoft Excel versions 5.x, 7.x and 8.x on stand-alone PC or LAN.
- It will identify charts, dialogs, and links in a Microsoft Excel Spreadsheet.
- Easy-to-use tabbed graphical user interface supporting 32-bit and 16-bit executables.
- User interface allows for various selections and reporting criteria, which is used by the spreadsheet analysis and reporting module.
- Supports the following environments: Windows 3.x, Windows 95, Windows NT 3.5x and 4.0.
- Either single user or network edition licensing.
- Use of wise installation system setup and uninstall routines.

ADDITIONAL FEATURES OF DATESPY PROFESSIONAL AND DATESPY PRO ENTERPRISE

- Scans files based on file date.
- Supports user defined file extensions.
- Scan for specific date values.
- Detect dependencies.
- Exclude list.

TEMPLATES

Various departments may need to use different combinations of filtering and search options and may look for lists of targets (a target is the value you are looking for i.e. the word "year"). In order to manage the various combinations, DateSpy Professional provides a template facility. Users can save this list of options in a template file and use the template file in future scans. This powerful feature facilitates electronic distribution of search options by administrators and managers. It also helps users manage and document the multiple scans they used to analyze a specific set of spreadsheets.

BATCH MODE

DateSpy can run in batch mode without any user intervention. It also enables DateSpy deployment via network logging scripts.

REPORT COLLECTION

Central and local collection of run logs, reports and summary detail files (up to 6 files per DateSpy run).

FILES

- Allow file selection by file date (<=, = or =>).
- Allow search for spreadsheets with custom filename suffix — allows scan of csv files etc.
- Exclude files ability.

SEARCHING

- Finds all Excel Spreadsheets on a specified drive
- Searches for:
    Date values in cells
    Date formats
    Date formulas

Dates in macros

Dates in VB for applications

- Offers predefined date formats and masks

- Allows user-defined date formats and masks

- Exclude search targets option.

- Target searching by value only option.

- Search for text dates.

- New date search options to allow search for specific dates within spreadsheets, i.e.: dates equal, dates after, dates before and date range include/exclude options.

- Search for 2-digit year formatted cells

FEATURES UNIQUE TO DATESPY PRO ENTERPRISE (REQUIRES DATESPY PROFESSIONAL)

- Supports input from DateSpy Professional

- View total number of users and spreadsheets impacted across an organization

- Capability to track 11 user fields that attach to each report

- Customized reporting with 47 different field options

- Capability to save the Summary detail csv files (locally and also on the network)

- Allows consolidation and management of csv files

- Provides for a few sample reports and an access database for subsequent user developed reports.

Requirements

- One of the following operating systems: Windows 3.x, Windows 95 or Windows NT version 3.5x or higher (Windows 95 or NT for DateSpy Pro Enterprise)

- A printer configured under Microsoft Windows environment

- Microsoft Excel 5.x or higher

- 4MB of free disk space
- Minimum of: 8MB of Memory & 4MB of free disk space (DateSpy Professional)
- Minimum of: 16MB of Memory & 3MB of free disk space (DateSpy Pro Enterprise)
- Microsoft Access 95 or 97 (DateSpy Pro Enterprise)
- DateSpy Pro Enterprise requires DateSpy Professional

Technical Description

- DateSpy is available in 16-bit and 32-bit versions to support Windows 3.x, Windows 95 and Windows NT
- Excel 5 is supported with the 16-bit version
- Office 95 and Office 97 are supported with the 32-bit version.
- DateSpy interface is written in Visual Basic 4.0 and requires some run-time files, All run-time files are installed during setup.
- DateSpy is available in stand-alone and network edition.

Year 2000— Excel Support

- DateSpy finds all Excel Spreadsheets on a specified drive
- DateSpy searches for:
- Date values in cells
- Date formats
- Date formulas
- Dates in macros
- Dates in VB for applications
- DateSpy offers predefined date formats and masks
- DateSpy allows user-defined date formats and masks

Reporting

- DateSpy produces detail, log file, and summary reports from workbook down to the cell level.

• Reports can be saved as spreadsheets for future statistical analysis and graphical representation of scan results.

Additional Reporting Features of DateSpy Professional and DateSpy Pro Enterprise

CUSTOMIZATION

Customization of reports in Microsoft Access.

SUMMARY FILE

Summary file documenting the grand totals of each scan. The summary file can be used to build an organization-wide database using DateSpy Pro Enterprise. The DateSpy Pro Enterprise database enables large-scale deployment and management of DateSpy.

USER PROFILE

The user profile is a collection of 11 user fields that attach to each scanning report. The profile identifies the user with location and contact information. Administrators can use the profile data to locate and assist users with complex problems. It can also be used for corporate-wide budgeting and cost management.

TOOL: DATEFIND

Purpose	Scans databases and spreadsheets for dates
To Order	AMS Group International Distributors, Inc.
Phone	(414) 352-4896
Fax	(414) 228-0487
Internet	*sales@amsgrp.com*

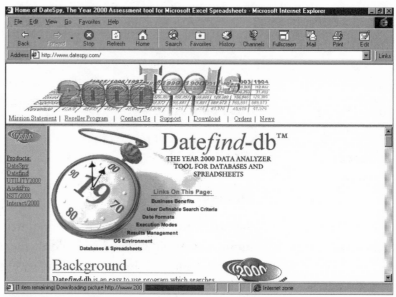

FIGURE *DateFind*

G-2 Copyright 1998, AMS Group International Distributors Inc.

Background

Datefind-db is an easy to use program, which searches PC, midrange and mainframe databases, spreadsheets and other file types, identifying any data that seem to contain dates which are NOT year 2000 ready. The year 2000 readiness is determined by a set of user-defined and/or predefined search criteria. This ensures that real data is factored into compliance checking processes.

Business Benefits

IMPROVED COVERAGE

Most year 2000 compliance processes to date have concentrated on "structural" tests, checking the source code of computer programs and other structures or processes, which may lead to the creation of "non-compliant" dates. These checks are clearly essential. If used in isolation they are to an extent hypothetical and incomplete, since they ignore the end product of these processes — the business data. Datefind-db therefore complements these checks and can be used stand-alone or in conjunction with any existing tools.

LONG SHELF LIFE

Whether an individual PC user or a major corporation, Datefind-db clients find the tool useful throughout the year 2000 compliance process, from initial impact analysis through ongoing and final compliance verification and beyond. Datefind-db can also be used to search for other (non-date) values.

REGULAR HEALTH CHECKS

Datefind-db can be continually optimized and re-run to check the compliance of new and updated operational systems and used together with backups, it is useful in providing regular or periodic health checks. This includes an "entire drive" scan option similar to the approach used by current virus checkers.

EASY TO USE

Datefind-db supports Wizard, Advanced and Unattended execution modes.

The Wizards guide the user through all set-up and execution steps, accompanied by explanatory text and notes. They can be used for initial tutorial sessions or for end users uncomfortable with technology or unfamiliar with the tool. In Advanced mode, Datefind-db provides the user with more rapid access to the search definition facilities. Full Windows context-sensitive help is provided throughout.

OPEN AND SCALEABLE

Datefind-db is usable on all platforms from a single PC to large organizations with multiple mainframe, midrange, mini and PC environments.

EDI AND EXTERNAL DATA PARTNER SUPPORT

Often ignored, EDI message data is as critical as that held in mainstream databases. Datefind-db can be configured to search entire EDI message strings (and, indeed, the other forms of unstructured text, and strings frequently used by external date or mailing list providers).

User-Definable Search Criteria

Datefind-db allows the user to create, store and recall multiple sets of search criteria as search templates. A sample database is shipped with the product and can be used for tutorial purposes.

TEMPLATES INCLUDE USER SELECTIONS TO CHECK:

- Databases and spreadsheets
- Predefined date formats
- Additional user-defined values
- Further inclusion / exclusion criteria

User-Defined Date Formats

In addition to the above predefined date formats, Datefind-db supports the entry of user-defined date formats, catering to system and client-specific needs. Examples might include 090999, often used in legacy systems to indicate end of file, and 999999, frequently used to indicate infinity.

Predefined Date Formats

The user can choose Datefind-db predefined date formats, each of which may be included or excluded as required, via Datefind-db's Template configuration facilities.

PREDEFINED FORMATS INCLUDE:

Format	Example
DDMMYY	01/08/97
MMDDYY	08/01/97
YYMMDD	97/08/01
DDMMMYY	01-Aug-97
YYMMMDD	97-Aug-01
MMYY	08/97
YYMM	97/08
YY	97

Multiple Execution Modes	Advanced users and system administrators configure Datefind-db via switches (at both a command line and default file level).

Results Management	Running a search produces a list of records/rows, which contain potentially non-compliant dates. Analysis information includes:

- Number of records/rows searched
- Ratio of records/rows to passing/failing tests
- Percentage of records searched
- Minimum/maximum years found
- Field/column type
- Date format believed detected
- Date last modified
- File size

The minimum reportable percentage of records containing these "invalid" dates, together with the minimum two-digit value to be considered as a "year," can be configured within the template facility.

The number of records/rows to be checked per file can be configured via the template facility, offering control over the trade-off between speed of execution versus depth of coverage. This may be continually fine-tuned to achieve the required balance.

Once Datefind-db has been used to identify the potential scale of the problem, further support is provided for verification and including:

Graphical Display of Summary Information	Output to screen, structured text file and comma delimited CSV file enabling export to EIS / OLAP tools, spreadsheets and word processors for statistical analysis and reporting Copy to clipboard option and Built-in record browser for further verification.

Operating Environment

DATAFIND-DB RUNS UNDER

- MS-Windows 3.x
- MS-Windows 95
- MS-Windows NT

ODBC database connectivity requires Level 1. Compliance supports both 16bit and 32bit databases and ODBC drivers. Data searched can be numeric or text (alpha).

Databases and Spreadsheets

Direct Connect most commonly used PC databases and spreadsheets including:

- MS-Access v2–v7
- dBase III / IV
- Paradox 3.x, 4.x
- FoxPro 2.0, 2.5, 2.6
- MS-Excel v2-97
- Lotus 123
- Quattro Pro
- Symphony

ODBC Connect midrange and mainframe databases including:

- Oracle
- Sybase
- Informix
- SQL Server
- Ingres
- DB2
- DB2/400
- VSAM

TOOL: CENTENNIAL 2000

Purpose   Test and fix hardware on PC, LAN, and WAN

To Order   Tally Systems

Internet   *www.tallysystems.com/tally/contacts/index.html*

Centennial 2000 simplifies the process of achieving year 2000 compliance in organizations with distributed networks (LAN and WAN), remote-user machines and standalone desktops. Now, the process is automated, eliminating the need to manually test each PC for year 2000 compliance: instead, you can test and fix non-compliant PCs and continually monitor all of them to ensure year 2000 compliance is maintained.

Centennial 2000 Performs the Following

Tests on every PC
- PC Firmware (BIOS) Test
- Real Time Clock (RTC) Test
- Leap Year Test

Fixes to non-compliant PCs
- Software Update
- Flash BIOS Upgrade

Continuous monitoring and updating across your network
Centennial 2000 provides detailed reporting on the status of year 2000 compliance of your PCs. This reporting is critical for demonstrating to shareholders, suppliers, customers and government regulators that your organization has performed the necessary due diligence surrounding the year 2000.

Simple Steps to Year 2000 PC Compliance

Install Centennial 2000 on a network server. You can install Centennial 2000 on as many servers as you need to best manage your IT infrastructure. Each installation will create and maintain a database of the PC population attached to that network.

Set-up user and system login scripts to activate a year 2000 test. As each user logs on to the network, PC information is registered with the server database. That machine is now ready to be tested for year 2000 compliance the next time the user logs on.

Automatically test the status of the machine. Centennial 2000 performs year 2000 tests on the hardware Real Time Clock and the BIOS. The tests include a roll-over reboot test and leap year test. This process is completely transparent to the end-user.

Collect and view test results. The results of the tests are stored in the server database and can be viewed from a central console. You can also filter the report to view subsets of the database — i.e., machines that have failed the Y2K test.

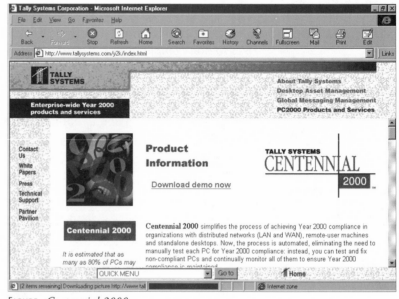

FIGURE *Centennial 2000*

G-3 Copyright 1998, Tally Systems Inc.

Activate the fix for non-compliant machines. To fix PCs that failed the Y2K BIOS test, you can either apply the Centennial 2000 Software Update or a Flash BIOS upgrade. This process can be managed from a central location and can easily monitor when the fix has been successfully applied to every machine in your organization.

Monitor to ensure all machines are updated and remain compliant. As your PC organization changes, Centennial 2000 provides a continual monitoring function to ensure that new and moved PCs are tested and added to the database. This feature also continually checks to ensure that all software fixes remain effectively in place.

Generate status reports. At any time, you can view the current status of all your PCs: Test Pending; Passed; Failed; Fix Pending; Fixed; Fix Removed; etc.

Product Highlights

The software update. The software update can be applied in cases where the BIOS cannot handle the roll-over to the 21st century. The software update advances the clock correctly at the appropriate time. Once the software update has been applied, Centennial 2000 automatically re-tests the machine to ensure that the update has been applied successfully. The machine status is updated within the database.

The Flash BIOS upgrade. For PCs that have Flash BIOS capability (and where a BIOS upgrade is available from the manufacturer), Centennial 2000 provides a fix wizard to automatically distribute a Flash upgrade. After the Flash BIOS upgrade has been applied, Centennial 2000 automatically re-tests to ensure that the PC passes testing year 2000 compliance and the status is updated within the database.

Testing and fixing non-networked PCs. To check and update the compliance status of stand-alone PCs, Centennial 2000 includes a separate program which can be run from a diskette. The collected information can then be merged into your database.

Remote or dial-in access.   Users with remote network connectivity can be tested upon login.

WAN capabilities.   Centennial 2000 can be used over a dial-in link to access repositories stored at other locations. This makes it possible to administer and manage year 2000 compliance across a distributed corporate network.

Detailed reports.   Extensive reports on the testing, fixing and monitoring phases are available and can also be exported for use in other applications, such as spreadsheets. The reports will provide you with information on whether the PCs passed or failed the year 2000 compliance test and whether a software update or BIOS flash can be applied to bring the system into compliance. Several filter options are available to view selections and sorts of the database.

System Requirements	*Administrator's Console*	
		Microsoft Windows 95 or Microsoft NT workstation
	ClientPCs	Windows 3.x, Windows 95, Windows NT, Windows for Workgroups and DOS
	Servers	Microsoft Windows NT® Novell NetWare® IntranetWare, Banyan Vines®

TOOL: NETCENSUS

(not available on the CD-ROM that accompanies this book)

Purpose	Conducts hardware and software inventory
To Order	Tally Systems
Internet	*www.tallysystems.com/tally/contacts/index.html*

Unparalleled Inventory for Your PC Enterprise

NetCensus is the most accurate automatic hardware and software inventory product available today. The first product of its kind to be introduced to the desktop asset management industry, NetCensus has since defined inventory service standards in the worldwide marketplace. Tally Systems has been awarded a U.S. Patent for this advanced data collection technology which provides you with the most comprehensive hardware and software recognition database.

NetCensus hardware recognition includes brand name PCs, add-on drives, communications cards, processors, hard disk configuration, memory utilization, peripherals, plus much more. Software recognition includes manufacturer, name, version, serial numbers, foreign language editions, application path and installation status (full/partial).

Inventory—Your First Step in Asset Management

Total Cost of Ownership. Use NetCensus to maintain an accurate and current record of exactly what you have and where it is. Use this to assign life cycle costs to your desktop assets.

Migration planning. Query your NetCensus database to determine what machines need the Windows 95 upgrade and what memory enhancements are required.

Y2K. Let NetCensus help you prepare your data systems for the year 2000 by performing detailed systems inventory of all company owned PC hardware and software.

Help your help desk. Keep current configuration details and machine profiles available to support staff to improve technician response time.

Purchase PC software in volume. Take advantage of software license discounts with documented usage information.

Eliminate software overbuying. Know who is using what software and avoid purchasing duplicate licenses for the same users.

Outsourcing. Define the level of service and deliverables required from your IT servicers and consultants.

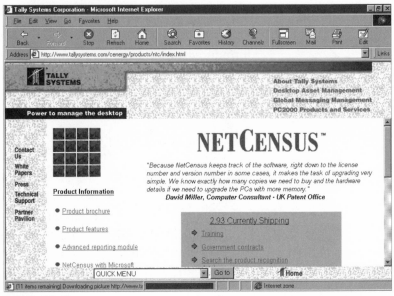

FIGURE *NetCensus*

G-4 Copyright 1998, Tally Systems Inc.

Enterprise Support

NetCensus works with you as your IT environment evolves to maintain a consistent method of information collection, storage and analysis across your entire organization.

Multiple Platform Support. Automatic hardware and software inventory on DOS, Windows, Windows 95, Windows NT and OS/2-based PCs.

Multiple NOS Capabilities. Works on any network operating system that supports DOS file sharing. Server inventory is available for Novell®, Banyan, LAN Manager, LAN Server and Windows NT networks.

Networked and Stand-alone PCs. Collections on home-based PCs, field-based laptops, and other non-connected PCs are as easily inventoried as those connected to your organization's networks.

Enterprise PlusPack. The NetCensus Enterprise PlusPack is a collection of modules designed to enhance the functionality of

NetCensus for the larger, distributed enterprise. These modules include the following:

- NetCensus Client/Server Exporter — export one or more NetCensus databases to a single Microsoft SQL Server or Oracle database
- NetCensus Process Controller — automate the transport of collectors and collection files across a wide area network
- Multiple Configuration Deleter — browse, tag and delete multiple configuration records at one time from the NetCensus database
- Local Products Reconciler — reconcile discrepancies in the classification of proprietary in-house products

System Requirements

ADMINISTRATION PC

IBM, Compaq or compatible PC with a 386 (or later) processor (486 preferred).

10 MB hard disk or server space

4 MB RAM

A disk cache

DOS 3.2 or higher

Windows 3.1 or higher

DOS COLLECTOR

DOS and Windows 3.x

WIN 32 COLLECTOR

Windows 95 or Windows NT Workstation or NT Server version 3.5 or higher

OS/2 Collector

OS/2 version 2.1 or greater with a minimum of 4 MB RAM

Server Census

Scans servers on Novell®, Banyan or LAN manager networks

Network Operating System

A Novell®, Banyan or LAN Manager LAN, or any PC LAN that lets you use a file server with DOS directories

Tool: CentaMeter

(not available on the CD-ROM that accompanies this book)

Purpose   Software Application Metering

To Order   Tally Systems

Internet   *www.tallysystems.com/tally/contacts/index.html*

Prioritize Year 2000 Compliance Upgrades with Metering	Once an organization has completed an inventory, the analysis phase begins. Metering software, such as Tally Systems CentaMeter, details user activity to help identify which applications are run most frequently and for the longest amount of time — helping you to prioritize your Y2K software project .
Increase Productivity	With CentaMeter, you can monitor and restrict access to games and Internet browsers such as Netscape. Plus, discover who is tying up valuable resources by monitoring and tracking inactive applications.

CentaMeter is Tally Systems' Best-of-class Netering and Monitoring Product	Use it enterprise-wide to meter, monitor, and track all your software license usage for greater cost efficiency and peace of mind. Approved by the Software Publishers Association (SPA) as an important tool to help keep your organization "software legal," CentaMeter is easy to use, flexible, and comprehensive.
CentaMeter—A Key Component in the Power to Manage the Desktop	On its own, CentaMeter is the superior way to manage your software licenses. For a *complete* desktop asset management solution, tap into the power of Cenergy™. Cenergy combines CentaMeter with two other best-of-class desktop asset management products: NetCensus™, an automatic inventory product for all your PCs; and WinINSTALL™ an award-winning software distribution product. With Cenergy, you get one point of purchase, one point of technical support, and one point of access on the desktop for all your asset management tools.

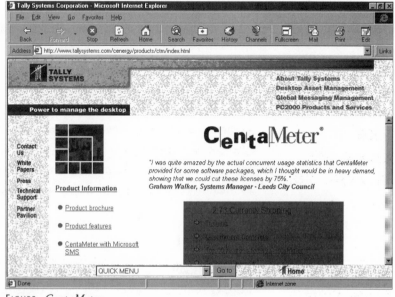

FIGURE *CentaMeter*

G-5 Copyright 1998, Tally Systems Inc.

Save Money on Software License Purchases

TRACK USAGE

CentaMeter provides real cost savings by helping you determine the optimal number of software licenses your company needs. Track and monitor license usage, and then analyze usage and trend data to support purchasing decisions. Stay in full compliance without overspending.

Share Licenses on the Network— Legally

Don't buy one license per PC when you can share licenses. Use CentaMeter to determine how many licenses will be used at any given time, then install enough licenses on your servers to create common access — legally.

OPTIMIZE SUITE LICENSES

CentaMeter automatically transfers suite package licenses to users working with more than one module, freeing up valuable single licenses. CentaMeter ensures that single and suite licenses are used efficiently and legally.

CentaMeter tracks end-user application usage and reminds users to free up and close inactive applications.

RESTRICT USAGE

To help increase productivity, you may restrict the use of applications, like game playing, by designating up to three separate time windows for each application. CentaMeter even tracks usage and restricts access to unauthorized applications installed on local hard drives.

CONTROL LICENSES

Allocate licenses to an individual, group, machine or any combination. Give priority access to priority users. Re-allocate licenses across connected servers on-the-fly for immediate, on-demand access.

NOTIFY USERS

Give users the option of joining a queue when all eligible licenses for an application are in use, and notify them as soon as a license becomes available. Remind users to close inactive applications. Flash a message about restricted game-playing hours.

COMPREHENSIVE REPORTING

Gather data about your company's software license usage, and create a single database from multiple locations. Query on user, application, group, and location. Create presentation-quality reports to help justify corporate software purchases, or to prove software license compliance. Use the charge-back reporting feature to determine the cost of application usage on a per access and a per minute/hour basis.

Enterprise Support

CentaMeter runs on virtually any network, allowing you to standardize across your entire corporation. With CentaMeter, you receive:

- *Local Hard Drive Metering* — optionally track usage and restrict access to applications installed on local hard drives
- *Multiple Platform Support* — Windows 3.1x, Windows 95, Windows NT, DOS
- *WAN Connections* — transfer licenses for applications across WAN connections
- *Multiple NOS Compatibility* — any NOS supporting file sharing and record locking

Support from All Sides

TECHNICAL SUPPORT

To ensure that you get the most from your Tally Systems products, we offer free, full-featured product updates, and unlimited technical support via phone, fax, or Internet.

PRODUCT TRAINING

For an even greater, in-depth look at how our products can help you manage your desktop assets, join us for training courses in either NetCensus or CentaMeter.

System Requirements

ADMINISTRATION PC

- 386, 486, or Pentium PC
- DOS 3.x+
- Windows 3.1x, Windows 95, or Windows NT

NETWORK OPERATING SYSTEM

- Any network operating system that supports file sharing and record locking, including Novell, 3.x and 4.x, Windows NT, Server, Pathworks, LAN Manager, Vines, LAN Server, LANtastic,, and Windows for Workgroups.

SYSTEM REQUIREMENTS

- 12 MB server disk space, plus 13 KB per metered application (plus 512 bytes per license) and 15-30 KB per monitored PC, depending on activity. For each PC monitored, 3 KB base memory for optional resident DOS CentaMeter Agent, plus an additional 2.5 KB while a DOS application is being monitored. The Windows CentaMeter Agent requires 202 KB of extended memory. No server RAM required.

TOOL: WININSTALL

(not available on the CD-ROM that accompanies this book)

Purpose   Software Application Installer

To Order   Tally Systems

Internet   *www.tallysystems.com/tally/contacts/index.html*

WinINSTALL is the most complete, foolproof and flexible way to install, uninstall, and upgrade Windows and DOS applications on a network.

On its own, WinINSTALL is the superior way to solve your file distribution problems. For a complete desktop asset management solution, tap into the power of Cenergy™. Cenergy combines the award-winning WinINSTALL with Tally Systems' best-of-class automatic inventory and metering forces, NetCensus™ and CentaMeter™. With Cenergy, you get the benefits of one point of purchase, one point of technical support, and one point of access on the desktop for all your asset management tools.

Easy Discovery— No Scripts to Write

WinINSTALL's DISCOVER feature saves time by eliminating the need for scripting languages. Without it, you could spend hours trying to figure out the changes that occur during an installation — if you're lucky enough to find them all. This foundation feature uncovers those changes quickly, easily, and more importantly, accurately — it even detects the intricate details of Windows application installs, including changes to the registration database or Windows Registry in Windows NT and Windows 95.

Fast Installs

WinINSTALL completely automates software distribution and makes quick work of adding new applications or upgrading applications to their latest release. In fact, it generally performs installations many times faster than the setup routines supplied with the applications themselves. Install a Windows or DOS application once, and use the DISCOVER feature to capture all the changes made during the setup process, including changes to .INI files, icons, the OLE registration database, and more. It's easy to use, powerful, and fast.

Foolproof Uninstalls	Remove applications safely to keep local configurations up-to-date and clutter-free. WinINSTALL can use install routines for uninstalls, so there is no need to develop a separate uninstall script.

Flexible Customizing Options	WinINSTALL's flexible tailoring options let you access environment variables, network user IDs, and many other types of installation-specific information. WinINSTALL's unique fill-in-the-blanks approach lets you easily customize every detail of any installation. Three ways to distribute software and upgrades from any network management system are:

1. *Automatic* — install applications automatically at Windows start-up or at specified dates and times.
2. *User Choice* — the user controls the timing of installs (and uninstalls, if you offer the option) with the click of a mouse.

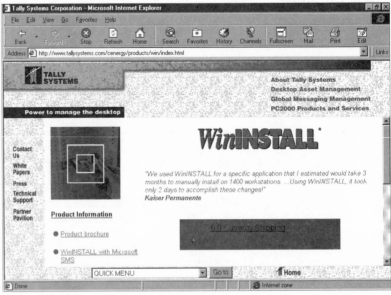

Figure
G-6 *WinInstall*
Copyright 1998, Tally Systems Inc.

3. *Electronic Mail*—send complete applications to users as self-installing attachments to any Windows-based mail system.

Integrated Desktop Asset Management Solutions	**INVENTORY AND METERING**

Cenergy combines WinINSTALL with Tally Systems' automatic inventory and metering products, NetCensus and CentaMeter. Use the inventory data collected by NetCensus as the foundation for your distribution and metering operations. Discover or remotely modify critical information about available PCs before performing an upgrade or uninstall. Schedule application deliveries using the embedded database to know which machines are ready. Access to CentaMeter from WinINSTALL allows registration of software before it is distributed. From the moment it is installed by WinINSTALL, an application will be metered and monitored by CentaMeter.

New Database Capability

Don't waste time learning new proprietary database formats. WinINSTALL supports many of them, including Access, dBASE, FoxPro, Paradox, and *any ODBC database*. WinINSTALL's database is centered on users' configurations.

- Track and record software distribution operations and diagnostic information in the WinINSTALL Log.
- View the Software Table to see entries for every successful installation of a .DAT file (an information file created during the DISCOVER process).
- Verify or analyze data about your PCs with information taken from the PC Data Table each time a WinINSTALL installer program is run.

Use Scheduling Groups Table to target applications to specific users, machines, or user/machine combinations, and to categorize users and user groups on almost any basis.

Complete Environment Support	Enjoy new, automatic electronic software distribution in the DOS environment, as well as the Windows NT and Windows 95 client registry updating capability.
WAN Support	It's as easy as installing an application at the desktop. Centrally create "Server Packages" and move an entire application, including all files necessary for installation, from one file server to another.
WinINSTALL Remote Add-on	Support your company's laptops and home computers not connected to the LAN with WinINSTALL Remote (sold separately). You can access the software distribution function over dial-up lines, electronic mail links and gateways, and other WAN connections.
Support from All Sides	**TECHNICAL SUPPORT** To ensure that you get the most from your Tally Systems products, we offer free, full-featured product updates, and unlimited technical support via phone, fax, or Internet.
System Requirements	• 286+ PC • DOS 2.0+ • Windows 3.x • 6 Mb server disk space if loaded on server, or • 2 Mb client disk space if loaded on a workstation WinINSTALL is not an NLM and does not require a TSR. It runs on any PC-based network operating system, including Novell,

3.x and 4.x, Windows NT, Pathworks, LAN Manager, Vines, LAN Server, and LANtastic. Support is provided for Windows 95 and Windows NT.

WinINSTALL integrates with any Windows-based E-mail application.

TOOL: KILLER

Purpose	Free BIOS and RTC/CMOS tester
To Order	Computer Experts (UK) Ltd.
Phone	+44 1273 696975
Fax	+44 1273 696976
Internet	*info@computerexperts.co.uk*

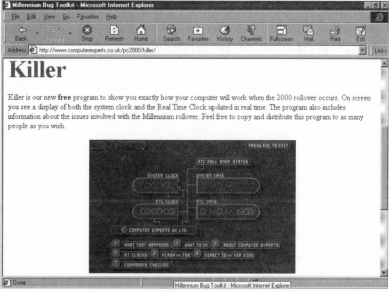

FIGURE *Killer*
G-7 Copyright 1998, Computer Experts (UK) Ltd.

Killer is our new *free* program to show you exactly how your computer will work when the 2000 rollover occurs. On screen you see a display of both the system clock and the Real Time Clock updated in real time. The program also includes information about the issues involved with the Millennium rollover. Feel free to copy and distribute this program to as many people as you wish.

Instructions	• Download the file from *www.computerexperts.co.uk/pc2000/killer/*
	• Double click on the file
	• Tick the "Run after extraction" box
	• Click on the Extract button
	• This will then extract Killer to your hard disk and run it

TOOL: MILLENNIUM BUG TOOLKIT

Purpose	Tests hardware and operating system
To Order	Computer Experts (UK) Ltd.
Phone	+44 1273 696975
Fax	+44 1273 696976
Internet	*info@computerexperts.co.uk*

Try The Millennium Bug Toolkit	Download a free trial of Computer Experts (UK) Ltd.'s Millennium Bug Toolkit

Millennium Bug Toolkit Demo

From here you can download a free trial of Computer Experts (UK) Ltd.'s Millennium Bug Toolkit. It's only 90K, so it's not going to take long to download, and you will have an insight to the millennium compatibility of your machine.

This demo version will carry out eight of the ten tests on your hardware to test for millennium compliance. If your PC fails any of these tests, then you should seriously think about getting the full package, or be prepared to wake up to a nightmare on New Year's Day 2000!

Please note that this version of the Toolkit doesn't work under NT.

THE *ONLY* MILLENNIUM TESTER THAT TESTS THE RTC-BIOS 2000 INTERFACE DURING POWER ON SELF TESTS

All other testers currently on the market (1997-08-14) assume that this will be OK, without testing for it. We consider this to be a very important test. Remember how surprised everyone was when they discovered the different results which came from virtually identical BIOS.

FIGURE *Millennium Bug Toolkit*

G-8 Copyright 1998, Computer Experts (UK) Ltd.

THE *SAFEST* SYSTEM FOR PROTECTING DATA & SOFTWARE

The Millennium Bug Toolkit is run completely from the floppy disk drive and does not interact with your hard disk during the testing procedure.

NUMBER *1* IN INDEPENDENT TESTS

An independent review of millennium products was initiated in July 1997 by the UK company Tecfacs @ *www.tecfacs.com*. Our toolkit scored 19/19 and came top out of the 6 products reviewed.

A copy of this report is freely available at *www.tecfacs.com/ year2000/internal.htm*.

Computer Experts Millennium Bug Toolkit	Our software will check and fix your hardware. The Millennium Bug Toolkit also contains useful information about how to test the software on your computer and the danger of viruses. It also has a feedback section should you wish us to help further.

TOOL: EON2000 PROJECT

(not available on the CD-ROM that accompanies this book)

Purpose   Develops Year2000 plan for PCs and LANs

To Order   Double E Computers
1111 S. 119th ST
Omaha, NE 68144

Phone   (402) 334-7870
1-800-464-8250, ext. 209

Fax   (402) 334-2195

Internet   *www.eon2000.com*

Because businesses today are increasingly dependent on their PC-based computer systems — and the accuracy and timeliness of the data these systems generate, store, and manipulate — a year 2000 plan is essential to your survival.

Eon2000 Project is a comprehensive tool-based management system designed to assist large and small organizations in developing and successfully implementing a year 2000 plan for their PCs and networked computer systems. It provides the necessary information to assess the risk of software, hardware and operating system failure in the year 2000 and generates an action plan for compliance complete with budget projections.

Project includes diagnostic tools and resulting impact analysis report; a management manual with recommended activities, priorities and due diligence; forms required to manage various phases of the process — data collection, application prioritization, software investigation, replacement analysis and meeting tracking; plus complete documentation for education and implementation by your technology team.

Three-Stage Management Process

Investigation/Impact analysis. Critical components (hardware, software and operating systems) are inventoried and considered for compliance. Eon2000 automates this inventory with a disk-based collection process. Data is captured directly on the diagnostic disk which is sent to Double E Computer Systems and analyzed on Double E's proprietary database system. The inventory of operating systems and all executable files are compared to a database of more than 7000 applications and each PC is checked for compliance status. A report is created to help with critical technical and business management decisions on hardware compliance, leap year rollover, equipment, software inventory, and more.

Analysis/Solution strategy. Eon2000 Project management procedures provide recommendations on the activities, priorities and due diligence documentation to implement a year 2000 plan.

Critical management activities covered include procedures to collect and organize hardware and software inventory; track management approvals; prioritize critical software applications; and notify and document contacts with key business partners such as software vendors, suppliers and customers. Sample legal language for vendor compliance notification is also included. Project helps determine what needs to be replaced, upgraded or re-engineered to achieve compliance; whether vendors have compliant versions or forthcoming releases and when they will be available; and other options. A network design, budget and timeline for management of resources are developed.

Preparation for execution and implementation. Eon2000 Project prepares you for the installation of new PCs and applications and subsequent software testing in the upgraded environment.

Eon2000 Project supports all major PC operating systems including MS-DOS, Windows 3.x, Windows 95, Windows NT, Novell, OS/2 and Apple Macintosh.

FIGURE *Eon2000 Project*
G-9 Copyright 1998, Double E Computers.

TOOL: EON2000 SUPPLY TRACKER

(not available on the CD-ROM that accompanies this book)

Purpose Tracks products' and suppliers' year 2000 status

To Order Double E Computers
1111 S. 119th ST
Omaha, NE 68144

Phone (402) 334-7870
1-800-464-8250, ext. 209

Fax (402) 334-2195

Internet *www.eon2000.com*

Eon2000 Supply Tracker is a project management system used to track the status of vendors and products for Year 2000 compliance on a PC-based computer system. It provides both large and small companies with an organized way to look at data that impacts their business on a continuing basis.

FIGURE *Eon2000 Supply Tracker*
G-10 Copyright 1998, Double E Computers.

**Product
Features Include**

Ease of access. The enterprise-wide database can be accessed by anyone in the organization and designated users can update information from any PC in the network.

Accountability. Individuals can be assigned tasks or areas of responsibility.

Sorts and lists. Information on compliant status is available in a number of categories by

- Hardware devices
- Software applications
- Embedded systems
- Department or sub-department
- Vendor or vendor group
- Compliant or non-compliant status
- Degree of criticality

Flags. Supply Tracker ranks compliance and criticality, sets flags and generates reports by

- Compliant
- Non-compliant
- Critical
- Important
- Low Priority Unknown
- Discard

Supply Tracker includes software; a management manual with recommended activities, priorities and due diligence; plus complete documentation for educational and operational use by your technology team.

This software runs on Windows 3.x, Windows 95 and Windows NT.

TOOL: ONMARK 2000

Purpose   Suite of Tools and Testers

To Order   ViaSoft Inc.

Phone   1-888-VIASOFT

Internet   *onmark-info@viasoft.com*

TOOL: ONMARK 2000 BIOS TEST & FIX

The OnMark 2000 BIOS Test is a date-safe test of the Real Time Clock (RTC) and Basic Input/Output System (BIOS) operation of personal computer. The test evaluates the ability of a system's RTC and BIOS to produce accurate dates as the clock rolls over from December 31, 1999, to January 1, 2000. OnMark 2000 BIOS Test also evaluates the ability of the BIOS to manage year 2000 dates after a system reboot.

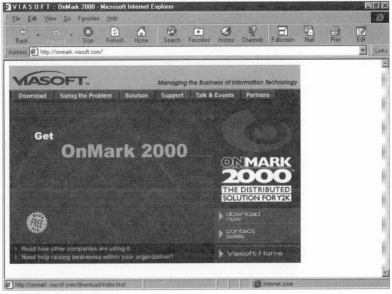

FIGURE   *OnMark 2000*

G-11   Copyright 1998, ViaSoft Inc.

BIOS Test produces a simple, easy-to-understand report about the BIOS handling of the century rollover and recommends one of three courses of action:

- No action is needed. The PC's RTC and BIOS fully support year 2000 dates.
- The user should install Viasoft's BIOS fix software to protect the PC against the change of date at the end of 1999 and/or to support system rebooting after December 31, 1999. BIOS fix is required to compensate for deficiencies in the RTC and/or BIOS.
- The user should replace the PC's BIOS with a later version, because the BIOS is incapable of supporting a date in the year 2000 and this situation cannot be fixed by software.

BIOS Fix is a Terminate and Stay Resident (TSR) program to correct Basic Input/Output System (BIOS) date management deficiencies, for year 2000 dates and beyond.

In most cases, installing OnMark 2000 BIOS Fix software corrects this problem and ensures that year 2000 system dates will be correctly set. BIOS Fix will correct the clock upon reboot and during operation of the PC.

In some cases, certain BIOSs simply assume the century is 19, and thus cannot hold a date with a century of 20, in which case the BIOS must be replaced.

For more information on how the free OnMark 2000 BIOS Test & Fix works, please download the PDF File from our website. Or, get the PDF bundled with the OnMark 2000 BIOS Test & Fix.

TOOL: ONMARK 2000 SURVEY

For 16-bit clients such as Windows 3.x, OnMark 2000 Survey requires up to 2 MB HD. For 32-bit clients, including Windows

95, Windows NT and OS/2, OnMark 2000 Survey requires up to 5 MB HD. The OnMark 2000 Survey manager requires at least 50 MB of HD and runs on the following servers:

- Windows NT Version 3.51 or higher
- OS/2 Version 2.11 or higher

OnMark 2000 Survey also supports MVS/ESA V4R 3.0 or higher.

OnMark 2000TM Survey provides an accurate and up-to-date view of distributed computer systems. It collects comprehensive data about an organization's hardware and software. OnMark 2000 Survey automatically collects this information at defined intervals and stores it in industry-standard relational databases. OnMark 2000 Survey includes a user-friendly interface that lets the user ask configuration questions such as: How many PCs are loaded with software that is not year 2000-ready?

Benefits

- Provides centralized repository of complete hardware and software in enterprise.
- Ensures accurate information with automated collection updates.
- Provides flexible reporting for tracking and analyzing user configurations.
- Streamlines desktop assessment through the ability to perform analysis from a central IT location.

TOOL: ONMARK 2000 ASSESS

OnMark 2000 Assess is an easy-to-use year 2000 analysis tool aimed specifically at the data and processing problems that will be encountered in the PC desktop environment. It analyses two-digit year problems in databases, spreadsheets and files, and highlights the results. Also, it generates reports that are immediately valuable for estimating the year 2000 problem size and impact, and for project planning.

After remediation is completed, OnMark 2000 Assess can be used to validate year 2000 readiness up to and beyond the year 2000. This information can be useful in satisfying both internal and external year 2000 auditing requirements.

Benefits	• Identifies corporate risk by assessing a broad range of commercial and end-user developed applications. • Empowers end users with a user-friendly, intuitive GUI interface that allows for easy identification and correction of problems. • Eliminates hardware date problems by correcting the PC BIOS and system clock. • Helps satisfy auditing requirements when used after remediation is complete to validate readiness before and after year 2000. • Facilitates corporate-wide information management with enterprise database for analysis, trend and summary reporting (requires Windows NT 4.0).
Spreadsheet Support	• Microsoft Excel (Versions 3, 4, 5, 95, 97) • Lotus 1-2-3 (Versions 1-5, 97) • Quattro Pro (Versions 1-8)
Database Support	• Microsoft Access (all versions) • dBase III, dBase IV • Clipper (dBase formats) • FoxPro (dBase formats) • Paradox (3.5, 4, 5, 7, 8)

TOOL: ONMARK 2000 WORKBENCH FOR EXCEL

OnMark 2000 Workbench for Excel is a complete, interactive workbench that performs a comprehensive analysis of Excel workbooks, identifying potential date problems and other inconsistencies that may produce errors. It highlights date-sensitive areas — from data to formulas — to create an environment in which the user can quickly identify and repair problems within the impacted cells.

With a user-friendly, year 2000 wizard interface, Workbench for Excel performs automatic discovery and impact analysis based on user-defined criteria. From the Repair Center, changes can then be made immediately. The system also detects and highlights cells that contain explicit references to Visual Basic application code and/or external functions, providing the user a complete picture of all corrections that need to be made that directly affect spreadsheets.

Benefits

- Provides a year 2000 wizard for discovery and analysis of potential date problems.
- Includes an easy-to-use Repair Center for quick remediation of impacted cells.
- Clearly identifies external references to functions and macro procedures.
- Features "warp" function that allows conversion of worksheet dates to future dates.
- Contrasts different versions of a worksheet cell by cell with its compare function, highlighting discrepancies and computational errors.

Specifics

MINIMUM CONFIGURATION

Workstation
- Pentium PC
- Windows 3.1 and 95 require at least 8MB RAM.

- Windows NT requires 32 MB of RAM.
- All three operating systems require 10 to 100 MB of free disk space, depending on the size of the workbooks to be analyzed.

PLATFORMS SUPPORTED

- OnMark 2000 Workbench for Excel operates in environments running Windows 3.1, 95 or NT 4.0 and is compatible with Excel versions 5.0 through 7.0.

TOOL: ONMARK 2000 WORKBENCH FOR ACCESS

OnMark 2000 Workbench for Access is a complete, interactive workbench that performs a comprehensive analysis of Access applications, identifying potential date problems and other inconsistencies that may produce errors. The Workbench for Access frees your staff from mundane and error-prone manual code analysis. It highlights date-sensitive areas — from data in tables, to code, forms, queries and reports — to create an environment in which the user can quickly identify and assess problems within the impacted application.

Workbench for Access performs automatic discovery and impact analysis based on user-defined criteria. Its application-specific knowledge parser understands the ins-and-outs of MS-Access and Visual Basic, and presents the results in a highly accessible, user-friendly environment. It acts as a detective, flagging areas that contain year 2000-related risk areas. The system also detects and highlights explicit references to Visual Basic application code and/or external references, providing the user a complete picture of all corrections that need to be made that directly affect databases.

Benefits

- Saves time and resources by quickly identifying date sensitivities that may result in miscalculations or errors.
- Increases analysis accuracy through its application-specific knowledge engine.

- Leverages information for reuse by creating an inventory port-folio of complex Access applications.

- Increases maintenance efficiency by finding errors that would otherwise escape detection, on any size application.

- Eliminates mundane and repetitive tasks by automating otherwise manual application inspection.

Specifics

MINIMUM CONFIGURATION

Workstation
- Pentium PC
- Windows 95; requires at least 16MB RAM.
- Windows NT 4.0; requires at least 32 MB of RAM.
- Both operating systems require 10 to 100 MB of free disk space, depending on the size of the applications to be analyzed.

PLATFORMS SUPPORTED

- OnMark 2000 Workbench for Access operates in environments running Windows 95 or NT 4.0 and is compatible with MS-Access versions 2.0, 95 and 97.

TOOL: ONMARK 2000 TEST

OnMark 2000 Test features VIA/AutoTest, a powerful tool that allows for enterprise-wide testing of GUI- and character-based applications. VIA/AutoTest provides the ability to capture/playback any number of applications, automatically build test scripts, and perform load, stress and regression testing. VIA/AutoTest allows testing scheduling and operating in unattended mode and provides the ability to share tests across any number of applications.

Save time by automating year 2000 testing

You can use VIA/AutoTest to automate test execution for all types and levels of testing, including acceptance, regression and integration testing. It easily creates modular, reusable tests that can be rerun as often as necessary, and its automated capture/replay functions allow a quick start to testing.

Better testing through planning

VIA/AutoTest provides a central repository in which to store business requirements, application tests and specific criteria to ensure that business functional equivalence is met. This central repository enables you to plan, manage and test applications from a single location. The repository stores all test results for easy reporting on testing success.

Ensure application performance

VIA/AutoTest allows you to test the response of an application under actual usage circumstances — from a central console — by processing and controlling multiple tests running concurrently. The tests may be run on a virtually unlimited number of workstations on a network, thereby providing a realistic estimate about the performance of your converted application in a production environment.

TOOL: NETKEEPER®

(a registered trademark of Multima Corporation)

Purpose   Inventories hardware and software while checking compliance

To Order   Multima Corporation

Phone   1-800-532-4862

Fax   (401) 885-2605

The Problem— Year 2000 Compatibility

As the Year 2000 approaches, the date compatibility of your computer related devices should be a major concern. It is important to know now the magnitude of the problem in your organization and to look for solutions now. You will be amazed at the number of software applications, files, operating systems, macros and date driven devices, you have even in a small organization. Many of these items will not operate properly after December 31, 1999. Many computers, even some relatively new ones will not work even if you fix or replace the software.

THE PROBLEM EXPLAINED

Most if not all modern PCs have two internal clocks: the System Clock and the RTC or Real Time Clock. The System Clock and the RTC are independent timepieces. One or both can fail to process year 2000 dates correctly.

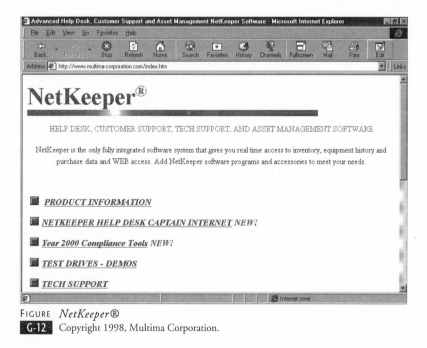

FIGURE *NetKeeper®*

G-12 Copyright 1998, Multima Corporation.

When you turn your PC on, the Operating System software (the software that runs your keyboard and your disk drives) reads the RTC and sets the System Clock's date and time. The RTC is read only when you power on your PC and won't be read again until you turn your PC off and then on again.

Usually the System Clock handles the year 2000 correctly though some older computers running older versions of DOS will not handle year 2000 dates correctly. Most RTC also handle the year 2000 dates correctly. Many PCs fail at reading the RTC and then setting the System Clock.

The Solution— NetKeeper® Year 2000 Automated Test

Now is the time for companies to take action. Companies need tools to diagnose the problem so that they can implement solutions before the Year 2000.

NetKeeper Year 2000 Automated Test is a valuable diagnostic tool for hardware that will determine the extent of the problem for you so that you make decisions now to update or replace equipment before the Year 2000 crashes your system.

The NetKeeper Year 2000 Automated Test program will check:

- The setting of the System Clock by the Real Time Clock.
- Leap year recognition — The Year 2000 is a leap year! The PC clocks may also fail to recognize that the year 2000 is a leap year but 2001 is not. NetKeeper Year 2000 Automated Test also tests this condition.
- That files are saved with the correct date when dated beyond December 31, 1999

The NetKeeper Year 2000 Automated program is also included in NetKeeper Express LAN Inventory program. NetKeeper Express documents the software that is year 2000 compatible and automatically inventories all hardware, software and configuration files. The data is also accessible in NetKeeper Help Desk Pro and NetKeeper Help Desk Captain.

Download from www.netkeeper. com	**NetKeeper Automated Year 2000 demo**

Execute manual and automatic year 2000 PC compatability tests. Fully working program, no time limit.

NetKeeper Express

Automatic LAN inventory program for hardware, software and configuration files. Includes NetKeeper Automated year 2000 Test and also allows you to document which software packages are year 2000 compatible.

NetKeeper Express

Powerful and cost effective Help Desk software. Includes NetKeeper Express LAN inventory with YEAR 2000 PC compatibility test.

Tool: RighTime

Purpose   Tests and fixes PC BIOS

To Order   *www.rightime.com*

Most PCs will not enter year 2000 without help. So, from the author of Y2KPCPro and Year2000.Com, here's Test2000.Exe — a simple, complete and free PC hardware year 2000 diagnostic.

Test2000.Exe Will Easily, Quickly and Reliably Determine:	• if your machine is compliant by BIOS or software fix

• or if your machine is truly year 2000 hardware compliant

• or if it can be made compliant with Y2KPCPro™,

• or if your machine cannot be made compliant without a BIOS upgrade.

Most PC applications get the system date from the operating system, whose software-based calendar is initialized at boot with the date from the BIOS firmware, which gets the date from the CMOS RTC, which is hardware. If the BIOS date does not make the 1999 — 2000 transition correctly — or if the machine loses the correct date after rebooting — it is not year 2000 compliant and will probably become a problem if it is not corrected or removed from service by the end of the decade.

Test2000.Exe will identify those machines with hardware compliance problems. You can read Test2000.Txt now, or download Test2000.Zip v2.23a (70K) which contains files Test2000.Exe, Test2000.Txt and ViewCMOS.Exe from *www.rightime.com*.

A utility that dynamically displays the contents of CMOS RAM and the three PC clock sources is also handy to see just what causes the problem. *Here's* ViewCMOS.Zip v5.13 (27K), it can be downloaded from *www.rightime.com*.

And, here's Year2000.Com — the *PC hardware year 2000 fix; this is an evaluation version of* Y2KPCPro *that's free for use by individuals in non-business service.*

For evaluation of Y2KPCPro, a small resident program for DOS (v3 or later), IBM OS/2™, and Microsoft Windows™ (except NT) that will cure the hardware aspect of the year 2000 problem on AT-class and later PCs, you may use Year2000.Com. You can read Year2000.Txt now, or download Year2000.Zip v2.32apub/year2000.zip (36K) which contains files Year2000.Txt, Year2000.Com and ViewCMOS.Exe, from *www.rightime.com*. Contact us or a licensed distributor for Y2KPCPro licensing information.

Windows NT handles its own century, but if you multiboot to other operating systems too, you might need *NTupDate (1MB)* to keep the CMOS RTC century correct, this can be downloaded from *www.rightime.com*.

Y2KPCPro and Year2000.Com are offspring of *RighTime* — the learning high precision resident system clock corrector —

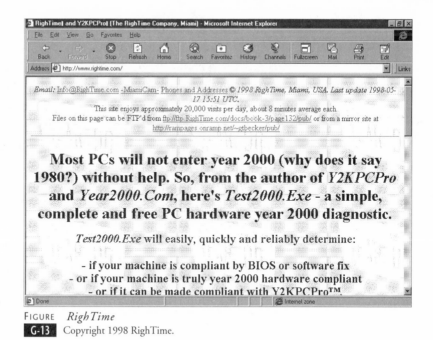

FIGURE *RighTime*

G-13 Copyright 1998 RighTime.

which can bring stability, accuracy and security to your system time-of-day clocks. *RighTime* makes possible sustained clock accuracies on the order of tens of milliseconds per day, easily and automatically. There are many other problems with the PC system clocks; RT2@PTTI.Txt is a detailed discussion of them and how *RighTime* solves them; this can be downloaded from *www.rightime.com*.

Here are the *RighTime*™ and *TimeSet*™ Evaluation Packages	Here is RighTime.Txt, the documentation from the full RighTime v5.06 evaluation file RITM506.Zip (316K) for DOS through Windows 95, and TimeSet.Txt, the documentation from Pete Petrakis' TimeSet v7.21 evaluation file TSET721.Zip (172K). *TimeSet*, from Life Sciences Software, is an excellent DOS-based international telephone time setter that works exceptionally well with *RighTime*. They can all be downloaded from *www.rightime.com*.

Tool: Check 2000 PC

Purpose   Hardware and software test and fix

To Order   Greenwich Mean Time-UTA, L. C.

Phone   1-800-216-5545

Internet   *www.gmt-uta.com*
sales@gmt-uta.com

Flags and Fixes Year 2000 PC Problems.

What Check 2000 PC Does For You	• Finds and fixes year 2000 hardware (BIOS) problems on the spot
	• Tells you how your data and software will be affected by the year 2000 changeover
	• Gives advice on avoiding problems inherent in thousands of popular software programs
	• Helps prioritize software and data problems for timely repair
	• Free customer support for 90 days
	• Lets you run the program as many times as you like to keep monitoring year 2000 status
Technical Data	Check 2000 PC is easy to use and can be run on most PCs. It is supplied on a 3.5" high density diskette (1.44 MB). To run it you need an IBM compatible PC with one of the following Microsoft operating systems: Windows 3.x (including Windows for Workgroups), Windows 95, Windows 98, Windows NT 3.x, Windows NT 4.x.
Attack Year 2000 Software Problems	Check 2000 PC is the only program of its kind. Its extensive knowledge base is built on years of detailed investigations of thousands of both old and new software programs. So you can depend on detailed advice for all your critical year 2000 software needs.

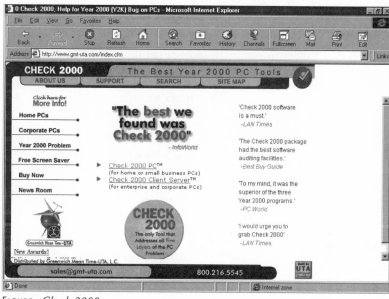

FIGURE *Check 2000*

G-14 Copyright 1997, Greenwich Mean Time-UTA, L.C.

Eliminate Year 2000 Hardware Problems

Your hardware is exposed to the millennium bug every time it tells you the date and time. Check 2000 PC finds and fixes these critical BIOS (basic input/output system) level problems.

Tool: Check 2000 Client Server

Scans your network to find and Fix Year 2000 PC Problems.

Check 2000 Client Server Does All This and More

- Performs a detailed hardware and software audit of your network

- Scans spreadsheets and databases for year 2000 problems, drilling down to individual cells

- Finds and fixes critical (BIOS) problems on your network

- Collates network data into one common database
- Supplies a top-down view of your year 2000 readiness
- Provides detailed reports for all levels of your enterprise, from management to technical
- Prioritizes software and data problems for timely repair
- Offers ongoing risk assessment to maintain your protection, as you change and add to your network

Technical Data	Check 2000 Client Server is supplied on CD. It can be run on standalone PCs or PCs networked with Novell NetWare, Microsoft Windows NT 4.0, Microsoft Windows Networking, OS/2, UNIX, and other common PC interconnectivity systems. The client server software will run on the following operating systems: DOS, Microsoft Windows 3.1x (including for workgroups), Windows 95, Windows 98 and Windows NT 4.0.
Flag Critical Data & Software Problems	Check 2000 Client Server analyzes software applications and provides detailed advice. And Data Scanner (included) scans years of your valuable data-in spreadsheets and databases-to find potential problems.
Powerful, Concise Reports Provide Action Plans	A top-down review of your network's year 2000 status helps you make informed decisions. Plus, separate detailed reports for every vital level — from executives and management to finance, technical and end-users — make it easy to plan and prioritize repairs.

TOOL: PROVE IT 2000

Purpose   Hardware and Operating System Test and Fix

To Order   Priority Data Group

Internet   *www.prioritydata.com*

Prove It 2000

The Eight Tests of the Prove It 2000 software are used to test year 2000 compliance on PC products using the following criteria:

1. Powered on RTC Rollover Test: This test allows the real time clock to rollover from December 31st 1999 to January 1st 2000 and the date is read from the RTC. If the date stored in the RTC is not January 1st 2000, then a failure is reported.

2. Powered on BIOS Rollover Test: This test allows the real time clock to rollover from December 31st 1999 to January 1st 2000, and the date is read through the BIOS. If the date read through the BIOS is not January 2000, then a failure is reported.

3. Powered on OS Rollover Test: This test allows the operating system clock to rollover from December 31st 1999 to January 1st 2000 and the date is read through the operating system. If the date read through the Os is not January 2000, then a failure is reported.

FIGURE *Prove It 2000*

G-15 Copyright 1998 Priority Data Group.

4. Leap Year 2000 Test: This test allows the RTC to rollover from February 28th 2000 to February 29th 2000 and the date is read from the RTC. If the date stored in the RTC is not February 29th 2000, then a failure is reported.

5. Non Leap Year 2001 Test: This test allows the RTC to rollover from February 28th 2001 to March 1st 2001 and the date is read from the RTC. If the date stored in the RTC is not March 1 2001, then a failure is reported.

6. Powered off RTC Rollover Test: This test allows the real time clock to rollover from December 31st 1999 to January 2000. Then the PC is turned off and on again and the date is read from the RTC. If the date stored in the RTC is not January 1st 2000, then a failure is reported.

7. Powered off BIOS Rollover Test: This test allows the real time clock to rollover from December 31st 1999 to what should be January 1st 2000. Then the PC is turned off and on again and the date is read through the BIOS. If the date read through the BIOS is not January 1st 2000, then a failure is reported.

8. Powered off OS Rollover Test: This test allows the operating system clock to rollover from December 31st 1999 to January 1st 2000. Then the PC is turned off and on again and the date is read through the operating system. If the date read through the OS is not January 1st 2000. It is important that all of the system clocks are checked properly, as different software applications read their date formats from different hardware components. The hardware may also perform in a different way depending on whether a power supply is maintained to the motherboard. This is why the powered on and powered off tests are essential.

Prove It 2000 defines an IBM compatible PC as "compliant" if it performs in exactly the same way with regard to date related issues after the year 2000 as it did in 1999, 1998 and 1997. If your PC fails any of the above tests, then the free TSR fix may be installed in order to achieve year 2000 compliance.

TOOL: YES2K

Purpose	Hardware Test and Fix For Single PC or LAN
To Order	SafetyNet Inc
Phone	(973) 467-1024
Internet	*www.safetynet.com* *safety@safetynet.com*

Yes2K—The Year 2000 Hardware Solution

Time is running out — Download Yes2K for FREE, before it's too late. . . .

ZDNet Gives Yes2K a 5 Star Rating! — "*Outstanding in all respects. One of the best of its class.*" Rating: The second most popular download in the Windows System Utilities category, with over 11,000 downloads per month.

New — Version 2.01 is now shipping. We've added a lot of your ideas.

What is the Yes2K Solution?

Yes2K analyzes PC hardware for year 2000 incompatibilities and automatically repairs systems as needed. If Y2K compatibility is not achieved, data corruption and loss may occur. For detailed information about year 2000 incompatibilities, see Yes2k FAQ below.

Free Reseller Promotion — Get the word out! Give your customers a customized version of Yes2K with your company message

ATSASMITS

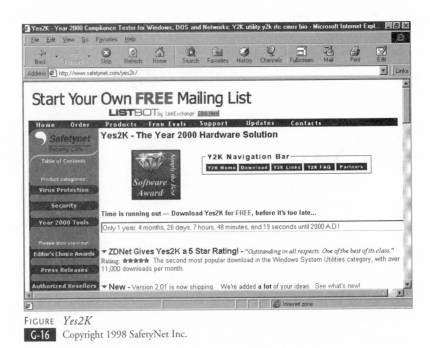

FIGURE Yes2K

G-16   Copyright 1998 SafetyNet Inc.

embedded in the interface. Fill out the Yes2K Partner Application form and we'll customize Yes2K with your message for Free!

Cost Effective Protection

Home Users.   Download Yes2K and use it for FREE on your home PCs (it does NOT expire).

All Other Users.   Download Yes2K for a free 30 day evaluation on up to 5 standalone PCs or network workstations. Register Yes2K to unlock its central management features. Orders placed before September 1, 1998 have an introductory price of US$5/PC (min $50). On September 1, its regular price of $10/PC takes effect.

Yes2K Advanced Features

Year 2000 Hardware Scanner
- Includes Windows and DOS versions, making Yes2K very easy to use.

- Built-in monitor to automatically fix any correctable problem that Yes2K detects.

- If a problem cannot be fixed (this occurs in a very low percentage of PCs) Yes2K will determine if the PC BIOS needs to be replaced.

- Simple interface requires little user intervention.

Central Network Control The Yes2K central management features are ideal for large organizations.

- Automatically test all networked workstations for Y2K compliance on system startup.

- Detect and fix year 2000 hardware problems without having to visit each workstation.

- Import test results from collection diskettes and remote workstations, enabling central analysis and reporting.

Fully functional network console:

- Generates statistical reports
- Summarizes the Y2K compliance status of the enterprise
- Prints comprehensive assessment summaries
- Capable of handling thousands of workstations

What's New in Yes2K v2.01

Since its introduction in April, Yes2K has been downloaded by over 150,000 users. It's quickly becoming the hardware compliance standard for companies, schools, government agencies and consultants.

Its success has given us a deluge of ideas from users with all types of needs, ranging from large companies and government agencies to individual users. We're listening (a lot!) and are working to make Yes2K the ideal solution to the Year 2000 PC hardware problem.

Based on your suggestions, we've added the following features to Yes2K v2.01.

Import capability   The Yes2K Compliance Manager can now import data from collection diskettes and remote network directories into a master results list. As always, this list shows full statistics on the pass/fail rates of each test, and can be sorted by individual tests. Since the workstation results file is in tab-delimited format, it can be easily imported into a spreadsheet for graphing and further analysis.

More complete leap year testing   Previously, Yes2K would test for leap year compatibility in the year 2000 and 2004. Now, in addition, it also checks to make sure the hardware doesn't interpret 2001, 2002 and 2003 as leap year dates.

Automatic testing of DOS, Win3.x, and Win95/98 PCs from a network login script   Many customers have a mixed environment DOS/Win3.x and Win95/98 PCs, and would like to scan, fix and centrally report the results for all workstations without having to visit them individually. We've included the Y2DOSWIN.BAT file which can be run from a network login script. Y2DOSWIN determines the workstation operating system and runs the Windows compliance tester or the DOS tester.

New command-line switches

    /REMOVE Available as a switch for the YES2KDOS.EXE, /REMOVE will remove all references of the YES2K monitor (YES2KMON.EXE) from the workstation CONFIG.SYS and also from the C:\YES2K directory. To automate the monitor's removal from networked workstations, add YES2KDOS /REMOVE to the network login script.

    /NOCMOS Instructs the DOS (YES2KDOS.EXE) and Windows (YES2K.EXE) Y2K-compliance testers to skip the CMOS compatibility test. This enables Yes2K to pass workstations that are sold as being "100% Year 2000 hardware ready." Without this switch, these "Y2K-compliant PCs" often keep the CMOS century byte at 19 (e.g. 19xx), even though the year changes to 2000. This switch can be safely used when the PC runs standard Windows-based business programs. However, since the source code is not available for

all commercial programs, determining which programs get their date from the CMOS is not possible. When /NOCMOS is used, a "n/a" will appear in the CMOS Century column of the Yes2K Compliance Manager.

/PN Prompts the user for a workstation name to uniquely identify the workstation in the central test results list. /PN can be used in conjunction with /WC (gets computer name from the Win95/98 Network Properties) and /WE= (gets computer name from an environment variable). When used with /WC and/or /WE=, /PN is a fallback position if the other two methods return a blank workstation name. In that case, the user will be prompted for a unique workstation name.

Yes2K FAQ (Frequently Asked Questions)

The DATE command shows my PC is Y2K compliant   A common, but extremely misleading way to test for Year 2000 compliance is to set the date in DOS or Windows to 12/31/1999 and the time to around 23:59:50. After waiting 20 seconds or so, the date shows 1/1/2000 and therefore the PC hardware is Year 2000 compliant. Maybe, but probably not. In most cases, the PC will not change the date properly when the Year 2000 arrives.

Why not? While recent versions of DOS and Windows support year 2000 dates, they only display the correct date when the system is left on. However, over 70% of PCs do not have Year 2000-compliant hardware. On these systems, when the computer is powered on in the year 2000, DOS and Windows get an incorrect date from the hardware. There are other problems with Year 2000 leap year support, Real-Time Clock compatibility, Y2K BIOS support and CMOS century settings. Yes2K detects these problems and when possible offers an automatic correction.

What is the Year 2000 Problem?   The year 2000 (Y2K) problem is a combination of hardware and software oversights that may result in data loss and corruption in the year 2000. Both issues are explained below:

Hardware   At the turn of the century the system date will be set incorrectly because of an error in the computer CMOS, BIOS and/or RTC (Real-Time Clock). With the date set incorrectly, many applications such as databases and scheduling utilities will behave unexpectedly, possibly causing data loss and corruption.

Software   Many applications are not equipped to properly handle a four digit year. If a database uses a two digit year, in the year 2000 all data that is calculated using the date (i.e. age, interest calculations, retirement qualifications, payment schedules, etc.) will be corrupted and all data that is deleted automatically based on the date may be lost. To demonstrate how data gets corrupted, let's take a person's age for example. Age is calculated by subtracting a person's date of birth from the current date. If a person is born in 1930, they would be 70 at the turn of the century (2000 - 1930 = 70), if the computer uses a two digit year field it will calculate the age by subtracting 30 from 00 and come to the incorrect conclusion that the person is -30 years old (00 - 30 = -30).

Important.   In order to have a Y2K ready environment, hardware and software issues must be addressed before the year 2000.

How many companies are prepared for the Year 2000?

Many companies have done nothing to make their PCs Y2K ready. Less than 15% of the companies interviewed have completed their year 2000 initiative.

How much money will it cost to fix the Y2K problem?   Hardware:

Safetynet's Yes2K application can detect and repair the CMOS, BIOS, and RTC glitches on almost every computer running Windows 98, 95, 3.x or DOS. Yes2K is FREE for home users. For business, government and educational users, Yes2K is promotionally priced at US$5 per PC with a minimum order of $50 until September 1st. After September 1st each copy will be US $10 per PC.

Software: According to Gartner Group, most major corporations are expected to spend about $50-100 million on Y2K issues. The Gartner Group estimates "A medium size shop with approximately 8000 programs will cost in the range of $450 to $600/program or $3.6-$4.8 million for the entire initiative."

How can I determine if my computer has a Y2K hardware problem?
Download Yes2K, the remedy to the year 2000 hardware problem. In almost every case Yes2K can fix your system if a Y2K hardware error is detected. If Yes2K cannot fix the error, it will generate a report stating what needs to be done in order to make the computer Y2K ready.

Why doesn't the system date get set to 2000?   Every computer (AT class or higher) contains a CMOS, BIOS and RTC (Real-Time Clock). The CMOS, BIOS and RTC are responsible for maintaining the system date and time when the computer is turned off. This is why the computer knows the date and time when it is booted.

The RTC stores the date in a two digit field and does not have the ability to increment the first two digits of the year. Therefore the century remains constant at 19. At the turn of the century only the last two digits will roll over to 00 and the system date will be set to 1900 instead of 2000. Because many BIOSes recognize 1900 as being out of range, the system date, will be set to 1980, 1984 or some other incorrect date dependent on the BIOS and operating system being used.

TOOL: MILLENNIUM BUG COMPLIANCE KIT

Purpose   Hardware Test and Fix

To Order   Planet City Corp.

Phone   (800) 219-8785

Internet   *www.planetcity.com*
             info@planetcity.com

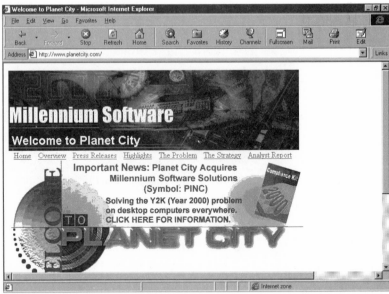

FIGURE *Millennium Bug Compliance Kit*

G-17 Copyright 1998 Planet City Corp.

Planet City (Software) has acquired Millennium Software Solutions, Inc. (MSS) of Montreal, Quebec. MSS holds the rights to software that diagnoses and fixes the inherent error caused by personal computers' inability to recognize the change from the year 1999 to 2000. It also identifies what software the user has, proprietary or purchased, and whether or not it is Y2K compliant.

Every PC manufactured before 1996 will need to correct this problem. The *Y2K Millennium Bug Compliance Kit* offers a simple, thorough, and inexpensive remedy that will meet year 2000 compliance standards. MSS holds the exclusive worldwide marketing rights with the exception of Australia & Asia. . Analysts are extremely concerned and suggest that the *Y2K problem* will cost billions of dollars and negatively impact world economies. To date, the computer industry has concentrated its efforts on solving the Y2K problem on larger mainframe and server systems, leaving the desktop computer market virtually untouched.

Planet City's *strategy* is to attack this huge market aggressively, entrenching MSS software as the industry standard for year 2000 compliance on PCs. The Company has initiated a massive marketing effort including distribution through leading national software retailers and catalogs channels, trial versions of the *Y2K kit* through on line services, and distribution through leading OEM's. Initial sales should begin impacting Planet City September 1998. Planet City has developed other software and is seeking strategic alliances and potential acquisitions that would compliment their core business.

"Anticipated Retail Price will be less than $50"

- The Millennium Bug Compliance Kit is the premiere software available for personal computers designed to fix the hardware problem resulting from the date change from the year 1999 to 2000 — the "Y2K Problem".

- Planet City holds the exclusive Worldwide marketing rights (with the exclusion of Australia & Asia) to the Millennium Bug Compliance Kit software in the United States, South America, and several European countries.

- Sales agreements through major software retailers, catalog channels, direct marketing and OEM's forming rapidly.

- Demand for product overwhelming as the PC market searches for immediate solutions to the Y2K problem.

- Imminent time line as all PCs manufactured prior to 1996 (early Pentium 1 or less) will require Y2K modification / upgrade within the next two years or risk system failure.

- Affordable pricing for complete software kit: suggested retail price under $50.

- Opportunity to capture the lion's share of the PC market which has been ignored by the computer industry. Few companies have approached the PC market, opting instead to focus on Y2K problems in larger systems.

- Attracting veteran management members such as internationally respected Dr. John Kendall to its board. Dr. Kendall recently retired as Dean of Science at a major university, has written several books, over sixty papers and holds three patents on computer related technologies.

The Y2K Problem

The Year 2000 or Y2K Problem is a result of computers' inability to recognize the date change from the year 1999 to 2000. The "bug" or "glitch" occurs because, for the past twenty five years, computer operating systems have relied on a two digit figure to indicate the year of their internal clock. Systems using this method at the end of 1999 will hold an incorrect internal year of 1900, which is then interpreted by most operating systems as 1980, since that is the first year that most PCs recognize themselves as existing. Since all computer files are coded by date, the clock error would lead to disastrous results, corrupting data and the computer's hierarchical order.

The ramifications of this problem are enormous and far reaching. Every PC in existence prior to 1996, including Pentium I, will require a repair/upgrade to fix the problem. The costs associated with Y2K compliance represents billions of dollars and an overwhelming effort by programmers to fix. According to Business Week (March 1998), the diversion of resources required to fix this problem could result in a 0.3 percentage point drop in total economic growth in 1999 and cut half a percentage point off of growth in 2000 and 2001.

The Millennium Y2K Bug Fix Kit

The Millennium Bug Compliance Kit identifies if a personal computer's (PC) hardware system, more specifically the BIOS processor clock and real time clock, has a potential year 2000 problem. The program fixes these problems by applying a removable "patch" or additional program over the BIOS' existing program. The computer will then recognize the year 2000 as well as leap years, which were not previously recognized by computers. A diagnostic tool that accompanies the patch will identify any existing or future non-year-2000 compliant software on the system.

The MBC Kit is the first Y2K software solution available for PCs through mass retail marketing. In Australia, where it was developed, the MCB Kit has gained wide acceptance with prominent corporations, government agencies, and individuals, selling about 14,000 units per month.

Planet City's Strategy

Planet City management has devoted all efforts towards the immediate rapid delivery of the Y2K product to market. The Company has a jump on competitors and will use the lack of participation by the computer industry to sew up its position in the PC market segment. There are millions of PCs requiring Y2K compliance within the MSS license regions. Planet City plans to gain complete immediate penetration to these users.

Initial contracts with major retailers such as Programmers Paradise, which will feature the software in several million catalogs, will ensure the mass roll out of the product. The Company will also utilize direct marketing via internet and online services, agreements with major software retailers and ventures with OEMs who wish to provide a Y2K fix for their various computer hardware systems.

Summary

At present, the general lack of concern about desktop PCs has computer analysts and reviewers disturbed. They are warning the PC market to act immediately. Planet City has the opportunity to establish itself as the premiere Y2K solution software for PCs. In order to reach this goal, it will need to react swiftly. The market for Y2K software is exploding and consumers will not wait. Planet City is poised to produce outstanding profits from a simple, valuable, well-timed product.

The Company's future will be determined by the ability of management to use its resources to launch itself from an initial breakthrough product in the likeness of forerunners such as Netscape, Corel, and others.

TOOL: FIX2000

Purpose   Hardware and Software Test and Fix

To Order   Intelliquis

Phone   (801) 553-1127

Internet   *www.intelliquis.com*
sales@intelliquis.com

Fix2000 is a software application that was designed to find and fix year 2000 date problems in PC software applications. Fix2000 will scan applications created in Visual C++, Delphi, Visual Basic, MS-SQL, Oracle, Access, Paradox, Fox Pro, dBase, Excel, PowerBuilder, and Sybase.

Fix2000 Pro contains all the features of Fix2000 and a PC CMOS clock repair utility known as the "Rosenthal Year 2000 Hardware Fix".

Use Fix2000 to find and fix software related year 2000 problems and Fix2000 Pro to find and fix software and hardware year 2000 related problems.

TOOL: MISCELLANEOUS

The following is a list of additional tools, that we were unable to gather extensive information for before the date of publishing:

Venture 2000 Inc.	*Tool*	PCAP
	Internet	*www.venture2000inc.com*
	Phone	1-888-642-2060

NSTL	*Tool*	Ymark2000
	Internet	*www.nstl.com*
	Phone	(610) 941-9600, ext. 401

UniComp Inc.	*Tool*	Date-A-Fix
	Internet	*www.unicomp-products.com*
	Phone	(770) 424-3684

WRQ	*Tool*	Express Suite 2000
	Internet	N/A
	Phone	(206) 728-8300

McAfee	*Tool*	ToolBox 2000
	Internet	*www.mcafeemall.com*
	Phone	1-800-338-8754, ext. 7984

NeoMedia Technologies	*Tool*	ADAPT-PC
	Internet	*www.neom.com*
	Phone	(941) 337-3434

Wincap Computer Development	*Tool*	Wincap Check and Change
	Internet	N/A
	Phone	(878) 392-3630

Nic Enterprises	*Tool*	Various Tools
	Internet	*www.nic-nz.com*
	Phone	N/A

Rob Harmer Constulting	*Tool*	Various Tools
	Internet	*www.pcprofile.com*
	Phone	N/A

ESP International	*Tool*	Millennium Buster
	Internet	*www.esp-international.com*
	Phone	44 1262 603 295

Footman-Walker Associates	*Tool*	Year 2000 Risk Manager
	Internet	*www.year2000riskmanager.com*
	Phone	44 1425 461 164

MFX Research	*Tool*	Millennium Master
	Internet	*www.mfxr.com*
	Phone	612 9231 3877

APPENDIX

H

Sample Letters

SAMPLE SOFTWARE SUPPLIER LETTER

(See CD-ROM \Letters\letter1.txt)

< date>

<supplier name>   <your name>
<address>   <address>

Dear XXXXXX:

I'm sure you are aware that the impact of the century change on existing software and hardware has recently become a much-publicized issue. I have purchased the attached list of products, which were manufactured by your company, and I am concerned they may not be year 2000 compliant. Please note I have included the release and version number associated with each of these products.

I am seeking information from your company to determine what the specific date-handling capabilities of these products are. I need to know whether the products accurately input, store, interpret, and process a full four-digit century/year date 100% of the time. If any of these products use a formula method to derive the correct century value, then please explain how the formula works. I also need assurance each product will correctly recognize February 29, 2000, as a leap year.

If any of these products are not capable of accurately handling century dates, I want to know what steps you are taking to address the problem. I need to know if the noncompliant products will be fixed, how I may obtain a corrected version, and if there will be any cost involved. Please complete the attached compliance questionnaire and return it to me within 30 days of receipt of this letter. Also, if your company has drafted a year 2000 position paper or product impact document, please remit a copy with the compliance warranties or questionnaire.

If your products are fully compliant, please advise me of this fact in writing.

I am relying on your products to meet my business and personal needs well beyond the year 2000. If they fail, I will be affected. I am certain you can understand and appreciate my concern, and I look forward to your prompt response.

Sincerely,

SAMPLE HARDWARE SUPPLIER LETTER

(See CD-ROM \Letters\letter2.txt)

< date>

<supplier name>   <your name>
<address>   <address>

Dear XXXXXX:

I'm sure you are aware that the impact of the century change on existing hardware and software has recently become a much-publicized issue. I have purchased the attached list of products from your company and am concerned they may not be year 2000 compliant. Please note that I have included the model and serial number for each product.

I am seeking information from your company to determine what the specific date-handling capabilities of these products are. I need to know whether the components used by your company to manufacture each of these products accurately input, store, calculate and process a full four-digit century/year combination 100% of the time. I also need assurance they will correctly recognize February 29, 2000, as a leap year.

If any of these products are not fully compliant, I want to know what steps are needed to ensure they will not fail before, during and after the year 2000. Can they be repaired? Will I need to obtain any component upgrades, and what, if any, costs will be associated with the upgrade or repair?

Please either send me a signed warranty stating the products are fully year 2000 compliant or complete the attached compliance questionnaire and return it to me within 30 days of receipt of this letter. Also, if your company has drafted a year 2000 position paper or product impact document, please remit a copy with the compliance warranty or questionnaire.

I am relying on your products to meet my business and personal needs well beyond the year 2000. Each of these products represents a significant investment to me and I am extremely concerned about this issue. I am certain you can understand my concern and I look forward to receiving your prompt response.

Sincerely,

Technology Supplier Year 2000 Certification Questionnaire

(See CD-ROM)

1. Have you fully tested these products to validate they process dates in all centuries accurately?

2. Which products are not able to correctly handle dates in all centuries?

3. Do these products recognize and will they correctly process February 29, 2000, as a leap year?

4. Identify those products that do not recognize, input, manipulate, compare, store and process all dates using a full four-digit century and year.

5. Identify products using formula methods to derive the century value from a two-digit year.

6. Describe the formula method used by these products.

7. Do products that use a formula method to derive the century calculate the correct century 100% of the time in all instances?

8. Are you planning to correct the products that do not handle dates in all centuries?

9. When will compliant/corrected product versions be available?

10. Can I obtain the corrected/upgraded products at no cost?

11. For software product upgrades, please identify associated hardware and operating system requirements.

12. Will the corrected/upgraded products be able to read data files created with the current product versions, or will the files have to be recreated or converted?

13. What tools or methods can you provide or recommend to help with any needed data file conversions?

14. Do you have a customer service hot-line or contact where I may obtain date problem resolution assistance for these products?

SAMPLE SERVICE PROVIDER LETTER

(See CD-ROM \Letters\letter3.txt)

< date>

<provider name>   <your name>
<address>   <address>

Dear XXXXXX:

I am seeking information regarding your company's state of year 2000 readiness.

I have recently become aware of, and am seriously concerned about, the approaching year 2000 date problem and the impact it will have on companies who depend on technology to deliver their products and services. I am speaking of the now well publicized problem caused by the use of two digits in many computer software/hardware products to represent the year and their resulting inability to correctly recognize the new century.

Attached is a list of the services I currently obtain from your company. These services are extremely important to me and I want to ensure that they will not be disrupted by year 2000 date problems. Also, I need assurance that your internal systems will properly calculate any interest or payments I make to your company.

In order to provide me with the assurance I need, please complete and return the attached questionnaire within 30 days. If I do not receive a response, I will assume your company is not being diligent about addressing this issue. I will start to investigate other companies who are willing to give me the information and assurance I am seeking.

I am certain you can appreciate my concern, and I thank you for your time and cooperation in responding to this request.

Sincerely,

SAMPLE BUSINESS PARTNER LETTER

(See CD-ROM \Letters\letter4.txt)

< date>

<partner name>   <your name>

<address>   <address>

Dear XXXXXX:

I am seeking information regarding year 2000 compliance.

I am very concerned about the approaching year 2000-date problems and am currently evaluating the impact it will have on our business operations. I am speaking of the now well-publicized problem caused by the use of two digits in many computer software/hardware products to represent the year and their resulting inability to correctly recognize the new century.

To evaluate the impact of this problem and develop a plan to implement changes to ensure that my business is not adversely affected, I need input from my business partners and product suppliers. Are you diligently dealing with the date issue? When will I need to test any anticipated product or interface fixes to ensure their year 2000 compliance? By year 2000 compliant, I mean that no product or data will be disrupted because of an inability to process dates into and beyond the year 2000.

Attached is a list of products and interfaces I rely on your company to deliver. They are extremely important to my business operations. Please complete and return the attached questionnaire within 30 days, so I may formulate my compliance plan and evaluate any business risks I may face.

I assume that you share my concern about this serious problem and that, as my business partner, you will take the time to promptly and candidly respond to this request.

Thank you for your cooperation.

Sincerely

SERVICE PROVIDER/BUSINESS PARTNER QUESTIONNAIRE

(See CD-ROM)

1. Which of the listed products and services are produced by systems relying on accurate data processing or date handling?

2. Which of the products and services are affected by known or suspected date-handling problems?

3. If they are affected, when do you plan to have them corrected?

4. How have you tested or how are you planning to test these systems to ensure that they will not fail?

5. Will you be making any interface or product changes that require me to modify the method I use to access your products and services, and when will this occur?

6. Please identify those products and services you guarantee will not be affected by year 2000 date-handling problems.

7. Have you developed a plan to ensure that your business partners and vendors are appropriately dealing with their year 2000 problems?

8. Whom at your company may I contact to discuss year 2000 compliance questions or comments?

9. Do you have a plan for addressing and correcting all of your year 2000 problems, and may I obtain a copy?

10. How long have you been working on a resolution of your year 2000 problems, and how much money and effort do you expect to spend to become compliant?

11. Has an independent auditor evaluated your effort to achieve year 2000 compliance, and are you willing to provide a copy of their reported findings?

12. How does your company define "year 2000 compliant"?

SAMPLE SOCIAL SECURITY ADMINISTRATION LETTER

(See CD-ROM \Letters\letter5.txt)

< date>

<agency name>   <your name>
<address>   <address>

Dear XXXXXX:

I am writing to request information about the Social Security Administration's state of year 2000 readiness. I also want to obtain a copy of my personal contribution records documenting my benefit entitlement to date.

As a longtime contributor to Social Security, I am extremely concerned about the impending century transition and the impact this will have on your systems. I realize the systems used by your agency are rather old and heavily dependent on date information. Therefore, I believe there is a strong chance the agency will experience some service failures as we move into the 21st century. I am referring to the well-publicized problems that will be caused by use of two-digit years in many computer programs and hardware platforms.

Please send me information about the steps your agency has taken to address this problem. I would also like to know what type of contingency plans have been developed to minimize payment errors and delays should serious problems occur. If there are no contingency plans, what assurance can you give me that your agency will continue to properly process its benefits? As I'm sure you realize, the security and well-being of a large number of citizens are dependent on the reliability of the Social Security Department.

(Continued on p. 385)

Also, how may I obtain a documented record of my past Social Security contributions? I have attached a completed copy of form SSA-7004 to request a statement of my lifetime earnings and an estimate of benefit payout. However, I do not know if this will include a detailed summary of my past contributions.

I view the year 2000 problem as an extremely serious issue, one that should receive close attention from all our government officials. I am certain you can appreciate my concern, and I look forward to your timely response.

Sincerely,

Overview of CD-ROM

The enclosed CD-ROM includes a collection of software that will assist you in fixing your year 2000 problems. This appendix details the location of the applications on the CD and how to install and run them. Chapter 14 discusses the general use of tools and testers and Appendix G provides product pages for each application. Please visit these two sections of the book before installing any applications.

Each application is listed below along with a Setup Location, Setup Executable, and Application Executable. The Setup Location states which directory (folder) the setup program is located in on the CD-ROM and the Setup Executable states which file is used for installation. The Application Executable states which file is used to execute the application after installation.

Simply invoke the setup executable by double clicking it in Windows Explorer or File Manager, or by typing its name from the DOS command prompt. Follow the installation instructions as described on the screen. Refer to the product pages in Appendix G for operating system and machine requirements. For further instructions refer to the applications documentation, such as the readme.txt file, contained in the installation directory (folder).

This CD contains Adobe® Acrobat® Reader®, the free companion to Acrobat®. Some products included on the CD use a "Portable Document Format" or PDF file, for distributing documentation and literature. Portable document formats are created using Adobe

Acrobat and are viewed or read using Adobe Acrobat Reader. To view the PDF files you must install the reader.

Some applications allow you to perform a "Boot Test". This tests your computers hardware/firmware (BIOS and RTC/CMOS) upon start up (boot) for year 2000 compliance. Most require you to copy files to a floppy diskette or actually create a "Boot Tester Diskette". OnMark 2000, contained on the CD-ROM, will automatically create a boot tester diskette. See the section below titled "Creating a Boot Tester Diskette".

Following is a layout of the directory (folder) structure on the CD-ROM as it would be seen in windows File Manager or Explorer, utilizing long file names.

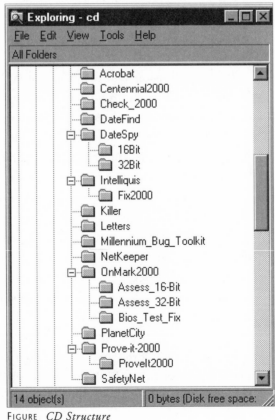

FIGURE   *CD Structure*
I-1

NOTE: The enclosed CD-ROM was created using a long file name structure. Some operating systems support long file names and others don't.

- If you are using DOS or Windows 3.x, refer to the short definitions.
- If you are using Windows 95 / 98 / NT, refer to the long definitions.

Following is a layout of the directory (folder) structure on the CD-ROM as it would be seen from a DOS or COMMAND prompt.

Long File Names	Short File Names
\Acrobat	\ACROBAT
\Centennial2000	\CENTEN~7
\Check_2000	\CHECK_~9
\DateFind	\DATEFIND
\DateSpy\16Bit	\DATESPY\16BIT
\DateSpy\32Bit	\DATESPY\32BIT
\Intelliquis\Fix2000	\INTELL~15\FIX2000
\Killer	\KILLER
\Letters	\LETTERS
\Millennium_Bug_Toolkit	\MILLE~21
\NetKeeper	\NETKE~23
\OnMark2000\Assess_16-Bit	\ONMAR~25\ASSESS~5
\OnMark2000\Assess_32-Bit	\ONMAR~25\ASSESS~7
\OnMark2000\Bios_Test_Fix	\ONMAR~25\BIOS_T~9
\PlanetCity	\PLANE~27
\Prove-It-2000\ProveIt2000	\PROVE-~29\PROVEI~5
\SafetyNet	\SAFET~31

APPLICATION LOCATIONS, EXECUTABLES AND DIRECTORIES

ADOBE® ACROBAT® READER

Long Setup Location:	\Acrobat
Long Setup Executable:	ar32e301.exe
Long Application Executable:	AcroRd32.exe
Short Setup Location:	\ACROBAT
Short Setup Executable:	AR32E301.EXE
Short Application Executable:	ACRORD32.EXE

CENTENNIAL 2000

(Resident running demo, need not install to Hard Drive)

Long Location:	\Centennial2000
Long Executable:	C2KDEMO.EXE
Short Location:	\CENTEN~7
Short Executable:	C2KDEMO.EXE

CHECK 2000

Long Setup Location:	\Check_2000
Long Setup Executable:	unpack.exe
Long Application Executable:	\c2kLite.exe
Short Setup Location:	\CHECK_~9
Short Setup Executable:	UNPACK.EXE
Short Application Executable:	C2KLITE.EXE

DATE*FIND*-DB

Long Setup Location:	\DateFind
Long Setup Executable:	Setup.exe
Long Application Executable:	datefind.exe
Short Setup Location:	\DATEFIND
Short Setup Executable:	SETUP.EXE
Short Application Executable:	\DATEFIND.EXE

DATESPY (16-BIT VERSION)

Long Setup Location:	\DateSpy\16Bit
Long Setup Executable:	SETUP16.EXE
Long Application Executable:	DATESP16.EXE
Short Setup Location:	\DATESPY\16BIT
Short Setup Executable:	SETUP16.EXE
Short Application Executable:	DATESP16.EXE

DATESPY (32-BIT VERSION)

Long Setup Location:	\DateSpy\32Bit
Long Setup Executable:	SETUP32.EXE
Long Application Executable:	DATESP32.EXE
Short Setup Location:	\DATESPY\32BIT
Short Setup Executable:	SETUP32.EXE
Short Application Executable:	DATESP32.EXE

Fix2000

Long Setup Location:	\Intelliquis\Fix2000
Long Setup Executable:	Fix2000.exe
Long Application Executable:	Fix2000.exe
Short Setup Location:	\INTELL~15\FIX2000
Short Setup Executable:	FIX2000.EXE
Short Application Executable:	FIX2000.EXE

Killer

(Resident running demo, need not install to Hard Drive)

Long Location:	\Killer
Long Executable:	KILLER.EXE
Short Location:	\KILLER
Short Executable:	KILLER.EXE

Millennium Bug ToolKit

Long Setup Location:	\Millennium_Bug_Toolkit
Long Setup Executable:	setupmbt.exe
Long Application Executable:	DEMO.EXE

(The demo.exe file on your hard drive runs the application demo.)

Long Application Executable:	DEMO.EXE

(The demo.exe file on the CD-ROM runs a separate slide show demonstration from the CD-ROM.)

Short Setup Location:	\MILLE~21

Short Setup Executable:	SETUPMBT.EXE
Short Application Executable:	DEMO.EXE

(The demo.exe file on your hard drive runs the application demo.)

Short Application Executable:	DEMO.EXE

(The demo.exe file on the CD-ROM runs a separate slide show demonstration from the CD-ROM.)

MILLENNIUM BUG COMPLIANCE KIT

Long Setup Location:	\PlanetCity
Long Setup Executable:	SETUP.EXE
Long Application Executable:	\REPORTER.EXE
Short Setup Location:	\PLANE~27
Short Setup Executable:	SETUP.EXE
Short Application Executable:	\REPORTER.EXE

 Note. When this application asks you to insert DISK #4, simply insert a blank floppy diskette into your floppy drive.

NETKEEPER

Long Setup Location:	\NetKeeper
Long Setup Executable:	SETUP.EXE
Long Application Executable:	\Year2k1.exe
Short Setup Location:	\NETKE~23
Short Setup Executable:	SETUP.EXE
Short Application Executable:	\YEAR2K1.EXE

ONMARK 2000 ASSESS (16-BIT VERSION)

Long Setup Location:	\OnMark2000\Assess_16-Bit
Long Setup Executable:	Assess16.exe
Long Application Executable:	Assess.exe
Short Setup Location:	\ONMAR~25\ASSESS~5
Short Setup Executable:	ASSESS16.EXE
Short Application Executable:	ASSESS.EXE

ONMARK 2000 ASSESS (32-BIT VERSION)

Long Setup Location:	\OnMark2000\Assess_32-Bit
Long Setup Executable:	Assess32.exe
Long Application Executable:	Assess.exe
Short Setup Location:	\ONMAR~25\ASSESS~7
Short Setup Executable:	ASSESS32.EXE
Short Application Executable:	ASSESS.EXE

ONMARK 2000 BIOS TEST AND FIX

(You may do a CUSTOM or TYPICAL install)

Long Setup Location:	\OnMark2000\Bios_Test_Fix
Long Setup Executable:	Btestfix.exe
Long Custom Install Directory:	\Program Files\OnMark\ OnMark 2000 Assess\ BIOSFIX
Long Custom App Executable:	Makebtd.exe

Long Typical Install Directory: \Program Files\OnMark\
                                    OnMark 2000 Assess\
                                    BIOSFIX

Long Typical App Executable: Biosfix.exe

Short Setup Location: \ONMAR~25\BIOS_T~9

Short Setup Executable: BTESTFIX.EXE

Short Custom Install Directory: \PROGRA~1\ONMARK\
                                    ONMARK~1\BIOSFIX

Short Custom App Executable: MAKEBTD.EXE

Short Typical Install Directory: \PROGRA~1\ONMARK\
                                    ONMARK~1\BIOSFIX

Short Typical App Executable: BIOSFIX.EXE

PROVE IT 2000

Long Setup Location: \Prove-it-2000\ProveIt2000

Long Setup Executable: SETUP.EXE

Long Application Executable: DEMO.EXE

Short Setup Location: \PROVE-~29\PROVEI~5

Short Setup Executable: SETUP.EXE

Short Application Executable: DEMO.EXE

YES2K

Long Setup Location: \SafetyNet

Long Setup Executable: yes2kv20.exe

Long Application Executable: yes2k.EXE

Long Application Executable:	yes2kadm.exe
Long Application Executable:	yes2kdos.exe
Short Setup Location:	\SAFET~31
Short Setup Executable:	YES2KV20.EXE
Short Application Executable:	YES2K.EXE
Short Application Executable:	YES2KADM.EXE
Short Application Executable:	YES2KDOS.EXE

SAMPLE LETTERS

Long Location:	\Letters
Short Location:	\LETTERS
Long File Name:	letter1.txt
Short File Name:	LETTER1.TXT
Long File Name:	letter2.txt
Short File Name:	LETTER2.TXT
Long File Name:	letter3.txt
Short File Name:	LETTER3.TXT
Long File Name:	letter4.txt
Short File Name:	LETTER4.TXT
Long File Name:	letter5.txt
Short File Name:	LETTER5.TXT

CREATING A BOOT TESTER DISKETTE

OnMark 2000 provides a program that will automatically create a Boot Diskette. This boot diskette will perform a power-on and power-off BIOS and RTC/CMOS test. To create the diskette, follow these steps:

1. Format a diskette, see section below titled "Formatting Diskettes".

2. Close all open or running applications.

3. Install one of the following OnMark 2000 programs: OnMark 2000 Assess 16-Bit, OnMark 2000 Assess 32-Bit or OnMark 2000 BIOS Test and Fix. Refer to Appendix G to determine which of these is right for you. See the above list for the installation location and executable file. Make a note of the directory location the application was installed to.

4. Run the program "OnMark 2000 Make BIOS Test Disk" located in the directory you installed to.

   • DOS — Execute the file called MAKEBTD.EXE,

   • Windows 3.x — Double-click the group item called "OnMark 2000 Make BIOS Test Disk".

   • Windows 95 / 98 / NT — Click the Start/Program item called "OnMark 2000 Make BIOS Test Disk". This will be found on the Start/Program/OnMark/OnMark 2000/ OnMark 2000 Assess menu option.

5. Insert diskette into floppy drive and re-boot computer.

FORMATTING DISKETTES

Consult your operating system documentation for formatting diskettes or follow the instructions below:

DOS OR WINDOWS 3.x

1. Insert diskette into drive making sure it's not write protected

2. Go To DOS Command Prompt

3. Type FORMAT A: or FORMAT B: [enter]

Windows 95 / 98 / NT

1. Insert diskette into drive making sure it's not write protected
2. Click "My Computer"
3. Right Click The Floppy Drive
4. Click "Format"
5. Click "Quick" or "Full"
6. Click on "Start"

APPENDIX

J

Year 2000 User Groups In the United States

ARIZONA

ARIZONA MILLENNIUM GROUP

Contact   Michael L. Sperling

Address   City of Phoenix, ITD
251 W. Washington Street
Phoenix, AZ 85003

Phone   (602) 256-4190

Fax   (602) 534-1488

E-mail   *msperlin@ci.phoenix.az.us*

Meeting schedule   Third Wednesday of every month, 3:00 PM–5:00 PM.

CALIFORNIA

LOS ANGELES (CA) AREA USER GROUP

Contact   Bruce McCormick

E-mail   *bmccormick@sunamerica.com*

Alternate Contact   Niru Patel

Alternate E-mail   *NPatel3549@aol.com*

Meeting Schedule   The monthly meetings will be held on the second Tuesday of each month from 1900 to 2100 (7:00 PM to 9:00 PM).

SAN DIEGO (CA) YEAR 2000 INTEREST GROUP

Contact   Mike Lyons

Phone   (619) 552-0300, ext 3022.

E-mail   *lyonsm@sourcesvc.com.*

SF-2000 USER GROUP

Contact   Anthony M. Peeters

Web Site   *http://www.sf2000.com*

CONNECTICUT

"THE NUTMEG CENTURIANS"

Contact   Dave Roger

Phone   (203) 386-8074

E-mail   *year2000@caldor.com*

Web Site   *http://www.effectivebydesign.com/nutmeg/*

FLORIDA

CENTRAL FLORIDA HEALTHCARE FOCUSED Y2K USERS GROUP (ORLAND)

Contact	Sharon E. Stein
Phone	1-800-327-8402, ext.1137,
Fax	(407) 841-8884
Web Site	*www.orhs.org/year2000/*

MIAMI YEAR 2000 USERS' GROUP

Contact	Michael Rodriguez
Address	195 SW 15 RD, Suite 600 Miami FL 33129
E-mail	*miker@metroinfo.com*
Fax	(305) 860-2953
Phone	(305) 860-1467
Web Sites	*http://www.metroinfo.com/Y2K/miami_ug* *http://www.pprcorp.com/Y2K/miami_ug*

TAMPA BAY (FL) AREA USER GROUP

Contact	David Widlak
Phone	(813) 935-7332, ext. 102
E-mail	*DavidW@CMCNET.COM*

GEORGIA

WARNER ROBINS (GA) MILLENNIUM GROUP

Contact   David Hall

E-mail   *dhall@arinc.com*

ATLANTA (GA)YEAR 2000 USERS GROUP

Contact   Omicron Year 2000 Date Integrity Work Group

User Group Web Site   *http://www.se.commerce.net/atlyear2000/*

Alternate Contact   Al Jacobsen

Phone   (404) 255-0096

ILLINOIS

CHICAGO (IL) AREA YEAR 2000 FINANCIAL INTEREST GROUP

Contact   Tom Wilkie
Year 2000 Project Manager
Household International

Phone   (847) 564-6024

Fax   (847) 205-7439

E-mail   *USVCNKKB@IBMMAIL.COM*

Meeting Schedule The group meets on the second Tuesday of each month.

CHICAGO AREA YEAR 2000 SUPPLY CHAIN USERS GROUP

Contact	Ed Shapiro
Phone	(847) 295-0513
E-mail	*tkmethod@icsp.net*

INDIANA

CENTRAL INDIANA Y2K USER GROUP

Contact	Scott Kincaid
Internet	*scott.kincaid@aul.com*
	http://www.bus.indiana.edu/ima/2000site.html
Web Site	*Y2KIN@INDIANA.EDU*

KANSAS

WICHITA Y2K FORUM

Contact	Jo Luther
Address	Wichita Y2K Forum Chairperson
	Koch Industries, Inc.,
	4111 E. 37th N.,
	Wichita, KS 67220
Phone	(316) 828-4506
Internet	*lutherj@kochind.com*

KENTUCKY

BLUEGRASS YEAR 2000 GROUP (LEXINGTON)

Contact	Wanda Compbell Greater Lexington Chamber of Commerce.
Phone	(606) 254-4447 (606) 226-1618
Alternate Contact	Scott Setters
Address	Central Kentucky Chapter of Data Processing Management Association (DPMA).
Phone	(606) 367-5512
Alternate Contact	Bob Brown Central Kentucky Computer Society.
Phone	(606)255-2527.

LOUISVILLE YEAR 2000 SPECIAL INTEREST GROUP

Contact	Jim Samuels
E-mail	*jimsam@aol.com*
Phone	(502) 228-5266

MASSACHUSETTS

BELVIDERE NEIGHBORHOOD ASSOCIATION YEAR 2000 PREPAREDNESS COMMITTEE (Lowell)

Contact	Ian Wells
Phone Hotline	(978) 459-6325
Web Site	*http://www.tiac.net/users/mpadki/y2k.htm*

MICHIGAN

DETROIT MILLENNIUM USER'S GROUP

Contact	Bob Ross Systems and Applications Manager, Detroit Newspapers
Phone	(313) 222-2207
Meeting Schedule	Third Thursday of every month at various host member business locations throughout the metro Detroit area.

MINNESOTA

MINNESOTA YEAR 2000 PROJECT MANAGERS (Minneapolis)

Contact	Jane Erickson
Phone	(612) 726-4285
E-mail	*jericks@nwa.com*
Meeting Schedule	Second Wednesday of each month from 1:00 PM to 5:00 PM.

MISSOURI

KANSAS CITY (MO) Y2K CLUB

Contact	Andrew Ellner 3RD Millennium Consulting
Phone	(913) 262-6500, ext. 2047

Web Site	*http://www.triplei.com/3mc/kcy2k.htm*
Meeting Schedule	Normally the second Tuesday of each month, from 1:00 PM to 5:00 PM. For a recorded message call: (816) 395-3461, Courtesy of BC/BS of Kansas City

MIDWEST 2000 SHARING GROUP (St. Louis)

Contact	Len Schulte
Phone	(314) 827-2264
Fax	(314) 827-3148
E-mail	*SchultLF@maritz.com*

NEBRASKA

NEBRASKA Y2K USER GROUP

Contact	Kevin Zach
Phone	(402) 894-0468
E-mail	*infinity_associates@msn.com*
Meeting Schedule	Second Thursday of every month, 4:30 PM–6:00 PM. Call for meeting location.

NEW JERSEY

NEW JERSEY USER GROUP

Contact	James Kinder
E-mail	*james_kinder@es.adp.com*

Alternate Contact Mike Cervine

Alternate E-mail CervineM@Panasonic.com

NEW YORK

NEW YORK 2000 USER GROUP

Contact Martyn Emery
Corporation 2000, Inc.

ALBANY

Contact Kirsten Leblanc

Phone (518) 452-7277

Web Site *http://www.albany.net/~dmills/y2k.htm*

CENTRAL NEW YORK Y2K USER GROUP (Syracuse)

Contact Joan T. Budzinski

E-mail *joan.t.budinski@carrier.utc.com*

NORTH CAROLINA

RTP (NC) YEAR2000 USER GROUP

Contact Mary Anne A. Williams

E-mail *maw67085@glaxowellcome.com*

Phone (919) 483-4024

Meeting Schedule Third Wednesday of each month, 3:00 PM–5:00 PM.

OHIO

OHIO 2000 (Cleveland)

Contact Jeff Nicolet
Source Consulting

Phone (216) 328-5900

E-mail *jeff.nicolet@mci2000.com*

Alternate Contacts Dan Miller
Nordson Corporation
(216) 892-1580

Willie Kennedy Jr.
Key Services Corporation
(216) 689-9168

Paul Simmons
Cleveland Clinic Foundation
(216) 444-4510

Stephen Covert
Highlights For Children
(614) 487-2218

Ann Flory
Princeton Softech
(513) 533-4033
www.ccai.net/ohio2000

OREGON

PORTLAND (OR) YEAR 2000 READY

Contact Patrick Canniff

Phone (503) 499-2734

Meeting Schedule First Wednesday of every month.

PENNSYLVANIA

DELAWARE VALLEY (PA) YEAR 2000 SPECIAL INTEREST GROUP (Philadelphia)

Contact Andy Kaufmann
Chairperson

E-mail *andyk@rcgphila.com*

Phone (800) 244-9212

Web Site *www.libertynet.org/~dpmaphil/dvy2ksig*

Meeting Schedule See web site

PITTSBURGH YEAR 2000 USER GROUP

Contact Laureen Link

E-mail *lllst12@pitt.edu*

Meeting Schedule Meetings will take place the first Tuesday of every month.

SOUTH CAROLINA

UPSTATE SOUTH CAROLINA Y2K USER GROUP

Contact Bruce Hevner

WebSite *http://www.russkelly.com/*
          UpstateYear2000UserGroup/

TENNESSEE

TENNESSEE Y2K ISSUES GROUP

Contact Mike Kilbane

Phone 615-287-4907

E-mail *mkilbane@midtn.campus.mci.net*

TEXAS

TEXAS YEAR 2000 WORKING GROUP

Contact Shannon Porterfield

Phone (512) 475-4740

Web Site *http://www.dir.state.tx.us/y2k*

Meeting Schedule Meets the 2nd Friday of the month.

DFW PREP 2000 (Dallas)

Contact Bill Wachel

E-mail *wmwachel@onramp.net*

Web Site	*http://www.dfadama.org*
Phone	(214) 333-6221
Fax	(214) 333-6220
Alternate Contact	Charles P. Reuben, B.Sc., M.A.
Alternate E-mail	*buytexas@swbell.net*
Alternate Address	Hancock Properties DALLAS 8609 NW Plaza@Hillcrest S:434 Dallas, TX 75225-4229
Alternate Phone	(214) 369-9922
Alternate Fax	(214) 691-6760

UTAH

UTAH YEAR 2000 USERS' GROUP

Contact	John Horton
Web Site	*http://www.governor.state.ut.us/sitc/usergroup/ usergroup.htm*

WASHINGTON, D.C.

WASHINGTON, D.C. YEAR 2000 GROUP

Contact	Bruce Webster
Phone	(202)752-3979
E-mail	*g8ubew@fnma.com*
Web Site	*http://www.bfwa.com/bwebster/y2k*

WISCONSIN

WISCONSIN Y2K USER GROUP

Contact   John Reybrock

Phone   (920) 734-5721, ext 4075

E-mail   *John_Reybrock@aal.org*

Web Site   *www.apex-isg.com\wiy2kug*

Meeting Schedule Second Wednesday of every month, 9:00 AM to noon.

Index

Ask a Tough Question. Expect Solid Direction.

Help on the Horizon. Arnold Information Technology points corporations and organizations to information that get results. Access our experienced professionals who can help senior managers identify options and chart a course.

Since 1991, we've proven we can help in a range of capacities:

BUSINESS DEVELOPMENT
- Knowledge Management
- Competitive Intelligence
- Marketing & Sales
- Acquisitions & Mergers
- Patent Evaluations
- Technology Startups

INFORMATION TECHNOLOGY SERVICES
- Intranets, and Extranets
- Web-based Technologies
- Database Management
- Digital Work Flow Planning
- Information Engineering

ACTION FROM IDEAS. We helped build the service known as the Top 5% of the Internet, found at www.lycos.com. Our latest competitive intelligence tool can be explored at abcompass.com. It builds a personal daily news feed that only you receive.

A TEAM WITH STRATEGIC VISION. Our seasoned consultants can build, research, prototype, budget, plan, assess, and tackle some of the toughest jobs in information technology. Our managers have taken a leadership role in U.S. corporations and elsewhere in the world.

GET WHERE YOU WANT TO GO. TODAY.
We move corporations and organizations into the future. Our work spans a variety of industries, including publishing, telecommunications, government agencies, investment banks, and startups. We welcome confidential, informal discussions of your challenges and opportunities.

CONTACT:

Stephen E. Arnold, President
Arnold Information Technology
P.O. Box 320
Harrods Creek, Kentucky 40027
Voice: 502 228-1966
E-Mail: ait@arnoldit.com
Facsimile: 502 228-0548

JD Consulting LLC

We hope you found this book to be useful. We would like your feedback and ideas for a future edition or other material you would like to see offered.

E-mail our web site: *service@jdcllc.com*

Call: (860) 725-6433

Mail: JD Consulting LLC
                   P.O. Box 280506
                   East Hartford, CT 06128

JD Consulting offers other avenues of education and support to help you deal with your year 2000 problem evaluation and resolution needs.

➢ 1 day seminar: Designed to cover all areas and aspects of the problem. Learn what the problem is and focus on effective approaches for identifying, assessing, and resolving the issues.

➢ 2 day workshop: Covers the same topic areas as our 1 day seminar in a hands-on lab environment. Learn how to effectively test for problems. Understand how to obtain and apply solutions for hardware, operating system and common software problems.

➢ Customized Classes: Offered at client sites to meet specific needs.

➢ Consulting Services: To assist small business owners in identifying support needs and securing resources to evaluate and implement appropriate solutions.